PATHWAY
THE DYSLEXIC'S TALE

A Personal Account

DAVE CRAWFORD

Copyright ©2020 Dave Crawford

All right reserved. No part of this book may be used or reproduced by any means, graphic, electronic, or mechanical, including photocopying, recording, taping or by any information storage retrieval system without the written permission of the author except in the case of brief quotations embodies in critical article and reviews.

Because of the dynamic nature of the Internet, any web addresses or links contained in this book may have changed since publication and may no longer be valid. The reviews expressed in this work are solely those of the author and do not necessarily reflect the views of the publisher, and the publisher hereby disclaims any responsibility for them.

*To inform you of the state of everyone
Of all of these, as it appeared to me
And who they were, and what was their degree.*
                              Geoffrey Chaucer

Author's Note

IN THIS ACCOUNT, THE NAMES of persons and places that might help identify individuals have been changed. The exceptions are of my immediate family and a few cases where there was a need to maintain historic context or authenticity.

Preface

I HAD ANOTHER PHYSICS TEST IN the morning and a chemistry practical report was due the day after. But I was reasonably confident I had it all under control. My work desk was strewn with papers, and on my right, a pile of loose-leaf folders. I set about getting the paperwork in better order, the day's lecture notes duly filed for future reference.

It'd been a particularly busy day. But now relaxing before bed, I asked myself what had my day been like twelve years earlier.

Mud, mud, mud, out across the paddock stretched the green of a half-grown wheat while under foot, water and the red-brown mud. I'd taken off my boots and socks, rolled the trousers to my knees, and with long-handled shovel over the shoulder set out to see what the water had been doing overnight. During the hours of darkness, the outlet from the irrigation channel had been reduced to a trickle. But with even this simple precaution, problems were bound to have developed. For water, once let loose, has a mind of its own.

In this part of the world, long handled shovels were affectionately called *banjos*. This was the Riverina District of south western New South Wales, and after a relatively dry winter with no spring rain in sight, the irrigation farmers were out busily playing the water game with their banjos. My task, and that of John Spencer (Old Dunaway Station's foreman), was to rescue a wheat crop from the pending drought.

Many millions of years ago, this part of Australia had been covered by shallow sea. Now, some hundreds of miles from the coast, the region had retained a sea bed quality, a stark flatness crisscrossed by winding rivers with occasional sandy rises—the remnants of ancient sand dunes. The wheat crop, covering about 200 acres, had been sown on a section of slightly rising ground where the soil was somewhat sandier than the heavy black or reddish clays more typical of the region.

The decision to irrigate had resulted a rushed job. An existing irrigation channel had been extended using a tractor towing a channelling machine, a sort of plough with blade-like wings that formed the banks. Then the cropping area had been surveyed, and temporary check banks installed using a tractor and a small deep furrowing plough. The aim of check banks was to force the irrigation water to spread out, thereby achieving the maximum ground coverage. But making all this work meant hours of toil in mud and water from dawn to dusk. The new irrigation channel had to be opened in strategic places with outlets dug by hand. But it was the check bank that required constant attention, for these were not compacted, the water forever breaking through the loose soil. This resulted in a non-stop battle for control, the endless patrolling backwards and forwards along the furrows left by the plough, shovelling, and blocking the leaks as they appeared.

Once the water held within an irrigated bay had been spread out as much as possible, breaches would be opened in the check banks and so, the process repeated for the next irrigation bay, one at a slightly lower elevation.

It was 1961, I was 19 years old and this was my life. An existence of long hours, low pay and basic living conditions. I could look back at the road I'd come and see the twists and turns that'd brought me to this place, this wheat crop desperate for a drink. But trying to look into the future, I came to the conclusion that from now on, it would be hard manual labour and nothing much could change. This would be my life, a thought that left me depressed and deeply angry. Yet there seemed nothing that could be done. Fate had decreed it so. All this stemmed from being sort of intelligent but not in any way academic, or at least that's what I'd been led to believe. But how wrong all that turned out to be.

Chapter 1

In the Beginning

I WAS BORN IN ENGLAND HALFWAY through the Second World War. My arrival was beset by problems both for myself and my mother, but this had nothing to do with the turmoil of a world tearing itself to pieces. During the birth, my 22-year-old mother was haemorrhaging to the extent of putting us both at risk. It was also found after the delivery, that I had some sort of internal bleeding and was given vitamin K.

But equally, if not more serious, I had ABO hemolytic disease, something specific to first born children. This comes about when the father has AB blood type and the mother O. The mother's antibodies cross the placental barrier to attack the baby's blood cells. As a result, I was anaemic on arrival, seriously jaundiced, given a 50 percent chance of survival and baptised on that first night. But following the practice of the times, I was whisked away from my mum and not reunited until after the immediate crisis had passed. Of course, I only came to learn of this much later, but guess I must have come down on the right side of the ledger.

My earliest recollections stem from a time I got a splitter in my hand. There was this solid looking wooden garden seat and off I went, running across the lawn all set for a bit of a clamber, but then disaster. For some reason, the splitter wasn't really hurting, having barely penetrated the skin, but it looked large and truly terrifying. My mother, Molly, dad, Norman, younger sister, Gill, and the family dog, Kinder, were there in the garden. I rushed back to my parents, made a fuss, had the splitter removed and was then rewarded with a piece of chocolate, a rare treat in war-time Britain. But amid the fuss, Gill in her bassinet, started to cry and mum picked her up. This left me resentful that the attention I'd been getting was being directed elsewhere.

But unperturbed I threw my arms around the neck of Kinder, a black Labrador who towered over me. He showed his appreciation with a wide doggy smile. At this I put my mouth to his smooth black fur even though I knew that kissing the dog was really not allowed. Meanwhile, my parents had started talking about a large rosebush that was flowering profusely after an earlier pruning. I glanced at it briefly, noting the pinkish white flowers against a grey sky. But all this suggests earlier Autumn, in which case I would have been little more than two years old.

Soon after this, we moved to a larger two storey house. I have only a few memories of that place. These include the departure of Kinder on his final journey to the vet's, the appearance of my second sister, Hilary, and VE day which marked the end of the conflict in Europe.

Kinder was my father's dog and named after Kinder Scout, a high moorland plateau in the Peak District. In the years before dad met my mother, man and dog had roamed the rugged hills and valleys of northern England during holidays. My father had a difficult complex personality and before he met Molly, I suspect Kinder was his only enduring friend.

But Kinder had become old, was not well and the lease on the newly rented house didn't allow for pets. I remember overhearing a terse exchange between my parents in the kitchen as to what should be done. My mother was a level-headed rational person with considerable diplomatic skills, but I could sense the tension even though I didn't understand what was being said. Later that evening, I watched from my bedroom window as mum took Kinder for his final walk. In the morning, I was told the dog had died but was spared the details.

My sister Hilary arrived a few months later in the spring. I'd noticed my mum's expanding condition and it had been explained - yes there was a real live baby in there. What's more, I'd been started off in the same way, though the details as to how I got out wasn't entirely clear. Then one night, mum was off to hospital in a brown taxi and returned a few days later with this dark-haired little girl. I was glad mum was back but otherwise no big deal. Both me and my sister Gill are fairly close in ages and there was sibling rivalry that was to last for years. But by that stage, I'd got used to the idea that my parents' love and attention needed to be shared around, though I'd hoped for a brother.

At that time, I had no direct experience of the war and I didn't even know what the word *war* meant. But on hearing that the war was over (at the time not entirely true) I was puzzled by all the fuss. On that day a neighbour, Mrs Conn, arrived and she and mum were almost dancing around the kitchen at the news: 'The war is over, the war is over!' But then, with cups of tea in hand, Mrs Conn became teary eyed on recalling a friend and an uncle, neither of whom had survived to see this day. Then mum made some sort of reference to more distant enemies, *the others,* as she called them, and the mood in the kitchen became even more sombre. Later, dad arrived home with the exiting news of people dancing in the streets, but I still didn't understand other than it'd been a sort of great day at least for some.

There was a railway cutting not far from where we lived. I remember standing on the top of the cutting with other little boys spotting the steam trains far off in the distance coming down the line towards us. Though the trains passed some twenty yards away, the line running along the bottom of the cutting, I always made sure I was safely on the right side of the wire fence.

We must have lived in that house for about a year. The only memory of our departure was of the house being cleared of furniture, strange men taking things away and mum doing a last minute clean-up of the fire place. There was tension in the air and when I asked where we were going to live, I was told, 'Moving to granddad and grandma's house.' Later, I learned that my parents had some sort of dispute with the landlord. The rent was going up and the move was a stop-gap measure.

My grandfather Fred (mum's father) and my dad Norman never got on. The only memory I have of the time we all spent under the one roof was the two having a blazing row. What it was about I've no idea, only that we didn't seem to stay there very long. The next move was to a place with the odd name of Weston under Wetherley.

Chapter 2

Family Roots

FEW, IF ANY OF US, arrive in this world by immaculate conception. This means we not only inherit a set of hopefully marvellous genes but also a family culture. It's not just the life experiences and attitudes of our parents that matter, but also the collective endeavours, triumphs and tribulations of generations stretching back through time. Those long gone still speak to us in the present in subtle ways.

My dad Norman was born in 1908 into a military family and would have likely taken up a career in the army but for contracting polio at age 16. This left him with damage to both legs. His left knee was most affected and he was destined to walk with a stick for the greater part of his life.

Both my father's parents had died before I was born, as had several uncles and aunts. Norman had very little to say about those that had been closest to him during his formative years. Much of what I now know results from the research done by my sister Gill, who has taken on the role of family historian.

Dad's father, William, a professional soldier, had as a younger man served on India's north-west frontier. He'd retired from the army in 1914. But a few months later, with the outbreak of world war, went back and saw action as a non-commissioned officer for about five months on the western front. He then spent the rest of the war as an artillery officer, training gunners for the front. His loyalty to king and country seems beyond question.

William had married Alice, and Norman was their only child. Alice came from a large family. But on the relatively rare occasions my father did say anything of his parents, his comments tended to shed little real light.

Gill's research suggests that a significant part of Norman's childhood was spent with his mother. William was away in Africa between 1911-1912 and then at war from 1915 to 1919. A postcard sent by William for Africa and addressed to Norman reads in part –

> *A merry Christmas to you and dear Mamma.*
> *Your loving Dad*
> *W. N. Crawford*

But it seems the son wasn't happy when his father was home and taking over the reins of running the household. The man, who among other things, demanded to know where his son had been and what he'd been doing. As a result, Norman would often make up stories.

Norman seems to have been close to his grandmother, Louie, and his mother's youngest sister, Amy, who was 12 years his senior. There is a photo taken on Brighton Beach before the war of Louie, Amy and Norman, and as a five-year-old he looks very happy. Later, he was there when Amy married a wounded New Zealand soldier. The man was a supposed sheep farmer and Amy thought she was going to a farm in New Zealand. But in fact, she ended up in a shepherd's hut in the back of beyond, effectively cut off from her family. Her children and grandchildren were not to know anything of their English relatives until very recently.

But for Norman, polio at sixteen was a devastating blow, for at the time it was considered a dirty disease, akin to syphilis. Not something someone from a self-respecting household would suffer even though the cause and mode of transition were at the time a complete mystery. Norman said his father was upright, physically fit and very disparaging about his son's weak invalid status. This would explain that when Norman passed the age of 70, he considered it quite an achievement for he'd outlived his father in terms of years.

When Norman was 22, his mother Alice died of cancer - "missed but not mourned" was how he later describe the event.

After this, father and son shared a house but not their lives. They might not see each other for a week, yet they moved together from London to Bournemouth in 1938. William died in November the following year.

Looking at an old photo of my father taken when he was about seven, I sense a shy child. A kid who would try to avoid the teacher's eye in class, but be as far as possible from the rowdies and bullies at the back of the room. I know that he had bad memories of high school, and wished ill of the place. But years later during the war, it came as a strange surprise to discover the hated buildings had been demolished by a stick of German bombs.

Part of this could have stemmed from Norman being naturally left-handed. This was not acceptable in those years, so he was forced to use his right hand for writing. Furthermore, it wouldn't have helped when he broke his left arm which seemed to have been badly set. Another issue was the year spent in hospital with polio. This interfered with his education and he left school without matriculating.

However, in his boyhood, the time spent with the scouting movement had been a real positive. He used to talk about running down Webbs Alley and of the Hole-in-the-Wall. When I was told this story I'd no idea where these places were, but by an odd twist of fate, I was to get to know them quite well. But it would seem my father had spent summer camping trips with the scouts in the area around Sevenoaks and the nearby Knole Park.

But despite what seems to have been a troubled boyhood, Norman was left with romantic notions about earlier generations of the Crawfords. He would have been about four when his grandfather James died and could barely remember him. But James joined the army as a private, survived the Crimean War to rise through the ranks as an NCO, becoming Regimental Sergeant Major.

But other family stories Norman passed on to his children are not supported by subsequent research. More recent evidence suggests humble labourers or small business people who were able to take advantage of the 19th century and rise securely into the middle class. But with this came pretensions and raised class consciousness. My father's middle name was Frank, but he seems never to have been told that the Frances Crawford, after whom he was named, was a Scots-Irishman who worked in Edinburgh as a sawyer.

Norman, on leaving school, became a cash accountant, a pen pusher, a man who could add up a column of numbers with great speed and accuracy before the computer age. A skill learnt during the Great Depression that served him well in the years that followed. Though never a chartered accountant his work seems to have been more than keeping simple records of figures and paying wages.

At one stage, Norman worked for the Ministry of Supply, doing the audits of factories. He would tell the tale of a factory making pickles and sauces and of them tipping rotten fruit and vegetables into the mix which was why we, as kids, never had bottled sauces at home. The expression – *tomato sauce dead horse* - was something I was only to hear later in life but would seem to have some sort of historical resonance. My father also had an aversion to commercially produced meat pies, but it was never clear if this was the result of insider information or just the thought of what might have been.

Norman's disability kept him from active service during World War II, but even as a civilian, the war was not without its dangers. Soon after the outbreak, he and his dog, Kinda, had been using a footpath only to discover that the area had been turned into a recently laid mind field. A group of solders watched him and the dog's progress with bated breath.

'Hoy you, that were a mine field you just walked across.'

'Just following the foot path.'

'Really, what foot path?'

All part of the general chaos off that time.

On more normal days at this time, Norman was involved in the auditing work for the government, looking at companies supplying goods and services. Apart from the paperwork, he was also involved in serving court summonses, the papers having to be served in person. But being a harmless looking guy with a walking stick he was often able to get up close and personal, cornering the accused before they had a chance to bolt for the back door.

It was while engaged in this government work, he was involved in a serious incident at Hatfield north of London and he makes a reference to this when writing to Molly the following day. From other sources, I know it was 3 October 1940, a day of low clouds. A lone German bomber that seems to have lost its way, emerged from the clouds and flew over a flight training school. Years later, my dad described how bombs were dropped, but due to the low altitude they flat-bounced off the roadway before crashing through the roof of a nearby building and exploding. The aircraft then turned around and strafed the area with machine gun fire. Twenty-one people were killed but my father emerged unscathed.

Dad, in a good mood, would sometimes jokingly refer to himself as *Norm the Storm*. I gather this was a nickname that'd sometimes been applied to him at work, an apt title seeing he could be as changeable as the weather. He had a great sense of humour, a sharp witty observer of life. But when something or someone upset him, as happened fairly frequently, his thunder (like his laugh) was typically loud. However, despite having an excellent command of English, coupled with a very short fuse, I never once heard him using seriously bad language.

His views on many things tended to be strongly held, either for or against, and this often extended to meeting people for the first time. During the years after the war he seemed forever changing jobs. Sometimes, he would come home with tales of what a good team of people he was working with, but then a few weeks later something would set him off and he'd be looking for his next position. Despite his undoubted intelligence, he never progressed much above base grade. Though later, he seems to have mellowed to the extent that he was able to hold down a job for more than a few months.

One of his greatest fears was some sort of fall that would aggravate his already weakened knees and so render him unable to work. Over the years, he'd developed a technique of being able to fall without serious injury. On a couple of occasions, I witnessed such falls where he stayed loose and roll-cushioned the impact. No easy feat for he was a big man but this remained a constant source of worry.

He engendered a strong sense of family loyalty, loved my mother dearly, but when things were tough it was always the kids that came first, food and clothing top priority. This meant going around with holes in the soles of his shoes at times and walking an extra mile being unable to afford the four-pence-a-day bus fares.

In those early years there was no issues with alcohol; my parents drank on rare occasions. At one time, I was allowed my first sip of stout and didn't like it. A similar outcome when I tried my first wine. Later in life, my father's drinking started to become something of an issue, but that was not to be for many years into the future.

When me and my two sisters were small, dad would often play with us. But later, with the addition of a further two boys to the family, much of that activity ceased, though he still played cards and monopoly.

At times, he could he quite charming, but at others, strangely shy and socially awkward. On other occasions, he would thoroughly irritate my mother with some thoughtless remark. But when she would make her feelings known, he would quickly back down with child-like apologies.

But where did the eccentric *Norm the Storm* come from? The people who may have been able to shed real light on that question seemed to be no longer around. But did his encounter with the polio virus at 16 do more than leave him with damaged legs? Certainly, polio changed his life forever, could only have deepened a seemingly fractious relationship with his parents, or at least his father. Later, having started a family, here was a man who seemed to have severed his ties with the past or at least wasn't prepared to talk about them to his children. But more than half a century later, the strange story of Uncle Harry (his father's younger brother) came to light. I'd been told that Harry had died before the war in 1938. In fact, Uncle Harry and his wife, Millicent, had survived into the post-war era and had lived in London. Furthermore, Norman had stayed with them when he needed a base in the city. Harry died in 1951 and Norman was there at his funeral. After that event, Aunty Millicent wanted Norman's help sorting out her affairs, but he refused to have anything more to do with her. But apart from that, I can't help wonder if she knew that Norman had by that stage a wife and four kids living in Warwickshire. At the time I, the eldest, would've been nine-years-old.

But there had been two encounters during this period with Alice's side of the family. As a small baby, I'd been taken to see Norman's grandmother, Louise. Then on another occasion, Molly took myself, Gill and Hilary to meet two of Norman's aunts from that side of the family. I remember Hilary being in a push chair, the autumn leaves heavy on the ground. They said it was a pity that Will was no longer around to see his grandchildren. At the time, I didn't even know I had a deceased grandfather called William.

My mother, Molly, came from a line of mostly small business people and farmers with just a smattering of landed gentry. But unlike Norman, her life and family background had always been something of an open book.

A story that has been passed down is that of her grandfather George who seems to have been a bit of a wild lad in his day. He started out by joining the Royal Navy only to abscond. Later, he was on a sailing ship trading around the Black Sea.

The story goes that they were in port somewhere with the captain ashore, wining and dining with the local mayor, business people and other dignitaries. However, in the early hours, the ship's crew, who'd been half-starved and generally badly treated, set about rounding up as many of the town's chickens as they could lay hands on. But to cover their crime, all the feathers were wrapped in the ship's sails.

Then came the time to leave. All the captain's newfound friends were there lining the dock with cries of *please come again* and they even had a band playing. The ship cast off, the sails were unfurled and so departed amid a great cloud of chicken feathers.

Later, George was a foreman shipwright who was sent, with other foremen by the very prestigious firm, Armstrongs on the Tyne, to Pozzuoli in Italy to train Italians in a newly built shipyard. He then managed a ship repair shop before becoming the publican of a large pub. He was also a prominent figure in the local masons.

George had two sons and paid for a premium apprenticeship for both of them. Fred trained in ship engineering design and at the age of 25, was appointed joint-chief draughtsman for Smiths Docks in Middlesbrough, said at the time to be the largest firm of dry dock owners and ship repairers in the world. In those days, there was no applying for such a job, no interviews; these posts were by appointment only, and Fred had shown his abilities by winning a prize during his apprenticeship.

In World War I, Fred was sent by the Ministry of Shipping to Canada as an advisor on the building of cargo ships. Between the wars, he designed the engines for the Arctic explorer William Scoresby launched in 1925. In World War II, Fred worked for the Ministry of Shipping again, later to become part of the Ministry of War Transport in a department responsible for merchant ship repairs. He was also involved in the mulberry harbour D-day project. Merchant ships deemed beyond repair were sent over to be used along with the concrete blocks to form a temporary harbour on the Normandy landing beaches. This operation was under the auspices of Vice Admiral Ramsey.

After the war, Fred helped supervise the conversion of an old schooner into the whaler 'Pequod' as used for the Disney film, *Moby Dick*. Moving on, Fred became the manager of a ship repair yard in Hull - repairing trawlers.

But there were other major issues in my grandfather's life, one of which profoundly affected his children. My mother was 14 months old when her own mother, Lydia, died of pneumonia. My grandmother was only 32, but in the preceding years had lost a sister aged eight and then another sister and a brother to tuberculosis. Lydia was the last sibling in her family and such was the world before modern antibiotics.

With Lydia's death, Fred being the practical hardnosed business man he always was, wrote to an ex-girlfriend, Dot, explaining that his wife had died and would she like to become the mother of his four young children. He added almost as an afterthought, 'I'll make it legal and marry you.' His marriage proposal survives to this day and Dot, a trained nurse and much to her great credit, took up the offer. An action that probably saved my mother's life. During the crisis, little Freda, as she was then called, had been placed in the care of a cousin, and grieving over the loss of her own mother, was in a bad way. The cousin is reported to have said, when handing the child over to Dot, 'You won't raise this one.' However, my mother was destined to give birth to five children, outlive all her siblings and die at the age of 98.

When growing up, Molly must have become something of a diplomatic bridge in a divided household. Skills that would later serve her well while living with Norman and raising her own family. As a child, Molly formed a very good relationship with Dot and half-brother, Tom, while being close with two of her three older brothers, Jack and George. The older brothers never got on well with their step-mother. This doesn't seem to have been helped by Fred and Dot refusing the kids permission to talk about Lydia at home and destroying all photos in which she was depicted. Three photographs did survive, but only because the oldest boy, Jack, kept them hidden. A divided household, Dot may have been ably assisted by her mother-in-law, who'd moved in after Lydia's death. Molly used to tell the story of young Jack being pinned behind a kitchen door by a frustrated grandmother who cried, 'You little devilskin!' But she couldn't recall what devilry had prompted this particular confrontation.

The only one Molly found a problem was with her brother Norman (not to be confused with my father). When I was growing up, she never gave even a hint of this, only speaking of it towards the very end of her life when all else was failing.

Molly's experiences at school seem to have been positive. Her high school, Boulevard Municipal, was once attended by the famous aviator Amy Johnson, who'd been there about a decade earlier. Amy once revisited the school and Molly described how she and the rest of the girls lined the stairs while the honoured visitor climbed the steps. Amy was then shown into the hall where she addressed the boys assembly on matters of aviation. Some of the lads may have gone on to be spitfire pilots, but it says much about the attitude to girls education at the time.

Fred never seems to have had good relationships with any of his own children, though when I went to stay with him and Dot one school holiday, I remember a positive experience. But five years before I was born, there had been a bad falling out between Molly and her father. Finishing school, Molly was offered a scholarship at Reading University, but Fred didn't believe in women with degrees and flatly refused to give his consent. The only consolation was that he would fund her through teaching college and after that she would be on her own. Molly was never to forgive him, though there was a complicating issue in that Fred was by that stage out of work, a consequence of the depression. He was living on his savings, but Molly always maintained that her scholarship would have covered most of the costs.

Later Fred was opposed to her marriage, but as Molly was about to turn 21, he finally acquiesced. Molly and Norman were to remain married until Norman's death 49 years later.

One of the things that my parents had in common was favouring the left side of politics, but regarded anyone calling themselves socialist with suspicion. Yet, go back a generation and there on both sides was rock-solid right-wing conservatism. As a lad, Norman had, with parental approval, joined the young conservatives.

What changed my parents around was the 1930s Depression. But this difference in political outlook was just one of many points of difference between Norman and his father-in-law. My dad would sometimes claim Fred's successes were down to luck. But despite serious setbacks and shortcomings, Fred had largely made his own way, made his own luck whereas Norman saw himself as being more a victim. He would sometimes tell the story of how he was once sacked because the boss objected to the sound of his walking stick on the floor as he went past. But about this time, Fred was also sacked. It seemed my grandfather had applied for a senior position, but the company board had thought differently. Fred had promptly protested and as a result, lost his job. Fred then faced greatly diminishing job prospects in the shipping industry which was in deep trouble and didn't fully recover until the next war. Norman seemed to have continued to muddle through, but always somewhere near the bottom of the heap.

One of my father's other 1930s stories is of a firm he once worked for in which business activity was seasonal. During up turns, they would take on new staff but as activity decreased, staff would be laid off. The method of sacking was to slip notes into the intended pay packets on a Friday, saying the recipients needn't turn up the following Monday. Nobody knew from week to week who was going to get the chop, the atmosphere come pay-time thick with apprehension. Being out of work might mean trying to live off the dole, or, at worse, out on the street. But for the lucky ones, the lottery had been won, but in another week it all started again.

Sometimes, my father would talk about *the big boys*. The powerful people who sat at the top of the tree, those that dictated to the ordinary folks below. With stories like these, it's not hard to see where such simplistic ideas came from. Winston Churchill was, at war's end, seen as something of a national hero but my father never had a good word for him. Churchill was, it seemed, one of the big boys.

Molly would have been too young to have experience the full force of the depression, but her older brothers were not so fortunate. I think my mother's left leaning politics grew out of her strong conviction towards social justice and inequality. This is not to say that can't come out of the conservative side of politics, but the 1930s had starkly exposed the fault lines of British society. When times are bad, it is the poor who almost always suffer the most.

The late 1940s was another very political period, a time when I was starting to become aware of the world. During the war, the British people had stood as one against the common enemy. But the minute victory had been declared in Europe, the underlying differences came to the fore. The fact that the country was in an utter mess didn't seem to matter - the gloves were off.

This is illustrated by one of my father's other stories in which an electrician was called to a house that'd lost all power. The man asked how this had come about only to be told that the householders had been so incensed by the election of the new Labour government, they'd turned on every light and appliance they could find. The electrician promptly told them to *go to hell* and walked away.

Chapter 3

Weston under Wetherley

THE WARWICKSHIRE VILLAGE OF WESTON under Wetherley was strung out along a road that led away from the narrow flood plains of the Leam River. The name translates from the Anglo-Saxon as something like *below the western sheep flats*, but most locals referred to the place as *Weston*. My family lived there on the southern edge of the village for over five years, but I look back on this period with very mixed feelings.

Molly was an eminently sensible woman, though during the early years at Weston, she found me particularly difficult to manage. A little boy who was always into mischief, pulling the arms off my sister's doll's, crash-banging toy cars or playing with matches behind the outside toilet. If it wasn't that, I was teasing my sister Gill. But it was mum who first sparked my interest in science. Among other things, helping identify some of the local birds. She marvelled with me at the tiny fairy shrimps caught one day in a field drainage ditch. As a four-year-old, I saw something moving in the water, but not knowing what it was went home and got a glass jar. I then showed my mum the catch. Though my mother never acknowledged the extent of my dyslexic condition, as it later started to emerge, she played a critical role in steering my developing interests.

Soon after arriving at Weston, I met my first German. By this stage, I'd sort of worked out what the war had been all about. I remember my mother's shock at the news of the Nazi concentration camps, but was spared the details. And later, I'd looked out the bus window at the bomb sites of Coventry. The piled acres of rubble, the shattered walls and the crumbling cellars blasted open to the sky. But by that stage, weeds and brambles had started to creep across the carnage. However, the war itself was like a drama that everyone knew about, spoke about but I'd somehow missed.

But one day, mum was chatting with a girl from a nearby farm. Also present was a young red-haired man who spoke with an odd accent. Molly was asking how he was and of his plans for the future. The man had been a German prisoner of war who'd worked on the farm as a volunteer, but with the end of hostilities had become a valued employee. On that particular day, he'd gotten good news: the Red Cross had located his older sister in Germany. She was living in a garage with her kids, the family home having been destroyed. But I was surprised to discover that this German was a real live human being and at my mother's totally relaxed friendly attitude. She explained afterwards that most Germans were hard-working decent folk and only a few were really bad. I was left confused. What had this war thing been all about?

Another memory I have was being given daily doses of orange juice concentrate and cod liver oil and the screw top cough mixure bottles they used to come in. This was a government run scheme, the aim of which was to lift the general health of the nation's young children by boosting vitamin C and D levels. So, in a time when rationing was still being enforced, bottles of this stuff were issued to all mothers with young children. I never liked the fish oil, but this had to be swallowed first, followed by the orange reward to take away the bad taste.

The rituals of Christmas and birthdays were closely adhered to in the household. Christmas meant decorations and socks hung on the end of beds in which sweats, fruit and little toys would magically appear. Then there was always a tree with wrapped presents. There was also cake, jellies and mince pies. But cakes with icing sugar would always attract the attention of the mystery mouse who could be relied on to nibble at the edges when no one was looking. Who was the chief among the mice? I've no idea, but I suspect it was more often than not someone who looked remarkably like me. My mysterious double who only appeared when icing sugar and cake were on offer.

But on the relatively rare occasions when ice cream was brought home, the three little house mice made short work of it, for we had no refrigerator. The nearest thing to a fridge was a cold shelf in the pantry room. The shelf was a concrete slab with a little mesh-covered window behind which opened to the outside. There was probably more to it than I remember, for the idea was to draw air up from the ground outside and ventilate it out again via some sort of flue.

Happy games played with my sisters included them sitting in a tea service trolley that I'd push around the house. At other times, we would play trains, three or four chairs would be lined up. With me, the engine driver, sitting in the leading chair. Gill as the train conductor would sit behind, and after her would come Hilary as the only real passenger. Then with all the usual train sound effects, off we'd go, at least in our imaginations.

When we were a little older, social activities included card games like *Happy Families* and *Snap*. Then there were the wind-up toys that could be sent whizzing across the floor and toy soldiers made of brightly painted lead. At about age seven, I was given a meccano set, the basis of which were metal strips with holes which allowed them to be bolted together with nuts and bolts. A tiny spanner was supplied, but the more intricate bits, like cogs and wheels, were generally lacking. Then there was the train set, a working model of the Flying Scotsman. This used to speed around on a circular electrified track until one day it stopped never to go again. I guess the motor had burnt out but was never fixed. However, it stayed with the family for many years but was eventually given away to someone with a collector's eye.

During this period, we had visits from my mother's older brothers, George and Norman, plus their families. I remember my cousin, Rodger, who was a year younger than me as being particularly lively company. On at least one occasion, my grandmother Dot from Hull came, though Fred stayed away.

When I was seven, my brother Jonathan was born. I was excited on hearing the news. But having forgotten what new born babies were like, I imagined here would be someone to play with on the first day home. Play there certainly was, but a bit of patience and growing time was needed first.

We also went back to see our grandparents in Hull, but only mum came, while the train journeys there and back turned out to be the most exciting part of such trips. In those days, all trains were steaming monsters, much more exciting than the boring types that came later. Steam trains have a distinctive smell, a hard to describe watery chemical smell that was almost pleasant in a mildly pungent way.

The village of Weston had an imposing church made of red stone, but when we were there, there were no shops, not even a pub. The nearest main shopping centre was the town of Leamington Spa which we, as a family, visited quite frequently. Such excursions were always by bus, something to which I always looked forward. But Gill, who was by far the most gregarious of the family, would often get chatting with a stranger, while me, I'd be mostly looking out the window.

A small mystery for me at this time concerned the driving of buses. Typically, there would be a windowed partition between the driver and passengers. I would often sit up behind the driver and watch how it was done. I worked out the function of the steering wheel, brake pedal and the gear stick, but the clutch pedal was a complete mystery. When I asked my father, he didn't know either and the mystery was to remain until years later when I learnt to drive.

One day while sitting on a park bench in Leamington, I overheard two old ladies. They had posh accents and were talking about the good old days of the eighties and nineties, that is the 1880s and 1890s. 'You can't get the servants these days,' they were saying. 'When you do they expect to be paid a fortune but are no jolly good.' I guess things really were different in those days.

But the Leamington of my childhood had other interests for me. This was a place where ice cream was on sale. Apart from that, a place with real shops that sold all sorts of things, everything from cakes to toy soldiers, and by saving the threepence a week pocket money, all manner of goodies could be obtained. Saving money and then spending up big was something I was quite good at, a pattern that was to be repeated during other times in my life.

Weston's local church, St Michaels, was attended once a week. Our mum always took us kids. Apart from the singing, I found the church services rather boring.

Dad never ever expressed an interest in anything to do with religion. This seems another example of Norman trying to shut out anything to do with his childhood. On the other hand, he never said a word against the church, nor did he claim to be an atheist. Many decades later nearing the end of his life, he asked that his remains be cremated with neither ceremony or memorials. His wishes were complied with but after his death in 1990, I formed the view that funerals are far more about the needs of the living than the dead. People attend funerals to ostensibly say goodbye to the deceased.

At Weston, the house was a single storey brick with a front feature of pseudo-Tudor dark wood and white plaster. This along with the bay windows made the house quite attractive when viewed from the front. But I remember the wall around the back door, bulging outwards in rather an alarming fashion. The wall never collapsed while we were there, though the back of the house in general was rather shabby.

There were three bedrooms, a lounge room, kitchen, scullery and entrance hallway. Out the front, there was an almost non-existent garden - a rockery and then a wide gravelly verge leading up to the sealed roadway and a sharp S bend that led down into the village. On the other side of the house, the kitchen window opened directly out onto a field and on a couple of occasions, a cow almost put its head through the open window. A side-back door opened into a long narrow garden bounded by hedges that ran parallel to the road. Here in the garden was the outside toilet and a water pump. Though the house had electricity, it was dependent on bore water that had to be pumped by hand into a large storage tank set below the roof in the scullery. Pumping water was my father's job, though on the few occasions as a small child, I tried, only to discover it really hard work.

The outside toilet had a small storeroom attachment but there was no electric light. Night time visits were made using a torch and in the depths of winter could be an ordeal. At the far end of the garden, past the veggie patch, was an old corrugated iron garage set on a concrete slab, but as we never owned a car this became our junk and forget it shed. It was in the garage at aged four that I encountered the *Snazzer*, a one legged monster with long curved neck that on less imaginative occasions looked surprisingly like one of my dad's old walking sticks.

After arriving at Weston in late spring, it wasn't long before I was exploring the local fields and hedge rows, sometimes accompanied by one or more of my sisters but generally, I much preferred to be on my own. The country was gently rolling farm land, a mix of dairy and cropping with a criss-cross of hedges and some patches of woodland.

This should have been a totally safe environment for kids, but as I discovered during my second winter, this wasn't always the case. There had been particularly severe overnight frost. I, with an urge to wander, left the comforts of home, and, rugged up against the cold, set out to explore the wonders of the frozen countryside. But on this day not only was the grass covered with crunchy frost, but the whiteness extended up into the leaves of the hedges making the spider webs stand out as never before.

Having crossed a field, I was able to clamber through a farm gate before following a hedge line up the gently sloping ground to a pond. But here was the day's real wonder for the pond was frozen over. The pond had a retaining bank at one end and at the other, a cluster of overhanging beech trees. Caught up by the exciting novelty of the moment, I stepped off across the ice, gaining an entirely new perspective. Then I decided to set out for the far bank, only to be brought to an abrupt halt by a cracking sound. I took one more step and the sound came again. The ice under the overhanging trees was much thinner. I now noticed it was a different colour, and the vibrations I was setting up while walking was making the ice crack along the water's edge. I knew how painfully cold water was when overlaid by ice, having earlier explored a few frozen puddles. I had visions of falling through, of being immersed in bitterly cold water, and suddenly, the day wasn't fun anymore. Frightened, I turned around and started to retrace my steps. Only then did I notice the patches of ice-free water around several clumps of reeds. How had I not noticed these before? With thankful steps I reached my starting point, a place where the cows came down to drink.

Though in subsequent winters the pond froze over, I never again ventured out onto the ice. But there was one further twist in the story. One summer afternoon, Hilary went missing. She was about two-and-a-half, but this was quite uncharacteristic for she seemed to have no inclination to go off on her own. A frantic search got underway and I remember wandering across the field adjacent to the house calling her name. I looked across towards the pond but thought she would surely not have gone that far. We had sometimes gone on walks, but I didn't think she'd ever been there. Half an hour later, to our parents' huge relief, Hilary was sighted walking across the field towards the house, but she'd lost her shoes. We were unable to discover where she'd been, but some two years later, I discovered a small pair of children's shoes in the water at the edge of the pond.

Winter snow that might lie for a day or two occurred most years. Snow was always a great novelty for it meant snow ball fights with dad and my sisters. Then there was the fun of making a snowman. These would be started by rolling a small snowball across the ground picking up more snow as it went. By the time the ball was two feet across, it would be tipped on its side to form the body of the snowman. Then a smaller ball of snow would form the head. Further innovations, such as buttons and a carrot, would give the man a face. A hat and scarf might also be added. But once the thaw set in, the snowman would linger, the last to melt away.

In the winter of 1948, there was a very heavy dump of snow across Britain. For us at Weston this meant snow drifts, some as high as the hedge rows. The local bus got stuck outside our house and the driver and passengers were invited in to be given cups of tea. All these strange people invading the place and I remember the bus driver, a solidly built man with balding head, using our phone to ring his depot for help. A couple of hours later, a tow truck arrived and our visitors departed.

Next day, the worst of the storm had passed and dad went out the front and did his best to clear a path for the traffic. In those days, he claimed not to like cars or the people who drove them, having never learnt to drive himself. But buses were different, they needed to get through, for real folk travelled on buses.

During the summer, wasps were a problem. These were European Paper Wasps, as distinct from the other sorts that I was to encounter later in life. These were everywhere and into just about everything and us kids were forever being stung. Though after a while the stings didn't seem that bad, unlike the occasional bee sting which really were painful.

We never found the wasp nests, football sized structures often constructed underground. I remember hunting through the large blackberry bushes growing near the kitchen window but found nothing. Though looking back, I suspect the attic of our house might have been worth inspecting, the black and yellow striped enemy much closer to home than we realised. But we used to make wasp traps that were set up on the kitchen window sill. These were jam jars with traces of jam and partly filled with water. The wasp would fly into the jar, the top would be quickly put back, and the insect would end up in the water and drown.

As a family, we didn't seem to have a great deal to do with the neighbours. But for me, old Earnie Edwards, was the exception. Earnie was well into his eighties and had worked all his life for the Whiteheads, one of prominent farming families in the district. Earnie lived with his wife on the other side of the road in an old house about twenty yards from our door. The house had a thatched roof and no electricity supply. I only ever went inside on a couple of occasions, but even in the daylight, the cluttered interior was strangely dingy. Earnie spent a lot of time in his vegetable garden, on occasions scything down the long grass and nearly always seemed to be raising a pig or two. Furthermore, back at the house were legs of smoked ham, dangling from the rafters.

On one occasion, a large pig was slaughtered in the garden, shot with a bolt gun before being cut up for meat. I watched with morbid fascination. I'd never seen the insides of an animal. I wondered what all the bits were called and their function in life. Gill, who was also there, was quite upset, telling mum afterwards that Mr Edwards was doing terrible things to a piggy across the road.

On arriving in Weston there was talk of me attending school. I didn't know what that meant but wasn't sure I liked the sound of it. Through the summer, there was no further talk and I thought all had been forgotten. But come early September, school was suddenly back on the agenda.

What I didn't know at the time was that if I'd been born just three weeks later, I would have been on the other side of the cut-off line and school could have been up to a year away. Even today, I wonder what that extra year at home could have done for me. But for better or worse, I was launched into the school experience just a few weeks after my fourth birthday.

School was at semi-rural Cubbington, a bit over a mile away. On that first day with new school bag and shoes, I was taken by my mother on the bus and after that came a further walk from the bus stop. Unlike some of the kids, I wasn't overly distressed at being left there. I met my new teacher, mixed with the other kids and had quite a fun morning. At lunchtime, we were let out and had the playground to ourselves, but it was then I decided to be very naughty. The gate had been left open and I decided for no reason that I can remember to go home.

At that stage, I'd only travelled through Cubbington a few times on the bus, but in my mind the route was quite clear. An hour or so later out along the road, I remember looking down at my tired four-year-old legs thinking this was going to be more difficult than I'd thought. I was seriously contemplating dumping the school bag to lighten the load but then a red van pulled up and a man in some sort of uniform got out. He was a postal worker who asked if I would like a lift. So, I was given a ride the rest of the way home, but only then did I start thinking what would happen next. The man dropped me off near the garage, but there was a twist, for while I hid in the garden he went on to report my arrival to my mother. Damn!

Mum was sort of furious but also, I now realise, hugely relieved that her four-year-old had gotten home, when there was a potential to end up just about anywhere. That afternoon, I was taken back to

Cubbington where the staff at the school hadn't even realised I'd gone AWOL.

Next day I was back with mum, having promised never to skip school again, an undertaking I was to keep for the rest of my school days. But for my mother, there was a problem, for on taking me she'd to have someone minding my sisters. She wasn't entirely comfortable with this. So, after a couple of days, I was allowed to regularly catch the bus on my own. Though later, having become bigger, stronger and aware of my family's fiscal problems, I voluntarily started walking.

But at the very start of my school days, there was another far more serious problem. On day one, the place had seemed almost fun but come day two, the school had transformed into a truly threatening place for the older kids were back. Cubbington was a middle school that catered for children from four to fourteen. To a four-year-old, kids of thirteen and fourteen are like young adults, rowdy giants but without the cares and restrains I'd come to expect from big people. From then on, the classroom became something of a sanctuary whereas the playground, an asphalt jungle, for all the kids were mixed together. The situation was made ten times worse because there was usually no staff to be seen anywhere. Bullying was a major issue and it wasn't long before I was being targeted by some of the alpha males. I also witnessed my first playground fight. A pair of thirteen-year-olds lying into each other, fists flying with a ring of supporters standing around and chanting, 'Fight, fight, fight!' I'd never seen anything like it and only then did one of the teachers appear to break up the melee.

I quickly learned that it was safer to be around some of the older girls, and though physicality between them did occur, it was rare. Later still, I developed better strategies for staying clear of trouble.

I was to attend Cubbington Middle School for four years, though I never felt at ease in the playground. Looking back, I guess the older bullies I encountered had themselves been picked on as little kids, so the culture had proliferated year after year. In later life, I was to have a lot to do with schools but I have never known an institution having so little regard for the physical and mental wellbeing of its students as at Cubbington. I am sure there are kids, then as now, destined to grow up in far worse circumstances. But during the late 1940s, there was a management problem at Cubbington that could have been so easily rectified. Play times could have been separated, the younger kids from the bigger kids, with one or two staff outside on duty.

Chapter 4

The Day Dreamer Condemned

THE GIRLS AT CUBBINGTON SPENT a lot of time skipping in the playground. Of all the schools I attended as a kid I've never known rope skipping to be such a popular pastime. Typically, they would work in teams, two at either end of a long rope with another pair skipping in the middle. In the age long before mobile phones, the girls of my early childhood had a little song they used to sing as the skipping rope was spun around to a steady beat.

> *The wind, the wind, the wind blows free*
> *The wind comes scattering down the street.*
> *She is young and she is pretty*
> *She is the girl of the golden city*

At the age of about seven, I was briefly smitten by classroom love. There was this new girl ,Irene, nice face, lovely smile and long dark hair who captured my attention. One day the class was doing some modelling when an opportunity arose to express my genuine heartfelt interest. I got hold of some brown plasticine clay, shaped and presented it as a piece of chocolate to my intended. Irene took a bite, pulled a face and promptly spat it out, while I laughed loudly at the silly prank. A few days later after school, I was walking up the road to catch the bus and there was Irene. I gave her a smile and a nice hello, but she responded with a sour look before walking away. It seemed I'd a bit to learn when it came to issues of the heart. She didn't attend Cabbington the following term and alas, life moved on.

Later in the year, when walking home from school, I noticed a modern looking caravan half hidden from the road, pulled in behind a line of trees. Having not seen it before, I went a little closer to investigate. There was a boy about my age. He was startled at seeing me, seemed about to run, but then decided I wasn't such a threat after all and approached.

'Thought you were the green goblin,' he claimed, a distinct Irish accent.

'No,' I laughed, thinking this some joke.

'The green goblin is about,' the boy assured me, looking around. 'Comes and goes he do, but you've got to keep an eye out.'

I was puzzled, was this kid being serious? 'What does he look like?'

'Green,' the boy told me, 'sort of all green.'

'Never seen anyone like that.'

'Got to watch out 'cause he takes things.'

'Serious?'

'Aye, shoes, clothes off the line, anything.'

At that instant there was a gust of wind that sent the nearby tree tops shaking. At this the boy started off towards the caravan, but when he saw me standing my ground, he turned and called, 'Dragon, didn't you see the dragon?'

'No dragon,' I replied, an edge of mockery. 'Just the wind in the trees silly.' Imaginings I well understood, but this kid was blurring the lines between fantasy and the real world in ways I found unsettling.

Then the caravan door opened and a large woman with long dark hair appeared. She called the boy over before giving me a furious look. I returned to the road and resumed my walk home. The caravan wasn't there when I passed that way the following day.

On a couple of occasions, gypsy wagons like small decorated houses on wheels pulled by horses, had rolled past the house. These were curiosities, as were the people that drove them. Though there was no talk against ethnic minorities at home, occasionally it did crop up at school. In English society, gypsies and other so-called travellers were often regarded with suspicion and sometimes outright hostility. But on this occasion, the caravan looked to have been towed there by car. But there would come a time when I and my family were being labelled by some as gypsies, which to this day I find extraordinary.

Apart from the occasional gypsy there were the tramps. In fact, he may have been the same man who wandered past the house on two or three separate occasions. Middle-aged, dishevelled clothing, battered hat, a frightening figure to a small child. On one occasion, he went up to our front door and asked my mother for a drink of water. She obliged before sending him off with a couple of apples and a bit of bread and cheese. A small gesture of charity for which she was thanked, a quiet voice, an almost cultured accent. But perhaps I should have been asking how anyone could get into such a predicament in the first place.

Years later, on Old Dunaway Station, the homeless turned up one day at the main house only this time they were a trio and driving an old beaten up car. One claimed to be some sort of motor mechanic, or as he put it, a *doctor of motors*. 'Doctor of bullshit,' exclaimed Robert the boss. 'But give 'em some meat, milk and any bread you can spare. Better to feed the starving than have them knocking off sheep in the back paddocks.'

It was during the first year at Cubbington I had my first bout of middle ear infections. In the years that followed this was to land me in nearby Coventry Hospital for up to three weeks at a time. On that first occasion, I was really distressed at being left in this strange place even though my dad came to see me every day. But during subsequent stays, I got used to the routine. Many of the nurses were from southern Ireland and I still remember their distinctive way of talking.

My last stay in hospital resulted in a mastoid drainage operation. Looking back, I suspect a lingering infection in the spongy mastoid bone had been the primary source of the problem all along. When I was almost recovered, the surgeon on his rounds came to see me and I was given a special injection. The barrel of the hypodermic syringe was torpedo shaped and oddly metallic. I was told that this was very special and would ensure I'd never ever have ear troubles again. In truth, it may have been just a saline solution, but whatever, the magic really worked.

But apart from all that, once I and then Gill started to attend school, we were hit with what was considered in those days the usual range of childhood diseases, measles, mumps, chicken pox and whooping cough. Often, I would get what seemed a fairly mild dose of whatever, then pass it on to my sisters. With measles, I only had a few spots and my parents weren't sure until my sisters broke into rashes a few days later. I remember the pair of them sitting up in bed utterly miserable, poor things. As a very small child I'd been vaccinated against smallpox, I still carry the scare, but other such precautions were not available at that time.

Our parents had always been good at reading to us but I'm not sure when that started. Later in life as a parent myself, I started to look at books with my son soon after his first birthday, a time when it had become clear he was able to understand simple sentences and concepts.

But years earlier as a small child I came to appreciate *Winnie the Pooh, The Wind in the Willows* and Kipling's *Just so Stories*. But my favourite character was Beatrix Potter's Sly Todd, that disreputable country gent who ends up locked in battle with the working class, but equally roguish, Badger. Later, the stories broadened out to include ones I could read, but with difficulty. These included comics like *The Eagle* with Dan Dare, the pilot of the future. But my childhood world was also dominated by radio, but no TV, mobile phones or video games. The only thing that came close in visual entertainment were infrequent visits to the movies.

Often, I would retell these stories in my head, inserting my imagined self into the action. But at other times, making up new stories, adding fragments from elsewhere and then re-running them with different mixes and different endings. In other words, a day dreamer who, to avoid distraction of the house, combined this activity with strolling across the nearby fields. Kipling's, 'I am the cat who walks by himself and all places are alike to me', took on a special meaning. I was indeed walking by myself, wearing my Wellington boots and all places were alike to me. A sort of reflection on the real world from which I was sometimes trying to disassociate. By escaping this boring sameness, I was entering an imagined world full of exciting possibilities. But in doing so impaired my ability to seriously concentrate on day-to-day demands. This could induce a feeling of being half asleep which could linger for hours after the daydream session had ended. But the troubles from which I was increasingly trying to dissociate were not at home, but at school.

At age four I'd found the playground environment of Cubbington threatening. But I did have my friends, Mike, a small dark-haired boy who was being raised by his grandmother, and Daniel, a larger fair-haired kid.

Then for a while there was Peter, a new kid who'd arrived at the school and in my class. A lively intelligent red-haired boy who reminded me of my cousin Rodger. Out in the playground, he soon joined our trio. Unfortunately, he was only at the school for a term, but on his last day he and his older brother walked with me partway home. To this day, I still remember them standing at the side of the road waving goodbye for the last time.

But it was important to have friends, not only someone to play with but also to watch each other's backs when out in the playground. Kids in such situations need to be territorial, and knowing which areas to avoid is an important survival stratagem. But these territories were subject to change year by year as the older kids left and the younger ones arrived.

For me, the classroom was at first a good place. There was storytelling, letters and numbers learning, and fun things within a structured environment. I learnt to chant my numbers tables, something I can still do 70 years later. On one occasion, we were asked to draw a picture of our families, the people we lived with at home. Pencil in hand, an image of my father's face came to mind, but I totally lacked the skills to get that sort of detail down on paper. But then, I glanced at the kid next to me, who, tongue out the side of the mouth, was busy drawing stick figures. *Oh yes*, I thought, *not that real but a way around the problem.* But then we were asked to put labels on our pictures saying who was who, a far greater challenge.

Though my school reports were largely positive, even the last I had from Cubbington, there was a dark cloud starting to develop, for I was seriously struggling to read and write. Even at the age of seven I had difficulty writing my own name. But at the same time there was a bird book at home with bright illustrations and despite my difficulties, I learnt by heart the common names of the forty species that were shown there. Similarly, I was starting to glean facts and figures from other sources, such as radio programs and pictures in encyclopaedias with attendant paragraphs that could be deciphered, though this might entail seeking parental help.

But overall, I knew something was wrong and my self-esteem starting to suffer. With this came an increasing sense of frustration and my day dreaming became more prolific to the extent I was too often not paying proper attention in class. But the imaginings had started to change, a shift away from straight storytelling to facts and figures on the wider topics that were beginning to interest to me. Sometimes, these verged on short lectures, but the idea that I would ever stand up in front of a real audience and speak was a total anathema. All very private, not something to be shared with others. And even today, as a published writer, I can sometimes feel awkward explaining a story's plot line to someone who hasn't read my books.

It was also about this time, aged nine, that my perceptions of God started to change. Before, I had no difficulty in believing in Father Christmas and God in equal measure. I was getting some religious education at school but was starting to see the creation stories in Genesis as far too simplistic, far too much like fairytales. This, in turn, led to a questioning of other aspects of Christian faith, though terms like *atheist* and *agnostic* were not known to me or at least not understood. Over the years I was to settle firmly on the side of agnosticism but with the bible retaining a degree of fascination that persists to this day and influences my writing. As an example, in the first book in the *Beyond the Silence* trilogy, the character Ushea presents a blend of astro-physicist, higher mathematics and Christian fundamentals – *I am the universe, I will cease only at time's end.*

When I was about nine, someone asked me what I wanted to be when I grew up. I replied a scientist because that's where my interests were starting to focus. But then dismissed that idea, for as a dumb kid I could never make the grade. One of the stories I had read to me a few years earlier was, I think, called *Mike the Muck Shufter*. The theme, Mike who wasn't overly bright - having tried and failed at just about everything - finds his niche in life driving a bulldozer. Even at that stage, I was starting to see myself in the future as a digger of ditches, a shufter of muck. But I remember thinking that the best Christmas present I could ever hope for was to be able to read and write really well. Both my parents were highly literate and my younger sister Gill was making good progress, but why was I so different?

In those days, the term *dyslexia* was more than a decade away from making a serious debut into the public consciousness. But at the time, my personal problems were being attributed to time lost to school due to sickness. Certainly, that hadn't helped, but even today as an old man the ghost of childhood dyslexia still haunts me. On occasions, I'll reverse sequences of letters or numbers, will stumble when asked how to spell a word even though I am able to write it down with ease and I am utterly hopeless at crosswords or similar word games.

It was about this time in the late 1940s I moved schools, a seemingly good idea, but looking back, an educational disaster. My parents had become increasingly concerned about my lack of progress in the reading and writing department and continued unhappiness with the Cubbington environment. After discussing this with me it was decided that at the beginning of the next school year in September, I would be attending Hunningham Primary School.

Hunningham is another small village on the banks of the Leam River. To get there required a walk of well over a mile but during all the time I'd been in Weston I'd never been there. I was told, 'Go down through Weston village then across the hump-backed bridge into Hunningham, past the Red Lyon Hotel and the school is on the left.' Almost right, except there was an unexpected T junction which meant having to decipher the names on the sign post and then a half mile walk before I came to the bridge.

The school (no longer there in 2010) was a set of temporary classrooms, quite different from the solid 19th century brickwork of Cubbington. There were about 50 kids attending from the surrounding area including the nearby village of Eathorp. But being a proper primary school, there were no thirteen- or fourteen-year olds, no alpha males in short grey trousers and socks around the ankles, dominating the playground. I was one of the older kids and tall for my age, but even so, saw no signs of bullying. But there certainly were serious and totally unexpected problems.

I'd arrived at Hunningham Primary not knowing the kids nor the teachers. That first morning with the weather being fine, the roll call was done out in the playground with the kids standing before the teachers. Then at the end, the head teacher called out my name. Being a shy child among strangers, I sort of put up my hand but failed to call out when she at first failed to see me.

Finally, I was seen and soon thereafter found myself sitting at the back of one of the three classroom. But not then or later was an assessment made as to my abilities as a student. Furthermore, as I discovered later, no school reports had reached them from my former school at Cubbington.

It seemed that the teachers at Hunningham had come to the view I was mentally retarded. On being totally ignored by everyone, I spent much of my time day dreaming both in class and out on the playground. I did do some work in class but only when I felt like it, and was never challenged. Among the kids, I made no friends. I, of course, was aware something was very wrong, but confused and the fear of being sent back to Cubbington prevented me from saying anything to my parents.

On one occasion, coming home from school, I saw an old man standing by the side of the road. He looked to be a farm worker by the way he was dressed.

'Been to school lad?' he called. 'What did you learn today?'

'A few things,' I replied, head down recalling another day of not very much.

'You work hard lad,' he advised. 'Do what the teachers tell you. A good education, you can't fault that.'

No doubt good and well meant, but at the time just adding to my sense of doom. My education was going nowhere.

On one occasion at Hunningham my teacher got some of the kids to read aloud to the class while the head teacher stood at the back observing. After this had gone on for perhaps half an hour the school head called out. 'That's right Miss, get the better children to read. They're the ones who'll be the lawyers, the scientists, the business people, the leaders of the future.'

Looking back, what an extraordinary thing to proclaim in front of a class of primary kids. Those who'd read were no doubt elevated by being labelled *the leaders of the future*. But what about the non-readers, those who'd not taken part? At the time the remark simply deepened my growing despair - condemned to a lifetime of failure at age nine.

During much of this time Gill, who was a year behind me in terms of school years, had been attending Cubbington. This continued until the last term when our youngest sister, Hilary, was due to start school. By that stage, Norman had found a job in London and there were plans to move the whole family south. So, in that last term before our departure from Warwickshire all three of us attended Hunningham Primary, walking to and from school. I remember not being entirely happy with this arrangement, having visions of carrying little sister Hilary on my back after she'd been worn out by all the walking. But in the event that was never necessary.

On the last day before the start of the long summer holiday, my teacher held me back after class. She presented me with a book and asked me to read aloud. This I did, slowly, haltingly but nevertheless surprising myself with the improvement for I'd been struggling along at home.

'You're a bit slow,' she observed. 'Only now do we get the report from your last school. Pity you're not coming back but now that we know, it would all have been much better next year.'

At the time I saw all this as a total put-down. I'd been asked to read and failed yet again. But recalling these remarks as an adult it's obvious that here was a belated apology for wasting an entire precious year of my education.

But at this time, there was one bonus with my first trip to London, what's more on a train by myself. With my father working in the city, the idea was for him to meet me at the train terminal. I remember worrying what to do in case he wasn't there. I decided in this event I would sit and wait, hours if needs be, but after that go in search of the station master. In the event there was no problem.

The excursion meant being on the London underground for the first time, a wondrous experience with all those electrified worm-trains racing through darkened tunnels. It was like stepping into a different other world. Then came the even more marvellous visit to the South Kensington Natural History Museum. The building itself was truly imposing, more like a cathedral than a museum. But being able to see actual dinosaur skeletons for the first time was beyond awesome. Then there were the galleries of stuffed birds that included such avian wonders as the Pied Goose, Wedge-tailed Eagle and Red-tailed Black Cockatoo. Species that I could never have hoped to see in real life. But a place of magic where science was far more than just pictures in a book.

The whole family moved south a few weeks later. But for me, this was to be a small turning point, though real lasting improvement was only to be found half a world away and many years into the future.

Chapter 5

The Family Goes South

I'D NEVER BEEN INSIDE A caravan before but over many minutes accompanied by a salesman, the three of us, mum, dad and myself had looked through several. I was impressed by the clever compactness of the internal designs. The way everything could be folded away, seats converted to beds, tiny cooking areas made to disappear behind sliding panels, then there were the tables that popped up from nowhere.

'With house rents being astronomical these days,' declared the salesman, 'caravan living is the way to go. Yes, since the end of the war business has been really booming to such an extent we can hardly keep up with demand.'

'If we decided to buy, where could you make a delivery?' asked my mother.

'Most parts of England,' replied the salesman. 'We've branches in many of the major centres.'

'What about the southern counties?' asked my father.

'Absolutely no problem,' came the reply.

With dad's job in London the family was only seeing him on weekends but now there were plans to move all of us into a pair of caravans.

So, a couple of months later, the family took up residence in a caravan park at Kingswood, Surrey on the edge of the commuter belt south of London.

The only casualty in all this was Dinah, the family cat. At Weston, the cat had become half wild, a house full of boisterous young kids too threatening. Sometimes the cat would be missing for days only to turn up with a mouse or young rabbit in its mouth. But on the day we were leaving, the cat appeared on the doorstep and was duly placed in a box with food and water. Dinah survived the journey but when the box was opened, bolted off never to be seen again. Hopefully the poor thing found sanctuary somewhere.

We had two caravans, the Mallard, a larger all-purpose van, and a smaller Willerby used exclusively as the children's bedroom. Us kids soon got used to living in such cramped conditions, but I think our parents found it a strain. The Mallard had a settee and table that could be transformed into a double bed. There was a small sink and a stove that ran off bottled gas. There was no electricity and at night the main source of light came from a Tilley pressure lamp that ran on paraffin. To get this started, methylated spirits had to be poured into a heat cup. This was lit, heating the mantle until it glowed. Then a pump was used to increase the air pressure inside the fuel tank at the base, thereby delivering fuel to the mantle. We used this device for years and the only servicing required was the periodic replacement of the heat mantle.

Water had to be hauled over to the caravan in buckets and carting water became my job. If hot water was needed, it had to be heated on the stove. We had no refrigerator, very few people did back then. Perishables such as meat and milk had to be kept in a meat safe.

Our parents slept in the larger caravan as did little brother Jon until he was older. Me and my two sisters slept in the smaller Willerby caravan. The girls in the double bed up one end and me in the single bed near the door. This caravan had a sink and a wardrobe but no cooking facilities. I don't remember it being cold in winter but there may have been a gas heater with ventilation that may have been turned on for a couple of hours before we went to bed.

Washing and laundry were done at the facilities block. It was here I used showers for the first time, prior to that it'd always been baths. The hot water didn't come free, a coin had to be inserted into a meter to ensure the water heating came on for a set period. Though there were male and female bathroom areas, we always went over to the block as a family.

When we first arrived, our nights were sometimes disturbed by domestic rows or parties going on in adjacent caravans. The bad language was of particular concern, but soon thereafter we were able to move our caravans to a quieter spot.

Kingswood is on the North Downs, chalk-limestone hills and quite unlike Warwickshire's rolling mid-lands, and I wasted little time in exploring this new environment. Bordering the caravan park to the south was heath land, in part dominated by gorse bushes with the occasional small stunted Rowan Tree. Apart from that, here were many flowering plants along with the small Chalk Blue Butterflies the likes of which I'd never seen before.

At night, the lights around the camping ground attracted Deaths Dead Hawkmoths, so called because of the skull-like pattern on the thorax. Also, in the area was the Privet Hawkmoth. I found one of their caterpillars, bright green with white and black stripes along the sides. This one was about two inches long and I kept it in a glass jar, fed it fresh privet leaves until it pupated. But then when nothing much seemed to be happening, I buried it in dead leaves under a privet hedge.

One day, I came across a brain fungus about six inches across. The fruiting bodies of brain fungi that erupt from rotting logs were quite common in nearby woodlands. They have a hard and rubbery texture, but as the name implies, look like small mammal brains in both shape and colour. But this specimen was about ten times the normal size and we sent it away to the Natural History Museum. A month later we got a letter back, thanking us for our interest but they were unable to explain why this thing was so large. This was before the DNA molecules had been described and the sort of analysis as to what had produced this mutation was perhaps beyond the science of the time. Nevertheless, Surrey compared to Weston was a different and more exciting landscape in which to wander, in which to observe things.

One day in early autumn we went as a family out across the heath to the edge of the downs. Here were very steep slopes covered by short grass. From this high vantage point, we could look out across the open country, the farm lands of the Weald, a great patchwork of fields that lay to the south.

The day was warm and humid, but when thunderstorms started to threaten, we began heading back. Watching the clouds, I thought at first we were in no danger, but, quite suddenly all changed and the six of us caught in a deluge. Soaked to the skin and cold we tried to find what shelter we could. Dad was for sheltering under a tree saying he'd been caught in storms before, but mum who was carrying two-year-old Jon, was having none of that. After a few short sharp words, she set off for a large house we could see about a hundred yards away. Reaching the door, she rang the bell and after talking to the lady that answered, signalled us over.

All dripping wet we were ushered into the kitchen. The woman who let us in was the cook and here in the warmth were a couple of young servant girls.

'The owners are away,' we were told, 'but we can't have you out there in that weather.'

Soon we had towelled off and got into any sort of clothing that could be found, including dressing gowns and old-fashioned lady's bloomers. Then came the hot tea and cakes while our wet clothes dried in front of the massive wood burning kitchen stove. By the time we were ready to leave, our clothes were nearly dry, the rain had stopped and the sun was out. A piece of genuine kindness that is still remembered over 60 years later.

My memories of going to school in Kingswood are positive. It was a much larger school than I'd been in before but classes seem to be conducted as they should. Teachers and students were friendly. On arriving, me and my sisters had broad Warwickshire accents. This seemed a bit of a novelty amongst some of the kids, but we lost these within months. An awareness of how others spoke and the ability to change accents over a relatively short period is something I was to observe in myself at other times during my life.

But even before the year was out, we were on the move again. At Weston, Molly had done a little relief teaching at Cubbington, but now she'd a full-time job not far away at Juniper Park in the county of Kent.

Juniper Park was a Georgian mansion tucked in below the Ragstone Ridge just outside the town of Sevenoaks. A magnificent three storey house with massive bay windows looking out across the Kentish Weald. There were well kept flower gardens and lawns, a round summer house and a magnificent red flowering rhododendron lined drive way. At the back of the house were several Canadian Redwood trees.

When we arrived, the place was surrounded on three sides by slopes covered with a 400-year-old beech forest. Massive trees that left a deep carpet of leaves on the forest floor. The wildlife included red squirrels and birds like nuthatch, green woodpecker, jay, magpie and treecreeper. But my greatest impression on wandering the woods was of the sheer number and variety of fungi, not only of the toadstool and puff ball kinds but the shelf fungi that grew out of rotting logs. One fungi I found half hidden in a hollow log looked like a miniature cascading white waterfall. At Weston and Kingswood, I'd eaten many a wild mushroom, but here there was nothing familiar about what was on display. If anyone were to go collecting for the dinner table, they would absolutely need to know what they were doing.

Below the house on the flatter ground was a field and a small tree-lined lake that had been created by a raised embankment on the southern side. The lake water was full of roach, a small fish with reddish fins, related to the carp.

Friends of my father, with two land rovers, had towed our caravans over from Kingswood. The vans were parked on steeply sloping ground northeast of the main house, not far from a huge fallen beech that had come down in a storm a few years earlier.

Life in the caravans continued much as before. There was no electric power but there was a connection to the mains water supply, so I didn't have to carry buckets up the hill. We were able to use the bathroom and laundry facilities in the main house.

Juniper Park had been owned, so I was told, by the Spotway family, but recently sold to a group of investors who planned to turn the place into an exclusive country club and retreat for the wealthy living in London. When we arrived, the house was undergoing partial but systematic renovation with perhaps a dozen families, both staff and paid-up residence, living there. The place was financially struggling, trying to attract further investors, though I understand it has since flourished.

My mother's job as a fully qualified primary school teacher was to teach Juniper Park's primary kids, while dad continued his daily commute into London. But I and my sister Gill never attended the school there. We were sent off to a nearby school in the village of Underriver, which is a whole other story.

One night in February, the radio was on in the main caravan. Then a very solemn voice came on the air, 'This is London.'

My father looked up and said, 'What's happened?'

Then followed the announcement that the king, George VI had died peacefully in his sleep. At the time, a complete surprise, though it was revealed years later that the king had died of lung cancer. A smoker, he'd been sick for quite some time.

At Juniper Park there was a marked social divide between staff and residence. As a family, we tended to get on well with the staff, whereas the residence (many of whom were professional people) tended to be socially aloof. On the other hand, the kids tended to mix freely. A fair amount of bickering seems to have been going on between the residence, but us kids only got to hear about that second hand.

I still remained the day dreamer, but had started to come out of my shell. I made genuine friends with some of the kids. These included Kaden, who was about two years younger than me, and Darren, an older boy. Kaden was the son of a resident and destined for boarding school, whereas Darren was the son of Mrs James the cook. Golden haired Kaden was a particularly lively character whereas Darren was generally more serious and sensible.

One of the things we liked to do was get up on the roof of the main house. Here was a different world, with three separate tiled roof rides running north-south. Between the ridges were two walkways about three feet wide. Ideal for little boys to get away from it all without being seen from the ground. Access to the roof was via a small "secret" door, but care had to be taken because two of the third-floor windows opened out onto this otherwise hidden roof space.

It was while up on the roof one day we witnessed what can best be described as a private encounter. One of residents, be it one who used to come and go, was a woman I'll call Miss M. She was dark-haired and middle-aged, a Jewish lady who'd lost her family during the holocaust. I understand she was one of several professional stage and screen people associated with Juniper Park at that time. The others included Mai Zetterling and on one occasion Vera Lynn came to visit.

Another person who came and went was a young man I'll called Terry who was about half of Miss M's age. We used to like Terry because he was always bright and cheerful when talking to us, but what his exact role was around the place wasn't clear.

On this particular day there was six roof climbers, our trio having been joined by three of the younger kids. We'd clambered up and over the central roof ridge and were in the process of scrambling back when Terry emerged from the secret door. Under normal circumstances we may have called out to him, but we were not supposed to be there. So, we all lay on our stomachs, a line of heads peering over the roof at Terry as he made his way along the walkway. And there was Miss M standing at her open third storey window wearing a dressing gown. Terry climbed in, the window was closed and the certain drawn. We collectively gave a sigh of relief at having not been spotted. We carefully and quietly slid down the roof back onto the walkway before making good our escape through the secret door which it seemed wasn't as secret as we'd supposed.

On another occasion, me and the boys caught a harmless Grass Snake and brought it into the main house. But then, by way of a joke, the poor creature was let loose in a chest of drawers full of clothes. The aim being to get some unsuspecting person, one of the girls, to open the drawer and get a fright. But the grand scheme went astray for when the target drawer was opened the reptile had vanished. Only after a frantic search was it located under a nearby bed. After that the day's laughs were put aside and the snake duly returned to the wild.

Britain's only dangerous snake, the Adder, may have been around but we never saw it.

Another project that held our attention was burning out an old tree stump on the edge of the beech forest. The stump was huge with its top the size of a table. But there was split in the timber and so we started a small fire inside. At first, only a few burning embers, but over the next two weeks it burnt out the entire stump leaving only a bit of a shell. After it was finished, I felt regretful for we'd created a mess in an otherwise pristine environment, exciting though the fire had been.

A common practice among the professional people living at Juniper was to leave their kids in the hands of the staff while they went off to London or elsewhere, sometimes for days or weeks at a time. This didn't always produce the best outcome for the children, some becoming quite feral. My sister Hilary, who would have been about seven at the time, walked into a room one day to discover two silly boys barbecuing some soft toys over a small fire made from lit newspaper. She tried to stop them but when an adult was called, the boys tried to blame her for the fire. Furthermore, some of the adults were inclined to believe them. But later, she felt vindicated when one of the same kids started another fire, this time causing significant damage. It was this same wayward child that on another day was to tip half a bag of cement powder down a toilet.

Meanwhile, I was learning to ride a bicycle. Years earlier, a small red bicycle had been given to me for my birthday, but having fallen off a couple of times, I gave up on that idea. But despite the family moves, it had stayed with us though at that stage, neither of my sisters had shown any interest in learning to ride. But now after freewheeling down the driveway a couple of times, I was peddling like an expert, even though the bike was starting to get too small for me.

As the teacher at Juniper Park, my mother initiated a silk-worm project that with the kids' help proved highly successful. On the slope just below the caravans were two substantial mulberry trees. Molly ordered some silk-worm cocoons from the only silk factory in Britain. These were allowed to hatch and the brown moths mated and lay their eggs on freshly supplied mulberry leaves. The resulting caterpillars were then reared to pupation. I remember going to a room in the main house where all this was happening. Large flat trays were covered with fresh mulberry leaves. By that stage, the caterpillars were two to three inches long and the sound of their collective munching distinctly audible.

Once the caterpillars had spun their silk cocoons and pupated, they were all boxed up and sent back to the factory. A month later Molly received a letter saying that the silk produced had been of such high quality it was to be added to that used in the making of Queen Elizabeth's coronation dress.

But for me and the family, the coming of autumn was a time of further changes. I lost two of my friends, Darren, because his mother had found a job elsewhere, and Kaden, to boarding school.

More disturbingly, the simply magnificent beech forest that surrounded the great house was being felled. The Juniper Park investors were desperately short of money and as a result, the forest area had been leased or sold to the Forestry Department, who set about clearing the area to establish a commercial pine plantation. Within a couple of months, the hills around the house were turned into a waste land. There were a few voices of protest but they were told that it would all look quite nice once the pine trees had been established.

As a kid I made friends with the four men who were clearing the forest. The felling of such large beech trees was truly dramatic. They would start off with a wedge cut into the base made with an axe. Then they used a two-handled saw to complete the job, sending the enormous trees crashing to the ground. No machinery was used other than the trucks to cart the wood away, but the guys made it look easy. But certainly, work not without its dangers and on one occasion, I was told-off for approaching the team without calling out to let them know where I was. Knowing how they worked, I judged my line of approach safe but they were right, there was always the chance of something going wrong. Exciting though the felling of the forest had been, the sense of loss was considerable.

Another shock came with the news that my mother had been sacked from her teaching job. Something that left my parents absolutely furious. It seemed that the residence committee had come to the view that the presence of our caravans on the hill behind the main house was spoiling the tone of the place. But to add insult to injury, the staff member who'd be taking over Molly's job had little experience and no formal qualifications as a teacher.

Looking back, I would have thought the destruction of the ancient beech forest was vastly more damaging to the tone of Juniper Park than the sight of a couple of caravans. But this was England in the early 1950s.

Since coming to Juniper Park, my sister Gill and I had been attending the primary school at the nearby village of Underriver. It was there with our caravans that we as a family now moved. Later, a couple of fishing trips were made to Juniper's small lake, but I steered clear of the main house. This was no longer friendly territory.

Chapter 6

Social Engineering Village Style

UNDERRIVER IS A SMALL VILLAGE with a pub and a church, but in the early 1950s there was also a primary school. By 2010, this had been converted into a private residence. The village lies at the foot of River Hill and the name *River* being a corruption of the Anglo-Saxon word for ridge.

This continuation of the Ragstone Ridge was covered with forest but with cleared farmland extending up onto the lower slopes. In this part of the world, villages at the bottom of steep road climbs typically have pubs. This was because in the days before motor transport, extra horse power could be hired from the pub's stables to assist in the hauling of stage coaches and wagons.

When my family arrived at Juniper Park, it was to the Underriver school that my sister Gill and I were sent. Towards the end of the following year, after my mother lost her job, it was to a small farm on the northern edge of the village that we brought our caravans and Hilary also started to attend the school. We stayed there through the winter and into the following spring. Though I've some positive memories of Underriver, looking back, I think our time there was the real low point for the family as a whole. Our parents' decision to move into Underriver was influenced by the need to maintain some continuity in the kids' schooling, but a move they came to largely regret. Problems may be unlooked for, unplanned for, but on coming can take more than one form.

In the previous year, Norman had borrowed money to buy the caravans. But in those days, obtaining a loan from a bank was often difficult and I suspect my father had no option but to look elsewhere with the inevitable higher rates of interest. Norman had a good head for money but nevertheless, my grandfather Fred had been called to go guarantor for the loan. But when Molly lost her job, dad defaulted on the payments and the lenders went after Fred, demanding the money be repaid in full. This he did, but the issue turned an already fractious relationship between generations into a very bitter row. Fred had always been a proud man, saw himself as paying his way and viewed all this as a betrayal of trust. But my parents with four kids, ten and under, were in a desperate situation. Fred did eventually get his money back, but it led to Molly telling her father she never wanted to have anything to do with him ever again. Later, there was some reconciliation, but for us kids there was to be no more visits to our grandparents in Hull.

It was at Underriver that I heard the term gypsies being applied to my family. The first time was by the farmer Mr Hails on whose land we were camping, but this was said seemingly as a joke. The reasoning, caravan dwellers and gypsies were supposed to be one of the same, but we then discovered some in the village seriously believed this. On one occasion, we even had stones thrown at us on the way home from school. The lad throwing the stones was the older brother of one of the kids with which we attended school.

In British society, gypsies and other travellers form distinct sub-cultures to which we clearly didn't belong. Through the centuries, they've often been regarded with suspicion, sometimes outright persecution, but the boundary between who was and wasn't a gypsy had never been clearly defined. Then after the war, with a chronic housing crisis and people flooding into caravans, a further layer of complication was added, at least it seemed in the minds of some.

Another problem that came with the move to Underriver was that we no longer had proper laundry or bathing facilities. This meant using a large tub and members of the family taking turns. Two minutes in the tub in the privacy of the main caravan then out, dry off, get partly dressed and make way for the next one. I was again having to carry buckets to meet the family's needs, the water being obtained from a tap inside a nearby farmyard. But heating large amounts of water on the caravan's gas stove was an ordeal. But then in my wanderings, I discovered a good supply of firewood in a patch of woodland about half a mile away. There was an old convention in England called *by hook or by crook*. This meant that anyone could go onto private land and gather firewood, providing they didn't damage living trees or cause other forms of havoc such as leaving gates open.

So, for several months through the winter, I collected firewood and hauled it back to the caravans where it was used outside to heat large batches of water when needed.

But then one day in spring, dad said to me, 'When you next go over there, let me know and I'll come with you.'

I was puzzled for he'd never shown such an interest before. We walked across the field, him with his walking stick and me the ten-year-old at his side. But on arriving at the edge of the woodland, there was unexpected company, a small man in a dark overcoat. He approached with a demeanour that was far from friendly. But my father, who I now realised was expecting trouble, put on a jovial smile and greeted the fellow as if an old friend.

'This land is private,' replied the man, keeping his distance. 'Your damned boy has been here and a lot of fucking damage done.'

'We've been collecting wood,' answered my dad, 'by hook and by crook sir, and if there's been anything untoward it most certainly hasn't been done by us.' The big smile maintained.

The conversation continued on this theme for several more minutes, the man aggressive, angry, dad skilfully maintaining an outward show of friendliness. As for the accusation of damage, that simply wasn't true.

The outcome was that we left without the firewood, but with our dignity intact. But if the landowner thought to easily browbeat a couple of gypsies, he'd more than met his match. As my father said as we made our way back across the field, 'In situations like that keep it polite and friendly, throws them off balance, they don't know how to react. As for the firewood we'll have to manage without.'

On a couple occasions later in life, I've used my father's technique of being cheerful in the face of rudeness or threats. On one occasion outside Central Railway Station in Sydney, I saw two young coves eyeing me off as I came towards them. One was very large and on his feet, while the smaller guy was sitting on a bench besides him. As I went to pass, the big guy fell into lock-step behind me. At this I quickly turned around and said, 'How are you mate?' Gave him my best smile while he mumbled a response. I then looked across at the smaller of the two with a nod of recognition, but all the time thinking, *Yes you're the real brains around here.* Meanwhile, a young backpacker went past, locked in his own world with not a clue what was going on. But after this I was allowed to go on my way unmolested. However to quote from my words in *The Edible Machine Gun* - "*As in city streets particularly late at night, it's important to watch for signs, the spells both good and evil. Kindness and compassion there might be, but malevolence can take many forms be they meteorological, criminological or officio-logical.*"

But at other times at Underriver, I witness the irrational side of my father's personality. On one occasion, he and I went strawberry picking. There is some skill in this for the fruit needs to be left undamaged during the picking process. Any damaged fruit was downgraded for jam making. We amateur pickers made a start only to have all our efforts politely downgraded to jam quality. At this, dad lost his temper. Soon thereafter, he and I were out the gate - heading for home. On the way I was given a lecture on the useless nature of strawberries in general and of the people who grew them. The name of the road we were on was called Egg Pie Lane, but in sighting a large black and white Magpie, I thought the name Magpie Lane more appropriate. But I didn't think much of my father's desecration of strawberries. After all, I'd helped myself to more than a few that morning, a far from unsatisfactory outcome.

As a child, I did make friends while in the village. They included Phillip who lived in one of several government-built council houses. A quiet kid, I used to sometimes accompany him taking his dog for a walk after school. Also the kids of the O'Brian family.

The O'Brians lived in a large house on the other side of the lane not far from where we lived. The house itself was quite remarkable. Not only did it have a beautifully laid out garden but on going inside, it was like stepping back into the sixteenth century. It did have some concessions to the modern age like electric light, but I most remember the ancient ceiling beams, low doorways and an odd twisting staircase. They were a really nice family and I once attended one of their birthday parties.

It was during this time I took on an engineering project. There was a small stream running past the caravans. One day, I caught a fish, but at the time a mystery as from where it had come. It was a roach, a species not normally found in shallow running water. Later I deduced it could only have come from the O'Brian's spring-fed fish pond and if I had known at the time it would have been returned.

As it was, I had the fish, about four inches long, swimming around in a jam jar. But this called for further urgent action. I set about mining clay out of the stream bank and constructing a small dam to provide deeper water. But then I added a second dam wall with more elaborate spillways. Further modifications were made, but alas one morning the fish was discovered floating belly up, the cause of death unknown.

One of my other friends from school was Joe Hatfield, the son of one of the district's tenant farmers. I visited his farm on a couple of occasions. His mother was from Scotland, a nice lady, but I had great difficulty in deciphering her Scottish accent. On that first visit, Joe's cousin, Des, was visiting, a tough little kid but another one with a funny way of speaking. Joe and I started to tease him, but Des got really angry and we had to take shelter in a hay shed while kale storks were being flung at us. After this a truce was called and we became friends once more.

On the second occasion, I had my one and only lesson in sex education. A cow was in season and once bailed up a bull was brought around to do what bulls do best.

It was Joe who explained that this was how calves got started. During the rest of my school years there was no formal sex education and it seemed during that period, kids were expected to pick all this up by osmosis. Seeing the display of bovine mating behaviour for the first time, I was left confused as to which part of the cow's anatomy the bull had been able to penetrate.

The Underriver school at that time was a parish school and one of only two so, I was told, left in the country. My understanding was that a parish schools differed from private schools in that the parents were not required to pay fees, the money which also maintained the church next door, being raised from within the local parish. The term as used elsewhere seems to take on different meanings.

The school had about 25 primary students in two classes, the littlies and the older kids. The head teacher who took the older children I'll call Miss Cramer. She was to be my teacher from the autumn of 1951 to when I left the primary school system 21 months later in July 1953 .

On the surface, I found the classroom and playground environment orderly for Miss Cramer, a large middle-age woman, maintained a strict code of discipline even when not physically present. On our first day, Gill and I were assessed as to our academic abilities, my sister as expected scoring much higher than me. At that stage Gill could read well, perhaps ahead of her reading age, whereas I was really struggling.

But it was on the second day I was left wondering what sort of a school this was. By that stage, I'd experienced near normal classroom environments at Cubbington and Kingswood. The primary school at Hunningham had been odd at least from my perspective but I'd seen nothing quite like this. Miss Cramer stood up in front of the class and proceeded to expound her views on social politics, that is politics pitched at eight to ten-year-olds.

At that time in England, all students sat for what was called the eleven plus exam at the end of primary school. The results from this determined which kids went on to grammar school, or for the less academically inclined, into the secondary modern stream. However, in Miss Cramer's view, this was all about social class. The right sort of kids from the right sort of middle class, preferably from well-to-do backgrounds, needed channelling towards grammar schools. Whereas those from the working class, farm labourers and the like, needed to be found places in secondary modern schools. Furthermore, she saw herself as duty bound to ensure that kids coming out of Underriver primary followed these pre-ordained paths, regardless of what was going on in the rest of the country. This meant that some of her pupils would be encouraged to do their very best, whereas others deliberately held back as the situation dictated. I think she even managed to make some disparaging remarks about the terrible Labour government that had been voted out of office a couple of years earlier. This was Miss Cramer's manifesto, delivered that foggy autumn morning to a captive audience of kids. Whether we all fully understood what was being said was uncertain, but it left me unsettled. Furthermore, this message was to be repeated several more times over the coming months.

Certainly, I witnessed Miss Cramer encouraging kids she deemed worthy, while bullying and belittling those she judged needed to be held back. There were two, in particular, who were held up as the golden girls. But from the very beginning Gill found herself on the black list, the recipient of negative treatment. I didn't like what was happening to my sister, but the teacher's rule was absolute.

However, Miss Cramer wasn't sure what to make of me. In class, I was very quiet, withdrawn and frequently not paying attention. Not for the first time it was thought I was mentally retarded. This time my mother was contacted and I was taken off to see a specialist. But Molly, who knew what I was like at home, thought this a waste of time. The report came back, normal intelligence, imaginative, but poor reading skills. So, it became a case of I-told-you-so. Soon after this, Miss Cramer engaged me in a more normal conversation in class and I opened up a little with a short discourse on the fungi of the Juniper Park's beech forest. I remember her stepping back a pace with a look that said, 'Where's this coming from?'

Despite her failing as a teacher, Miss Cramer was of the view that even working-class labourers needed to read and write. So, taking advantage of the small class size she set about improving my reading. The strategy was very simple. 'You David have failed,' she declared. 'Therefore, you'll go back to the very beginning and start again.' I resented being given the first book in the *I Can Read* series, but for the first time in my life I was actually able to read fluently. I then progressed through the series with greatly renewed confidence to the extent that over the next twenty months I made genuine progress. There was still a serious problem, but under Miss Cramer's guidance I was again making positives steps upon the mountain.

One of the brighter kids on Miss Cramer's black list was Keith Gipps, the son of a farm worker. On one particular day, Keith, normally a quiet kid, was complaining of feeling unwell with stomach trouble. We'd just come in from the playground and Miss Cramer was about to start the afternoon lesson when suddenly Keith leapt to his feet cheeks bulging and rushed out through the open door. He'd vomited, but faced with the potential wrath of Miss Cramer had kept his mouth closed until he reached the sanctuary of the bathroom. On that occasion he was praised for his extraordinary self-control, but being on the black list this was not to last.

Molly, faced with an unhappy Gill and with Hilary about to move into Miss Cramer's class, requested a teacher interview in an effort to find out what was going on. Up until this time, I think our mother was of the view that teachers should be allowed to teach without parents looking over their shoulder at every step of the way. But from the memoires, left by of my late sister Hilary, she too had reasons to fear Miss Cramer. But on this particular morning, I was surprised on looking up to see both teachers and my mum talking to each other as they sat around the teacher's desk at the front of the room.

Then Miss Cramer left her seat and called the class to attention. 'I've just been accused of bullying,' she announced, arms folded. 'Of favouring some of you children over others. Now have any of you seen me doing anything like that?'

Furious, my mother was on her feet, and addressed the room. 'I came here for a private conversation on a serious matter,' she declared. 'I came here believing that I would be treated with respect. Not to have this issue thrown open to a classroom of children, who neither have the cognisant ability nor maturity to understand what is being asked of them.' Then turning to Miss Cramer, 'Of course none are going to put up their hands. They are children, could you expect anything different? But you, Miss Cramer, in attempting to make this an issue in front of such a group are not worthy of the position you hold.'

'Who are you to question my teaching,' replied Miss Cramer. 'You live in a caravan and. . .'

'Where I live, madam, is of no relevance,' retorted my mother. 'It so happens I'm a fully qualified teacher and your behaviour can only be described as grossly unprofessional.' More followed, words like, 'an absolute disgrace to the teaching profession.'

As a ten-year-old listening to all this my first thought was: 'Nobody speaks to Miss Cramer like that and lives.'

But if Miss Cramer had set out to publicly humiliate my mother she'd seriously miscalculated. And like all bullies once faced with a strong defence she partly backed down. I don't know how much of this got to the other parents out there via the kids, but there were already mutterings in the wider community.

But I was worried about the terrible retaliation that would befall me and my sisters. That never happened, though I arrived home that afternoon to find my mother absolutely fuming.

Gill was never sent back but moved to a government run primary school in nearby Hildenbougher. A more normal school environment where she did well, passed her eleven plus and later went onto grammar school. My youngest sister Hilary stayed on at the school but only for a few more days.

A week or two after this, farmer Hails on whose land we were parked, came around to tell us it was time we were moving on. He was a surly fellow and I remember him keeping his distance when delivering his decree. Perhaps he did view us as gypsies after all, saw the need to keep clear just in case something was thrown at him by us wild lawless types. On the other hand, all these years later I wonder what stories were flying around the village grape vine concerning my mother's recent confrontation. Perhaps not just a grape vine, for there would have been a parish council that would have, among other things, organised Miss Cramer's original appointment.

Our next move was to the village of Sevenoaks Weald about two miles away. But because Miss Cramer had proved positive for me, it was decided that I would continue at Underriver for the next three months until I sat for my eleven plus exam that would determine my fate over the coming years. This meant commuting everyday between villages, either on my red bicycle, which by that stage was ridiculously small, or on foot. My mother had a bicycle that I could have borrowed, but being a lady's machine, I refused the offer.

It was at about this time I became aware of the plight of another child, Mary, who was also falling through the cracks in the school system. She was an older child, about 14, but with parental consent had remained in the primary school because of her very low academic abilities. She lived in a house just across the road from the school. Though regarded as border-line mentally retarded, she was a nice girl who'd effectively become the teacher's assistant, most often helping with the younger children.

One day it was announced that all the kids at the school would have their eyes tested. It was only then it was discovered that Mary was chronically short-sighted to the extent she was effectively blind. I remember sitting at my desk observing as one of the testers went to the other end of the room and asked Mary if she could see him. 'You're just one big blur,' she said. A couple of weeks later she was wearing glasses and no doubt discovering a whole new world out there.

The only regular visitor to the school was the village's resident artist Miss Ball. She would appear once a week and took us older kids for art. Though I had some natural ability, she observed that my hands weren't steady enough. Later, I did go to art college, but I think her original assessment was correct.

Early June 1953, I was sitting in Miss Cramer's classroom and we kids were all listening to the radio broadcast from a loud speaker set high along a wall. The BBC broadcast called *Back to the Past* was the highlight of my day. The show was part of a series whereby a time traveller went back into Earth's geological history and what he discovered along the way. The programs were built around descriptive dialogues with a few sound effects, but with a dramatic twist or two at the end. On that day, our hero was back in the Cretaceous about a hundred million years ago and watching a large Iguanodon dinosaur munching on the vegetation. Seemingly munching and minding its own business, oblivious to the visitor from the far future. But then this idyllic pastoral scene was shattered when a predator appeared. With much roaring sound effects, a battle ensued in which the Iguanodon somehow won, having survived another day. At the age of nearly eleven I was very impressed, the imagination really fired up. Wow, what would it have been like if I had really been there, done that?

The show over, we were all let out in the playground. I ate my lunch sitting on the low wall that marks the boundary of the school yard. I retrieved a sandwich and apple that mum put in my school bag that morning.

A few days earlier had been the coronation of Queen Elizabeth II. A big fuss and Miss Cramer, a staunch royalist, made sure we fully understood the significance of this great historic moment. A time when the country with all its troubles and divisions came together.

At the school earlier in the year there had been something of a farce in the togetherness stakes. The new queen was scheduled to make a visit to a local racing stables and the plan was that a child representing the school would be there. Furthermore, it was decided that the name of the child would be chosen via a raffle. However, it was my sister Gill's name that came out of the hat. Miss Cramer was furious, but I don't know what happened after that, whether the whole idea was dropped or there was a re-draw. But certainly, Gill never got to meet the Queen.

On that day, lunch eaten, I joined in a game of handball until the bell rang, time to go back into class. The bell itself was set in a funny little bell tower sitting at one end of the school roof. Once inside, we older kids were set the task of doing some arithmetic, addition and subtraction, copying off the chalk board and divining the answers. But my mind was wandering; I was back with those battling dinosaurs. If I were really there would I have joined in? The predator from the description seemed to have been some sort of Allosaurus, though the narrator had given it another name.

I pencil sketched a picture of an Allosaurus in my exercise book. Perhaps, if I encourage the dinosaur to eat some of the arithmetic, I wouldn't have to do them? But then my mind came back to the real world, to the task at hand. I used my rubber to erase the dinosaur sketch. I thought if Miss Cramer saw it I would be in big trouble.

With things still not fully copied off the board I made a start on the calculations. What did nine minus five equal? I used my fingers under the desk in an effort to discover the answer. Yes, I thought it might be four but wasn't sure. Six more calculations were completed and perhaps I was getting the hang of this after all.

Then Miss Cramer announced that it was reading time. I got my *I Can Read* book from a box in the corner. We all sat there reading our books in silence and then the teacher called some of the kids up to the front to read aloud to her one at a time. I was called and sat stumbling along reading phonetically, breaking the longer words down into their components. Under her eagle eye I was really having to concentrate.

Then she looked up, attention directed elsewhere. 'Keith Gipps what are you doing?' she called.

The offending student had his head down looking at something being held below the desk top.

Miss Cramer got up and went over. 'What's this, a dictionary?' she proclaimed. 'Give it here. . . Yes now, you are supposed to be reading not looking up words in a dictionary. I will hold on to this until the end of the day and then you can come and get it. But in the future, I never want to see you in school with one of these again, is that clearly understood?'

She then returned to hear me reading.

School was over and I was on the way back to the caravans, walking down Morley's Lane, the village of Weald in sight. Then I spotted a small brown bird lying on the road. It would seem to have been hit by a passing car. I picked it up and it opened its eye, dazed but still alive. I identified it as a Linnet and after a few minutes I got the bird to perch on my finger, then it was off flying unsteadily into a nearby hedge row.

Home, mum and Hilary were back from school in Weald for my mother now worked there. Gill was expected soon but we wouldn't see dad until much later. I then hauled buckets of water over to the main caravan from a tap in a nearby orchard. A routine I did every day. Mum started to make the evening meal. Gill arrived she had homework and after we had eaten she set to work at that the table in the main caravan. I never had homework and, on that occasion, went for a wander, dreaming of death dealing dinosaurs. It was still light when dad arrived home. During the winter he left and returned in the dark. Later still, I got into a silly argument with Gill over nothing very much. Probably I started it as per usual but then Gill could be relied on to overreact to such provocations. However, mum as usual, had to intervene to break it up.

It was about this time that we, as a family, started to listen to a broadcast on the BBC third program. Here was the radio dramatisation of the first book in a trilogy by someone called J R R Tolkien. I'd missed some of the opening episodes, but here was a great story being told with a real poetic grasp of the English language.

The other great radio piece of that time was The Goon Show with its crazy satirical humour built around totally impossible plot lines. An exerciser in absurdity that stretched the imagination and took the art of comedy to new heights.

Ten days short of my eleventh birthday I sat for the all-important eleven plus examination. A continuing consequence of being born about three weeks too early. On the day we were given instructions by a special supervisor who'd come to the school. The exam had been printed on pink paper and was all multiple choice. At first, it seemed easy enough but then became harder, the questions more difficult to read. I didn't attempt a large chunk of questions towards the end. But of course, what I didn't know, and what nobody had ever told me, was that I should never leave multiple choice questions blank because a blind guess had a one in four chance of being right.

A couple of days later Miss Cramer and I parted company. Her words to me before I disappeared out the door for the last time were, 'David I never want to see you again, I never ever want to hear from you ever again. Is that perfectly clear? You can go now.'

At the time I was taken aback and a little upset for despite her many shortcomings, she'd really boosted me in the right direction. It was a given that my next step of the journey was secondary modern school. Beyond that, it was anyone's guess, but she clearly didn't want to know, the love-hate relationship was over.

A postscript to my Underriver experience; a couple of times in those last weeks, Miss Cramer said to me, 'When you get to high school, you'll find the teachers tough and they'll keep you in line.' At the time this made no sense because I'd never ever had a behaviour problem, inattentive yes, but never disruptive. Later, my father and I were interviewed by Mr Rose, the Head Master of my new school. Dad said afterwards he thought that Miss Cramer had sent in a bad report of my behaviour. I now conclude he could only have been right. It's never been normal in a government run school for a Head Master to interview an incoming student and a parent unless there are some real concerns. But it's hard to understand Miss Cramer's motivations behind all this.

Later I heard Keith Gipps did well during the rest of his schooling and went on to university.

The Underriver school was taken over by the Kent Education Department but some years later Miss Cramer got into serious trouble over her treatment of students. Later still, a small piece appeared in the local paper thanking her for her services and from that I concluded she'd left her job.

Chapter 7

Secondary Modern

THE TEACHER STOOD IN FRONT of us boys holding a large round bottomed flask of bright blue liquid. He looked to be in his forties and I guessed a veteran of the Second World War. From now on, nearly all my teachers would be male war veterans.

I remember this, my first ever science lesson, as being a show and tell. A talk about the various branches of science and what scientists did. The solution in the flask was copper sulphate, but at the time the name didn't mean anything to me. Looking back down through the decades, I know that the lesson could have gone that much better. All it would have taken was a Bunsen burner set up on the front desk with the addition of a sodium hydroxide solution and some concentrated sulphuric acid. And presto, there would have been some chemistry magic, a real show worth watching. Chemists have solutions to many things, but they need to be demonstrated, to be seen to be believed.

As it was, school science for the next four years was to consist of far too much talk and chalk with damned little else. Despite an early promise, there was to be no real chemistry while physics remained a total mystery. I'd endless lessons on biology, very little of it hands-on and I never saw a microscope let alone used one. But science was to play a very significant role in much of my life, but only because in those early years I started to find my own path, make my own way.

At school, I was put into a C grade class. If the grammar and secondary modern schools were to be viewed as a single entity and the classes graded from 1 to 10, with 1 being the top academic kids and 10 the lowest, then my class level would have been at the 8th level. Furthermore, I was to remain at that level throughout my high school years.

I started my secondary modern high school experience at Tonbridge, but I was only there for a year. I remember little of my English classes or the name of my female teacher and have no surviving school reports. I suppose my performance in English continued to be unremarkable. But what was it like for this 11-year-old dyslexic?

At the start of my schooling, I seemed not to have had any trouble mastering the basics of the written language. It was after the shift away from rote learning that the trouble seems to have started. When phonically breaking down long words, I recall struggling to the extent that I would often lose the gist of the sentence and sometimes of the actual word itself. However, phonics was for me, and still is, a very useful tool but it has its limits. Words like *were* and *where* I saw as spelling variants of the same word. There are of course genuine examples of English words having more than one accepted spelling, but in this case, it led to endless problems. Then there is *initial* which has a soft *t* and is full of interchangeable short vowel sounds that can be generated by imperfectly spoken English. Apart from that, *thorough* - the phonics having almost no relevance to the actual spelling.

The overall impression during my first seven years of schooling was that the goalposts of correct spelling were forever being shifted. This not only led to frustration and low self-esteem but an absence of trust of the teachers and the school system as a whole.

I made only one friend at school in Tonbridge. I'll call him Ralf, but looking back, I think it decidedly odd that we were friends. On one occasion, he stuck the blunt end of a pencil into my arm with such force it made quite a wound. Then he tried to make a joke out of it, saying he would never do that to a friend and furthermore, I was making things up. When he heard I wouldn't be returning the next year he said, 'You doing this to get away from me?' I assured him that wasn't the case, but looking back I suspect it was for the better.

Then there was the case of the lizard catcher. I once bought a lizard off a boy who'd brought the little reptile to school in a small cardboard box. I paid him a whole six pence, an inflated price by the standards of the day, but when he offered to capture more, I made it absolutely clear I wasn't interested. But he wouldn't take no for an answer and next day came back with half a dozen. When I said the answer was still no, and that there never had been a deal, he became really angry. The original lizard I let go, but the fate of those caught later, supposedly in my name, was unknown.

But my most dramatic memory of Tonbridge was being assaulted in the street by two boys I'd never seen before. I had been on my way to the bus station, day dreaming, when the blows and kicks came thick and fast. A bystander, an elderly man, challenged them but they walked away laughing. Their accents suggested the assailants were day trippers from London out for a bit of a bash in the country and I'd been an easy target. When I got home my mother did ask about the bruises on my legs but I said it was nothing much.

This was the time of the Kray brothers, notorious gangsters from London's east end who were known to have some association with Tonbridge. About two weeks after I was attacked, the head master addressed a school assembly saying that the Krays had been seen about town and that no one should have anything to do with them. Though my attackers looked like identical twins, they were far too young. Perhaps junior look-a-likes emulating their heroes.

The family's move to Weald was to be the start of an improvement in all our lives, though at the time it wouldn't have been that obvious. Mum became a full-time teacher at the local primary school while dad continued his commute into London.

The village was relatively new by British standards, the local church having been built in the 1820s. Quite a few of the inhabitants were descendants of labouring railway worker. Many of Britain's 19th century railways were built by Irish navies.

On arriving at Weald, there were the ongoing issues with bathing and laundry. At first, arrangements were made whereby us kids could take a weekly bath at a neighbour's house up the road. The trouble was the woman who'd made the offer hadn't talked it over with her husband first. The man of the house wasn't the least bit impressed with this arrangement. Mum told us to keep our use of hot water to the minimum and I remember tiptoeing through the house at bath time hoping not to be noticed. Then one evening, there was an incident. When I came to run the bath, I found the water barely warm, but took a three minute dip anyway. But next day, I heard that the man had wanted to take a bath directly after me only to find there was no hot water. Furthermore, it was all my fault and after this, bath times were cancelled. Looking back, there is little doubt somebody had pulled the fuse in the hot water service thereby manufacturing an incident.

But then another lady, on whose land we were living, proved to be a good Samaritan. Her house was nearby and hearing of our plight, let use her facilities free of charge. She was an old lady living in the house with her daughter, but I was thankful at not having to tiptoe towards the bathroom ever again.

Our caravans were parked in a small field on the southern edge of the village. A narrow strip of woodland hid our caravans from the Scabharbour Road and a similar strip of trees on the other side separated the area from adjacent fields. There was also a one room wooden chalet, in and around which we children used to play.

One of my past times was to make spears out of hazel saplings. These grow straight and long and when the wood is still green, they are stiff but with just enough flexibility to make them useful for all sorts of things. On one occasion, I was playing around the chalet when dad challenged me to throw a couple of spears at him saying he would catch them. I launched my spears and ducked out of sight expecting return fire at any second. None was forth coming and on looking out, found my father holding his face. One of my spears had caught him full on the chest and the other on the bridge of the nose. At the time we both laughed, but it had been a what-if moment. Though the spear ends weren't sharp, what if one had caught him in the eye? I was eleven at the time but even then, conscious of how close it had been. I never threw spears at anyone after that.

Tucked in amongst the trees on the southern side of the small field was what we called the brick pond. I'm not sure if it had ever been used for mining clay because the waters were shallow but a great place for small stickleback fish, frogs, newts and other aquatic wildlife. I used to catch the sticklebacks by lowering an empty jam jar tied to a long stick into the water. The jar would have a small piece of bread to entice the fish, but once inside the jar, would be quickly pulled from the water. Sticklebacks get their name from the spines along the back and the mature males typically have a red throat and under belly.

Moorhens used to nest in the pond and for a while a black Muscovy Duck lived there. I guess the Muscovy was an escapee from somewhere but its appearance caused some excitement amongst us kids. I became something of an expert at finding bird nests, mostly Blackbirds and Song Thrush, though on one occasion a Yellow Hammer's and another a Willow Warbler's. There was also a pair of Wrens that built their nest under a canvas awning leaning up against one of the caravans. We observed the process from incubation to the fledging of the young. During the spring, Nightingales used to sing after dark and though I saw the birds in daylight, the nests were never found. Apart from that there were rabbits, grass snakes, slow worms (legless lizards) and the occasional shrew. On one occasion, I found an old insect stray pump in a hedge. Thinking to have some fun, I filled it with water only to be suddenly confronted by a half-drowned shrew. Knowing that there was a bad-tempered furball with sharp little teeth, I respectfully put the spray pump down and let the shrew go.

Stinkhorns, a type of fungus, were quite common. I hadn't seen these before, but soon learned to avoid them. On reaching maturity they develop a brown gluey cap and as the name implies, generate a smell like rotting flesh thus attracting flies which assist with spore dispersal. There might be more than just the smell, for once fully ripe, they often killed the surrounding vegetation, producing a brown patch in the grass.

A look at the local map when we first arrived showed a stream, the Rumpumps near the main railway line about half a mile away.

I wasted little time in getting down there. Over the next eighteen months the Rumpumps provided endless fascination. It issued out from the side of the railway embankment, was fast flowing through a rocky stream bed. Hiding under the rocks were delightful things like mayfly and caddisfly larvae and small thorn-like water snails. Looking back, it seemed I loved this stream to death because I wasn't very good at rolling the rocks back into place. Things that hide under rocks do so for a reason and continued disturbance is bad for business.

During the spring, Millers Thumbs used to move into the stream to spawn. These are small brown fish with wide flattened heads that belonged to the bull head family. I used to find clusters of pink fish eggs attached to rocks. I got very excited when these weird looking fish started to make their appearance after months of no sighting. Several Millers Thumbs ended up in a horse trough, which I'd converted into an aquarium near our caravans.

Toward the end of the first year at Weald, another family with a caravan moved into the field. There was a couple with a boy about my age called Mike. For a while, he and I were friends, but then came a really bad falling out. Just across the road in bushes that covered a section of slightly higher ground, I'd built a "secret camp" out of hazel sticks and grass. It was just large enough to accommodate two kids and I was rather proud of this achievement. Mike was greatly impressed when I showed it to him, but days later the whole thing was completely wrecked. Mike told me some bigger boys had done this but it wasn't clear how the wreckers had found the camp in the first place. But I wasn't too concerned as all the building materials had been left scattered around. It was just a matter of gathering up and moving to a new spot.

But then a couple of days later, I caught Mike and a smaller boy, who I'd never seen before, hauling my precious hazel sticks away and overhearing him saying, 'We'll put these under my caravan, he won't find them there.' I then sprang out to demand what they were doing.

Later Mike and his parents moved on, but not before the boy tried unsuccessfully to rekindle our friendship. Betraying a secret camp was almost forgivable but stealing and hiding the building materials was in my mind the height of criminality. Perhaps not murder, but close.

Earlier, my father had taught me how to play draughts, but now I was playing chess with him quite regularly and would often win. My dyslectic condition has never affected my abilities in games like chess and later, contract whist. At that time, I used to play more simple card games like sevens and rummy with my sisters. But my mother, being a full-time teacher, was too often engaged in lesson preparation.

My father, having had a positive experience of the scouts as a boy, revived the local troop and became the scout master of the 10th Sevenoaks. I joined the troop which had up to a dozen members. The village had a scout hall, a small wooden building on the edge of the village sports oval. But the building hadn't been used since the former scout master had moved out of the district and the local troop disbanded. After the start-up had been advertised around the village, about eight boys turned up for the first meeting at the scout hall. They were a nice group varying in age from 11 to 16. I was one of the youngest but was to meet lads I was later to attend school with in Sevenoaks.

Dad put aside his eccentricities and made a good scout master, displaying the care and leadership that the role demanded. A few months after the troop was re-established, we went camping at a scouting jamboree in Knole Park on the eastern side of Sevenoaks. Knole Park is the name given to the extensive grounds of Knole House with its woodlands, grassy flats and herds of fallow deer. This gathering was not particularly large by scouting standards, perhaps two dozen troops from across southern England and one from Germany.

For the two hundred boys that took part, the jamboree was perhaps a positive experience. The summer weather was kind and the actives well organised. But me, being the son of a scout master, I got to hear about the disquiet behind the scenes. The problem centred on the German delegation and their scout leader. The man himself seems to have been a reasonable rational guy, but 1953 was just eight years after the end of the war. The dozen or so German scouts who'd been brought over had been carefully selected as might have been expected of boys representing their country. But the effect of this was that they were all fine-looking fellows around 17 years old and well above the average age of the English scouts. In fact, there seemed to have been no senior scouts from the English side of the camp. So, the German lads developed a bit of a swagger, engaged in showing off as young men are apt to do when an opportunity presents itself. But amongst the English scout masters, some of whom had seen active service only a few years earlier, this raised images of the Nazi master race. My father felt sorry for the German scout leader who he told me really tried to smooth things over, but to no avail. In the end, people weren't speaking to each other and the outbreak of World War III was a definite possibility. But for me, it was an insight into the working of politics, of how the best intentions can sometimes go badly astray.

One aspect of the scouts is they had all sorts of awards with badges that could be sewn onto uniforms. One of these was the backwoods man award. So, while I went through the process of becoming a scout third class, I embarked on this award project with parental encouragement. This entailed keeping a nature diary, periodic written entries of the natural things I saw around me. I also had my artistic ability, so my diary included illustrations. Once started, this was a practise I was to continue on and off for years. But in these initial stages I would write out a rough draft, dad would then correct the spelling before I'd copy directly into the book. I still have this diary and another like it over 60 years later.

At about 13, I started reading *Bevis* by the 19th century author Richard Jefferies. Though ostensibly written for adults, this is a story of a teenage boy and his friends, seemingly a reflection of the author's own boyhood. I loved it, though struggled, reading two or three pages at a time. In the following year my reading list started to included technical works on geology. Nevertheless, my progress in the reading and writing department throughout my high school years was to remain painfully slow.

Even in Weald, there had been a stigma attached to caravan living. Waiting at the local bus stop one day, a local woman made a remark to my mother to the affect that people living in caravans needed to have their children taken away because they couldn't look after them properly. I'm not sure if this retort was the result of us kids being more rowdy than usual, but Molly's response was justifiably furious. 'Do you see under fed, poorly dressed, neglected children here with me?' she asked. 'Madam how dare you level such aspersions against my family. Who gave you the right to pass judgement on a subject about which you clearly know nothing?'

Chapter 8

Kemsing and The Wilderness School

FOR YEARS, MY PARENTS HAD been on the waiting list for a government built council house, but finally the good news arrived. A four-bedroom house was being built for us in a new estate at the village of Kemsing, on the other side of Sevenoaks. I think us kids hadn't minded the caravan life but our parents had found it a huge strain. But now after four years we were moving back into a proper house and furthermore, one with an inbuilt bathroom, toilet and laundry.

The move to Kemsing (the name translates as Kem's people) occurred a few weeks before the start of the next school year. So, I became a student at what was then called The Wilderness Secondary School for Boys (Wilderness being a local place name rather than a reflection of what went on there). Since then, I believe it's been re-named the Seal Hollow Road School. In 1954 the buildings were about five years old, single storey with extensive sporting fields and play grounds.

The C grade class I was in certainly had the potential to be a management problem, given some of the characters within the group. But disruptive behaviour in class was rare.

In those days, teachers were allowed to hit wayward students with a cane, ruler or sandshoe across the hand or backside. This sometimes worked, but there were boys who sought greater peer acceptance by boasting of the number of cuts of the cane they'd received. Whilst the misbehaviour that got them into trouble in the first place was of lesser importance.

I was on the receiving end of corporal punishment on only three occasions. Once for running in the corridor and on another occasion because the physical education teacher was in a thoroughly foul mood. I got whacked as a way of encouraging me to move faster, to show a bit of spirit. In those days I was a tall poorly coordinated kid and jumping over vaulting horses simply wasn't my thing. However, a heavy welt across the backside did nothing to improve my day nor open my eyes to the wonders of PE.

On the third occasion, the punishment was truly justified and a salutary lesson never to be forgotten. Even now, 60 years later, I would gladly shake the hand that delivered that fateful blow. One day my class was off on a rare excursion, but I, the dreamy kid, had forgotten my permission note from home and was therefore unable to go. Instead, I was put into a D grade class that had the reputation for being the worst group in the school and they were having a really bad day. The young teacher who had the great misfortune to be in the same room with them soon found himself facing a near riot. At this, foolish me was out of his seat and joining in. But then the teacher spotted me. 'You're from the other class,' he cried. 'Bend down!' At this I received a mighty whack with a rubber soled sandshoe on the backside and it really hurt. I sat down much chastened. Soon after that the Head Master Mr Streeter arrived cane in hand and order was restored. But for me a life-long lesson: when others are buggerising about it's never wise to join in.

The Wilderness playground was not always a friendly place, but unlike Cubbington, the staff were on duty and watchful. Playground fights were uncommon but there was a distinct pecking order. I had my friends but of some of the alpha males, even if they were in the same class, I rarely spoke to. On one occasion after I left school, I was walking along the Pilgrims Way not far from home. There was one of the alpha males, arm in arm with his girl. I called out, 'Hi there John.' But he looked at me as if to say who the hell are you? Even though we'd shared a classroom for three years I genuinely think he didn't know who I was.

Lessons were generally basic and boring but sometimes caught my interest. School reports year to year were much the same, average or above average for most subject within my year group but poor in English and Physical Education. But it was English that seemed the absolute benchmark for all else. That is, if a student was deficient in English, all other subjects were dumbed down to that level regardless.

In maths, after four years in secondary modern, I never progressed beyond long division sums. So, no algebra, geometry and as for calculus, never heard of it.

Then there was my other weak subject, physical education. I was never good at sport. One of my worst memories was of the annual all school fun run. This was a winter time race of over a mile around the periphery of the school grounds. There was one lad called Pongo and something of an athlete. I would be running along at about two hundredth in the race, hating every minute and there would be Pongo, leaning his back to a tree. He'd the ability to be up with the front runners, but no desire to draw attention to himself. But then, as I finally struggled towards the finish line, Pongo would shoot past, having wasted fifteen minutes further back in the field.

My first full year at the wilderness school was the most difficult, the entries in my nature diary are sparse, a reflection of my troubles. Perhaps for me and my peers, puberty was at its transitional worst, often expressed as bullying, mostly verbal, sometimes physical. But in the following year, I got an unexpected lift in my standing amongst my classmates. Over a couple of lessons, our science teacher had delved into aspects of the local geology. I soon came to the conclusion I knew more about the subject than he did. But I chose to say nothing until I left the classroom. Chatting outside, I gave a brief dissertation on where the teacher had got it wrong. After this, I was given the nickname *Professor* and furthermore among my peers a little of the status that went with the title. Certainly, an improvement on Crawford Crackers, a reference to a well-known biscuit brand of the time. Then in the year after with some of the rougher kids turning 14 and leaving, I actually started to like the school.

There were two domestic features of that time which are no longer with us in the twenty-first century, the coal hole and the wringer. At the Kemsing house the coal hole was a small room off the walkway near our laundry. This was where the coal was stored, for each house had a coal burning stove used for heating. Two or three times a year a truck with hessian bags of coal would pull up outside. Then the driver would carry the bags in on his back to where they were needed, cut open and emptied. The used bags were always shaken out before being taken away. I used to think it the worst of jobs, among other things, physically demanding with the workers covered from head to foot in coal dust. No face mask, no nothing to keep the dust out of the lungs. A dead-end job I suspected that led to another sort of dead-end for some.

Though washing machines had come into general use after the war, they were not fitted with spin dry. At Weston, where all washing was done by hand, the wet clothes had been put through the double rollers of a hand operated wringing machine. At Kenning we enquired, for the first time ever, our own washing machine with built in wringer. But care was needed when putting the wet washing through lest the fingers get caught between the roller. As far as I know this never happened to members of my family, but at school it wasn't unusual to see kids with blacked fingernails, the result of wringer accidents.

The village Kemsing was in two parts, the older section centred around St Edith's Well and the Pilgrims Way, and the new housing estate where we lived. Behind the village on the north side rose Shore Hill, part of the chalk ramparts that formed the North Downs. On arriving in the area, I wasted little time in getting up there, exploring its forests and steep grassy slopes. Here were woodlands of beech, chestnut and ash with springtime displays of blue bells. Furthermore, here was an old chalk pit overgrown with dogwood, brambles and clumps of yew trees. The pit may once have had quite a substantial cliff face but erosion over a century or more had reduced this to a steep scree slope with only a section of cliff slowing at the top. All this to my eyes was a marvellous area in which to wander, the English countryside at its best.

Further along the valley to the west was the village of Otford and the Darent River. The Darent (sometimes called the Darenth) runs due north through a gap in the downs. To the south of the housing estate were fields, a stream and an old overgrown orchard in which we used to go scrumping. In that part of the world *to scrump* was to go into an orchard and eat the fruit off the tree. Most probably a crime but many didn't regard it as such.

It was while climbing around the old chalk pit with a group of friends that I had another of those dangerous what-if moments, only this time I must bear full responsibility. Me and two other boys were up near the top of the scree just below the cliff face. Three others were below, somewhat off to the right and scrambling up the steep climb, hands and feet tenuously gripping the chalky gravel. I thought, wouldn't it be fun to roll a rock down on these fellows, but with sufficient clearance for it to be safe? So a rock I was holding was let loose accidentally-on-purpose. But I hadn't counted on the erratic unpredictable way the rock bounced as it rocketed down the slope. It missed them by about twelve feet out to their right, flying through the air well above head height, but for a few seconds had me desperately worried. We all thought it a great joke, of course, but secretly I vowed never to try that again.

Soon after arriving at Kemsing, a new adult-sized bicycle was bought for me. It was black but like most bikes of that era had no gears. I used to ride to and from school, though it wasn't long before I was going further afield.

At about the age of 13, I started canvassing the neighbourhood, looking for after-school gardening jobs. In the scouts, I'd taken part in bob-a-job week and this gave me confidence at striking out on my own. I was usually conscientious, reliable and, over time, contributing a little to the household budget but this also provided funds for other activities.

I made my first long distant bike trip soon thereafter. Joe, a friend and a neighbour, and I decided to take my dad's old tent and ride about twenty-five miles to the Isle of Sheppey on the Themes Estuary. We camped there for the night before returning the next day. The date, according to my nature diary, was 21 May 1955.

On the way, we stopped at a service station to buy drinks and the lady behind the counter expressed surprise that two boys our age should be on our own so far from home. We didn't think this such a big deal but as it turned out there was a drama that even 60 plus years later leaves me puzzled.

Sheppey is a flat marshy island separated from the mainland by The Swale, a muddy channel which is crossed via a bridge. We arrived at our destination, the tops of low cliffs overlooking the Themes Estuary just on dark. We erected our tent, made a camp fire and had something to eat.

During the night, I thought I heard voices but on emerging in the morning discovered another two-man tent, a pinky-purple colour, had popped up a little distance way. During breakfast we paid it no attention. I then went for a walk, making my way down the tumbled muddy cliff face to the beach.

When I got back, Joe told me there were two small boys in the other tent on their own. We went over. One of the kids looked to be about seven with the younger no more than four. During the night, there had been rain and some of our gear had gotten wet. But here it was much worse with water everywhere. A box of breakfast cereal and a soft toy floating amid the bedding. But the tent itself seemed to be almost brand new. We tried asking the kids where their mum and dad were, but as strangers, could get not a word.

We came to the conclusion that a responsible adult couldn't be too far away, after all how did they get here, who'd put up the tent? But we had not seen nor heard any sign of a vehicle and this was a fairly isolated spot with not a house in sight across a flat treeless landscape, with only the road to Sheerness two hundred yards away. Surely with the flooding during the night whoever was with them must have gone off to get help. But if they'd arrived in some way via the road why hadn't they taken the kids with them? Sure, they could see our tent but we could be just about anyone, as it was, we were children ourselves.

What to do? We didn't want to delay our departure for there was a need to get home while there was still daylight. After talking it over, we packed up and set off, reporting the two at a service station along the way. I just hope we were taken seriously, but could we have done more? Looking back, I would say yes, but in the days that followed there were no reports of missing kids and so the mystery remains.

I also rejoined the scouts, this time a troop based in the town of Sevenoaks itself. The scout master of the 19th Sevenoaks was Charlie Weston, a soft-spoken and kindly man who'd fought in Burma during the war. But like most old soldiers he spoke little of his experiences.

We scouts spent a lot of time in Knole Park. It was then I got to know Webbs Ally and The Hole in the Wall, places that had been important in my father's scouting career. I eventually became the patrol leader of the scruffiest most likeable patrol in the troop. Our greatest triumph was winning the Garnet Cup award in 1956 for our presentation on trees and birds of the local area. I'd played a major role in that project but with a little help from my dad.

But, I wasn't universally liked amongst the troop. One boy in particular Herbert - his dislike bordered on the pathological, but I don't know what it was about me he found so objectionable. I wouldn't class him as a bully because he didn't pick on the younger kids, though he certainly had his sights on me. On one occasion in company he asked, 'If you have a hole in the ground and half fill it, what do you have left?'

After a few seconds, I replied, 'A hole.'

This was of course the correct answer to this trick question. But he was so intent on catching me out he went on about *half holes*, until someone else pointed out there was no such thing. He'd fallen into a hole of his own making. And all this was before my patrol won the Garnet Cup, something I know caused him no end of irritation.

But later he did get his revenge of sorts. After receiving the Garnet award I'd been told to take the silver cup home and look after it. This I duly did but the following year, there was some confusion as to where it had gone. Finally, someone got around to asking me and I was only too happy to hand it back, but then Herbert accused me of trying to steal it.

It was these sorts of people in my childhood, along with Mary Shelley's *Frankenstein*, that led to my science fiction creation of the Krarls, a nation composed entirely of dangerous psychopaths who's murderous inclinations are mostly kept in check by a rigid set of laws. A concept that became the vehicle for much black satire in books like *The Threads of Time*. However, in my boyhood I never found Herbert the least bit amusing, funny perhaps but never amusing.

It was in 1957 when I saw my grandparents Fred and Dot for the last time. My mother was again talking to her father and they visited us in Kemsing. But on their arrival, Norman refused to see either of them, retreating to his bedroom, only emerging after they'd gone. 'I'll not talk to that swob,' he declared, referring to Fred.

One of my companions in those days was a boy I'll call Leith who lived nearby on the Kemsing estate. The story that surrounds Leith, rather than the boy himself, has had a profound influence on my thinking over the years. I first met him at the Wilderness school, though he wasn't in my class. A slightly built kid he seemed a lost soul and I came to understand from him that life at home was utterly awful. Among other things, his mother had died and his father had remarried. Then at 14, Leith was effectively kicked out of the house, only to be taken in by a neighbouring family who already had five kids of their own. This worked for a few months, but then Leith was accused of stealing money at school. At this, he was kicked out a second time and became a ward of the state.

My mother had spoken to the family that had taken Leith in who in turn had talked with the boy's father. But because I was the kid's friend the story was passed on to me. It seemed that during the war, the man Leith thought of as his dad had been away fighting somewhere. His mother back in England had an affair with another man and Leith was the result. The husband had returned, but a few years later, the woman had died, Leith being about four at the time. This had left him to be raised by a man who wasn't his biological father, a man who may have had a whole set of issues as a result of his wartime experiences.

The last time I saw Leith, he was about 16 and on the run, having escaped from wherever they'd had him locked up. When I asked what it was like in the boy's home, he replied, 'You don't want to know.' In light of more recent revelation, I can only guess what that might have meant.

But on hearing the story, my conclusion, sex might be great, but irresponsible acts can sometimes have appalling consequences that roll on for decades. I can only hope that Leith eventually managed to sort out his life after what had been a terrible start.

Chapter 9

The Lullingstone Experience

SOON AFTER ARRIVING AT KEMSING friends of my mother, seeing that I was so interested in science, introduced me to the people running the archaeological dig at Lullingstone in the Darent Valley. But they thought I might be a bit young and added it wasn't for everyone. However, on being taken that first Sunday, I absolutely fell in love with the place. For me Lullingstone, four miles from where I lived, was a door into the adult world where I was treated as a useful member of a team, free from the foibles of school.

All archaeological digs set out to answer the same basic questions. Who lived there, when did this happen, what sort of lives did they lead and how and why was the site abandoned? The answers have to be built up by careful detective work over time. The Lullingstone site was that of a Roman villa which in the first century AD had started as a simple farm house. Then after a period of abandonment, it was developed into a substantial building in the third and fourth centuries before its final demise in the fifth, about the time the Romans withdrew from Britain.

I sometimes wondered what the last days of Roman Lullingstone was like. Perhaps the aristocratic family loaded their belonging into ox carts. Then set out with armed retainers heading for Londinium, 20 miles away while the surrounding countryside degenerated into chaos. They would have hoped the army would someday return, bringing order to this far flung province.

Then there were the unknowns who had, a century later, camped amid the ruins of the abandoned villa, the ashes of a small fire the only sign of their passing. Who were they? What language did they speak? What was their world like? Perhaps they were survivors of that climate related calamity that had wiped out half the population of Europe through famine, disease and war.

In the years before I appeared on the scene, Lullingstone's spectacular mosaic floor and most of the foundations of the main building had been excavated. Finds from the site included two marble busts and here was a very early Christian chapel. But the chapel with its wonderful painted walls had been upstairs while in the basement below was a pagan temple. But during the building's dying days, everything had collapsed during a fire into the basement, making for a pagan-Christian mix.

But it would seem the Romans who once lived there believed in having a two way bet, pray to the new god while maintaining respect for the old. It's not hard to see how so many pagan beliefs, symbols and practises were readily incorporated into early Christianity. The pagan-Christian mix not such a bad metaphor after all.

In the centuries after the Romans had abandoned Britain much of the villa's walls or the rubble thereof, had been removed by people looking for dressed stone. So, what remained was the foundations, floors and some of the deeper basement rooms that had escaped earlier quarrying.

The dig was run by Lieutenant Cornel Meates, a soldier in both world wars and second in charge was 'Curly' Rook, a veteran of the first world war. The other enthusiasts were of a younger generation, everyone from housewives to lawyers and students. But the place had a real sense of camaraderie, of people pursuing a common cause.

Serious excavation was only done during the warmer months. With the onset of winter, any exposed walls and floors had to be covered with straw and sacking to reduce the risk of frost damage. During my first summer, exploration was being expanded into the periphery of the site. I was the dig's teaboy and all-round helper, but in subsequent years, a small builder's trowel in hand, I became a serious Sunday archaeologist.

The contrast between the Lullingstone dig, home and school were stark. Three different worlds but at the time I never stopped to ponder the irony.

Early July 1956 and we Sunday archaeologists were just about to finish lunch sitting around the outside wooden tables on the high ground overlooking the dig. There had been a bit of friendly banter around the table but as a 14-year-old, I preferred to laugh at the wit but otherwise say little.

But then I reached into my bag and pulled out a fossil I'd found the previous day and handed it over to my geology student friend, Morkie, sitting opposite me.

'A Spondilus mussel shell,' he declared. 'Quite a nice one.'

'Biggest I've seen,' I assured him. 'Both the top and bottom parts are there. Came out of a large bump of rock at the bottom of the Kemsing Chalk Pit. All the underside spines are still in place. But why such long spines?'

'In some modern species of bivalves, spines are used to anchor the shell in some sort of substrate, like a piece of drift wood,' suggested Morkie.

'Okay,' I replied. 'But this thing was buried in chalky mud very soon after it died. That's how the two halves of the shell stayed together, but there was no sign of fossilised wood. In fact, I've never seen fossilised drift wood in chalk. The spines are really long - two inches, perhaps used to simply anchor it into mud.'

'Yes, could have done,' agreed Morkie. 'Anyway, time to get back.'.

The work involved carefully trowelling through dark compacted soil near the edge of a Roman well that we'd cleaned out the year before. So far that day we discovered very little just a few pot fragments, cheap undecorated kitchen ware that seemed to date back to the third century. Besides that, there were the oyster shells, for the local Romans had been very fond of oysters, the crumbling half fossilised shells being just about everywhere around the site.

An hour into our methodical scraping, Morkie called out, 'Come, have a look at this.' When I went over, he added, 'Thought I'd come across the bones of a small dog. That is until I started to uncover the skull.'

'Jesus,' I exclaimed, down on my knees for a closer look. 'Lying on its side - the weight of the soil must have crushed the skull flat, but that's no dog. Can you work the soil way so we can see the jaw?'

This was done.

'No teeth,' observed Morkie. 'The milk teeth never had time to come through before it died.'

'Shall I go find the Cornel?' I asked.

'Yes, I think so,' agreed Morkie.

I found Cornel Meates in another part of the site chatting with a couple of the other diggers. 'Sir, can you come?' I said, 'We think we've the bones of a baby.'

'A newborn indeed,' declared the Cornel, when he arrived. 'At best a couple of weeks old. In a society with high infant mortality that sort of thing wasn't unusual. The proximity to the well is significant, the mother's hopes being that the child's spirit would be reborn. The well a source of water and therefore a source of life. But this isn't a Christian burial. Don't do any more for now. Cover it over with a plastic sheet and put a note up saying the area is not to be disturbed. Tomorrow I'll let the authorities know, the police will need to check it out, make sure the death isn't a recent occurrence. Well done you two.'

That evening, I arrived home to that second world in which I said nothing of ancient tragedies, the bones of a long dead baby. But there was a new addition to the household. My youngest brother Adrian, born three months earlier and just starting to be fully conscious of his surroundings. Mum had taken time off work and was still breast feeding. I waved a little blue bunny at the new baby lying in his bassinet and got a nice response, a wave of the arms. *When he's older I'll take him in a push chair a little way up Chalky Lane and Shore Hill,* I thought. *Introduce him to the world of trees and wild flowers.*

Meals were set around the Sunday dinner table. My father had done the cooking. The radio reported massive floods in parts of Australia, two thirds of the Riverina region underwater. Farmers having to swim livestock across flooded creeks, the wheat crop left unsown because machinery couldn't get onto the boggy ground. But in this household, nobody was paying attention. Old Dunaway Station was unknown and lay years into the future.

An argument started up between myself and sister Gill over nothing much, while quiet Hilary kept out of it. Then later Gill, who was going to grammar school, had homework but stuck on quadratic equations called on mum's help. I never got homework, quadratic equations a total mystery, but my younger brother Jon wanted to play. Dad yelled at as us to shut the door, the house was cold even though it wasn't winter. Then told us to turn the lights off when we left a room, electricity was expensive. Later, I made cups of cocoa for myself and my parents. The cat, Pinky, who was earlier put outside wanted to be let back in before everyone went to bed. Financially, the household was managing but only just.

Come Monday morning, I rode over from Kemsing to the Wilderness school in Seal Hollow Road. Part of this journey was along an ancient footpath called The Ash Splash and after recent rain somewhat muddier than usual.

I put my bicycle in the school bike shed and as I locked up, the bells started to ring for roll call. I hurried with bag over my shoulder. Whatever happened over the weekend was of no importance. For the next six hours I was just another 14-year-old school boy. The end of the term was not far away and I was looking forward to the long summer break.

Our form master and English Teacher, Mr Oakley, transfixed us with a grim icy stare; in class he never smiled. Though on occasions, I'd spied him at parent teacher meetings where he'd transform, demonstrating he really was human after all.

When we are all settled, he read out the names, 'Algar, Barnet, Brooke, Connors. . . ' We answered as our names were called. There were a couple of announcements, the all school assembly had been moved to first thing Wednesday morning and John Everet was to report to the front office. As he went, Johnnie took the roll.

Then the bell went but we knew to stay in our seats. Mr Oakey, who we disrespectfully called *Annie Oakey*, would be taking us for English and first thing would be a spelling test. Blank sheets of exercise paper were handed around, we scribbled our names on top and then the words were read out and we wrote them down as best we could.

Of late, I'd been making up imaginary bird names, and during a free few moments my mind turned to the white-headed pygmy goose, sooty owl, green catbird. Now that was an interesting name, what would a green catbird look like? Was it a cat, a bird, or somehow a glossy green mixture of both?

Later that morning, our metalwork teacher, Mr Shepard, checked the roll and then disappeared into a storeroom only to reappear waving a large sword. All the boys grinned; they'd seen this before.

Mr Shepard stuck the tip of the weapon into the top of a work bench and promptly declared all German made steel to be rubbish. Nevertheless, the sword was impressive, a shiny two-edged blade, the handle black with a pummel on the end displaying a Nazi swastika. However, I knew, as perhaps few if any of the others did in that room, that the swastika was an ancient symbol. The mosaic floor at Lullingstone had swastika designs that had absolutely nothing to do with the Nazis.

But Mr Shephard had a story to tell. Some wartime tale as to how it came into his possession. A wild wicked tale of daring, the sword having been captured in battle from some German officer though the action had been done by a friend of our teacher's who had duly passed the weapon on to him. Show over, we returned to the more serious business of school metalwork.

The next lesson, geography, was sometimes interesting. Previously, attention had been on southeast Asia - Singapore was out that way somewhere. Malaysia wasn't there, a lot of trouble going on, an insurgency or something? The Sarawak River. What would it be like to visit Borneo? Be on a river boat chugging along a muddy river channel lined with nipa palms.

But today, the attention shifted further south to Australia. There was a short film, black and white projected onto a screen showing iconic views of Sydney and the bridge (always the bridge). But this, it seemed, was also the land of sheep for here were blokes in wide-brimmed hats putting Marinos through a drafting race, control gates moving left and right. Then the same guys were inspecting a couple of woolly rams, using hands to open the living fleece, showing its depth and quality. This looked like another world as indeed it was. As for the hats, John Spencer's observation that the wider the brim the bigger a man's bank mortgage - hence the expression *mortgage hats* - was also way off in the unknown future.

Lesson over, recess followed, a short break in which many kids ate their lunch. The government provided free milk in those days and I grabbed my half-sized bottle from the crate. I then collected with a group of friends at a designated meeting place, Coll, Soggy and Other Dave. The playground was not so territorial, but care still needed to be taken as with whom we mixed, but here we were all friends hanging out together.

'Look what I've got here,' announced Coll, showing the top of a cigarette pack just long enough for all to see, before stuffing it back into his bag.

'You can have those,' I declared, with a dismissive wave.

'You still don't like them?' asked Soggy.

'Sore throat,' I complained, 'expensive too.'

'Have one of mine,' proposed Other Dave, producing a little packet of confectionery made up to look like real cigarettes. These were half the size of the real thing, soft sugary white with a red food dyed tip.

'Don't mind if I do old boy, old chap,' declared Coll, an overdone posh accent. We all took one.

'I say, I say gosh these are not at all bad,' I proclaimed, a theatrical flourish, my version of a posh accent on display. Then I tossed the pseudo-cigarette in the air and tried to catch it in my open mouth, but missed so that it landed at my feet. The others laughed. But I added to the joke. 'Never leave cig butts unattended,' I declared, grinding the confectionery into the ground with my heel.

More laughs.

'Why did the owl howl?' asked Other Dave.

'Because, because the woodpecker, would peck her,' I replied emphasising the point by giving the other boy a series of friendly shoves.

At this, a retaliatory arm was flung around my neck. Then while I was in a headlock, 'I pinch and punch for the first day of the month.'

'Can't say that,' I protested, 'that was last week.'

But on breaking free I counter-attacked with, 'A kick and a flick for being so quick.'

'A swipe and a pong, for getting it wrong,' declared Soggy, joining the melee.

'That doesn't even rhyme, silly,' I protested, using a friendly shoulder to barge back.

Recess was over and it was maths. I didn't much like the subject, long multiplication and divisions were basically boring. But at times our teacher, Mr Silverside, could be fun. He was an intelligence officer during the war. Based in North Africa he would spin tall tales of his liaisons with the local Arabs. Being a bit of an actor, he could put on a show that was guaranteed to add a dash of ironic humour to the day.

Physical education then followed. This time we were outside and the teacher was someone other than the fellow who once whacked me for being too slow. Being summer, we played cricket, but what I hated most was the lead up to the game. Two team captains were named and these in turn selected the talent on offer. This became a popularity contest and it wasn't unusual for uncoordinated me to be picked last. On this occasion during the game, the lack of confidence of others was well-founded. I was painfully hit on the shin and out leg-before-wicket, second ball. I had a sore leg for the rest of the day, but enough to put a guy off such games for the rest of his life. Though in Roman times they had games too, but these games were far more awful.

The following year there was a real drama at Lullingstone. On 5 September, severe thunderstorms swept over south eastern England. It was Friday afternoon and I remember looking across from the school playground at the dense black cloud over the Darent Valley and the surrounding hills. On arriving home, the water coming off Shore Hill was still gushing down Childsbridge Lane. Tree branches and sizable lumps of chalk in the middle of the road were testaments to the earlier force of the flood.

Saturday morning, I rode my bike through Otford and up the Darent Valley. The road was deserted of traffic, hardly surprising with washouts and fallen tress across the road. On arrival, I discovered the dig underwater with only a few walls sticking above the brown flood. Cornel Meates and Mr Rook were there thoroughly shaken.

During the storm, a wall of water had come down what we thought of as an old cart track going up the hill just to the south of the site. Looking later and judging by the debris left behind, that wall of water would have been at least seven feet high. I had been channelled by the contours of the surrounding hills. Perhaps this wasn't a track at all but a drainage channel, for flash floods of this nature must have occurred in the past. Fortunately, the damage to the site wasn't as bad as first thought though some parts remained buried in silt for quite some time.

During the Anglo-Saxon period, the hillside above Lullingstone had been cleared for cropping, and as a result, what was called hill wash, compacted reddish clay with lumps of flint, had come down over the back of the site. This was up to eighteen feet deep but we archaeologists were keen to discover what lay underneath. At the end of my second season, work started at the beginning of winter to clearing away this hill wash. This was hard work with pick, shovel and wheelbarrow, carried out by a reduced team of workers. So, my Sunday work extended through winter and then into the winter after that. I became an expert at building barrow runs. The trick to a good barrow run - the wooden planks laid on the ground needed to really be firm so that they didn't vibrate as the loaded barrows went over them.

Despite all this winter work, not a great deal was found under the mountain of hill wash. In Roman times, there had been an area of flat ground below a steep embankment. Here someone had set up a clay oven or pottery kiln. But apart from that there was not much else.

But the hill wash itself had a distinctive occupation layer with the occasional fragment of Saxon pottery. In the summer before I left England, the remains of a little chapel were unearthed further up the hill. It seemed to have dated to the 10th and 11th centuries. The stones used in its construction had been borrowed from the ruined villa, and no doubt when the chapel fell into disuse the stones were recycled elsewhere in the district.

Just to the south of the chapel were bodies, a family gravesite, a man, woman and child. The small child must've been about two at the time of death for the skull plates hadn't fully fused. The child had died first for when the other graves had been dug this had let in water causing a slippage in the earth around the child's bones.

As these were Christian burials, it was decided to have the bones re-interned in the local churchyard at Eynsford. I was given the job of gathering the remains into three cardboard boxes. At the time, I went about this task with a degree of reverence. After all, if the couple had other children, ones that had survived them, they were likely someone's ancestors. I imagined the grieving mother laying flowers at her child's grave, a simple wooden cross now long gone. And knowing that when the time came, she too would be buried in this spot overlooking the river valley where she'd perhaps lived and work all her life.

What I didn't know at the time was that many of my ancestors from both sides were north Kent people. It wasn't beyond the realms of possibility that these were in fact my own ancestors. Perhaps if they had had a say they might have resented the disturbance. But on the other hand, if, in a thousand years hence, someone was to dig me up, there might be some satisfaction in knowing they were family.

However, their eternal peace could have been disturbed in another way. Some years earlier, a German flying bomb (otherwise known as a V1 or doodle bug) had exploded nearby. These signs of the Second World War were quite common around the North Downs. Usually a round crater 18 to 24 feet across, often with bits of bomb casing and engine fragments rusting in the bottom. It seems that after an impact, people would gather up the larger pieces of debris and contemptuously chuck them into the hole.

It was while working at Lullingstone I developed a real interest in fossils and geology. North Kent is full of quarries of one sort or another and I was adding to my knowledge by trying to read books on the subject. Soon, I had a collection of chalk fossils, mostly sea urchins and shells, but one shark tooth. The gault clay pit at Trottiscliffe was a delight, the amount and range of stuff to be had there extraordinary. There was also a special fossil bed which was only about two inches deep. It occured where the Folkstone sands met the overlaying gault clay. Here there were species of ammonites found nowhere else. I wondered what it was a hundred million years ago that had originally brought about this abrupt change in the environment so evident from the geology.

I finally left school about the time of my 15th birthday. Soon thereafter, I went on a ten-day fossil hunting trip along the south coast of England from Lyme Regis to the Isle of Wight. Britain is not a particularly big place but has the most extraordinary geology. However, that section of coast must rate as the absolute jewel in the fossil hunter's crown. By travelling from west to east a fossil hunting geologist traverses about a hundred and sixty million years of the Earth's history. As for the Isle of Wight, it's all there in vertical striations, a consequence of the same massive forces that built the Alps.

On the first day, I arrived by train with my bicycle at the town of Yoevil and then peddled my way to a youth hostel at Litton Cheney. From then on, it was rocks and fossils, cliffs and beaches. I'd learnt a lesson from my earlier expedition to the Isle of Sheppey. On that occasion, I had a rucksack on my back, hard work when riding a bike, and I'd arrived home after two days utterly exhausted. This time, I had a rack with panya bags on the back of the bike, a lower centre of gravity giving much better control. In addition, I had a tennis racket clamp on the front forks to carry my geological hammer, essential equipment for any serious geologist.

I stayed in other youth hostels along the way and met dad as had been pre-arranged in Bournemouth before staying for two nights with my Uncle Norman. We, that is me, Norman, Aunty Beryl, and cousin Pat had an interesting fossil-hunters picknick at a beach side exposer of Barton Clay. I returned home by train.

The following year I made another fossil hunting trip through East Anglia. This time I was away from home for 18 days. During the previous expedition I'd been lucky with the weather, but this time it seemed to rain every second day.

On my list of places to see was a supposedly interesting exposure of red crag in a disused quarry at Thorpe Next Norwich. The pit was in the ground of the local mental hospital and I'd to get written permission to visit the site.

So here I was, a 16-year-old turning up at the mental hospital's front office with the words, 'Good morning I'm a geologist, I believe you're expecting me.'

Perhaps not the best choice of words.

The man behind the counter gave me a slightly odd look and asked, 'Do you have a referral, were you asked to come here?'

'No, I wrote,' I replied, before adding, 'I've come to look at the pit in the grounds.'

'What is your name, please?'

'Crawford.'

Then turning to a secretary, 'Are we expecting a Mr Crawford?'

At this point on realising my admission was imminent I produced the letter that explained everything.

The quarry turned out to be different to what I'd expected, more clay than red shell-grit sand and not that interesting. Perhaps this was an overlay of glacial deposits and a bit more digging at the bottom on the pit was required. But then a couple of other fossil hunters appeared, a father and son. They seemed the perfectly normal sorts of enthusiast one could expect to bump into just about anywhere. It was only when I started to talk of other sites outside the grounds of the mental hospital that I was told, 'Oh no we couldn't go there.' It was then that I realised they were patients.

I'm glad to report that at the end of the day the mad fossil hunter made good his escape and was last seen pedalling his bike towards the youth hostel at Naughton Mill.

Six days later, I walked into another youth hostel at Felixstowe and someone said what a nice day it had been, an improvement on what we they had been getting. I replied, 'Not where I've been.' I'd just arrived from the Chillesford area having laboured all day it seemed under my own private low-pressure system. Such are the vagaries of the English climate.

Besides the weather and administrative misunderstandings, the only other mishap was a broken bike chain four miles from home.

Chapter 10

The Leaving of England

I REMEMBER THE CAREER ADVISOR AS being a young man with a very select private school accent. He briefly looked at his notes, then in a voice that suggested he found the current proceeding tiresome, stated that I was best suited for work as an agricultural labourer. He asked me no questions and the whole interview lasted no more than two minutes. I went away angry. I'd spent eleven years in the school system and now I was being shown the door and given a symbolic kick up the arse as I went. But the oracle had spoken, the life sentence delivered in an accent that denoted class and privilege.

Looking back, I can see where the man was coming from. My academic performance at school had been dismal, whereas my extra curriculum activities in science, if he even knew of them, counted for absolutely nothing. But there was one ray of hope for having some artistic ability; there were moves to send me on to art college. This duly took place but I don't think people who knew me well could guess what possibilities the future might hold. The situation is best summed by my school's head master Mr F R Streeter, whose letter reads in part:

> *To whom it may concern,*
> *David was an individualist who showed remarkable intelligence in matters concerning nat-*

> ural history and art but whose responses to intelligence tests were unrepresentative. His Kent Standard Score of 81 reflected his academic standard rather than his real intelligence.
>
> I have no hesitation in saying that David's character was most excellent and he was most co-operative and helpful both in school and out.

The Standard Score seems related to the standardised system still widely used in UK schools where the average score is set at 100. With a standard deviation of plus or minus 15, this meant that on leaving school I was falling just below the bandwidth around what constituted average intelligence.

The testing for this was done in the months before I was due to leave school. I remember it being conducted in class time, there was no warning and we were given a test paper, told to do our best and not to worry. Mr Streeter in his letter dated June 1959, two years after the event, was the first and only time I was to hear about the results of this assessment.

A couple of weeks after I left school, I went on that fossil hunting expedition along the south coast. But during this time, there were two important developments. I'd been accepted into art college and my reading difficulties that for years had been the absolute bane of my life just vanished.

While away on my trip, I'd made a point whenever possible of reading roadside billboards. I still remember one slogan: *Stop for Super Shell and Go* that seemed to be just about everywhere. All I could think of was that the Shell Oil Company had somehow magically waved the wand and worked their *super go* on me. But in these more enlightened times, it was my understanding that with some types of dyslexia sudden improvements in reading ability during the mid-teens could occur. I also understood that dyslexia was often treatable with specialist tuition. More recently, a colleague of mine had a nine-year-old son who was about three years behind in his reading age and, so discouraged, was refusing to even try. After six months of tuition, lo and behold he was two years in front. Back then I'd perhaps got there the hard way by finding my own path, pursuing my own interests. But reading is one thing, spelling another and even today, I remain deficient in that department.

With my new found ability, I set about reading anything I could get my hands onto. This not only included Orwell, Wells and Steinbeck but also weighty volumes on history and of course, science. J Z Young's *Life of Vertebrates* became one of those heavy must-read tomes I used to cart around.

It would have been interesting to know if my intelligence test for the Kent standard score had been run at this time what the results would have looked like. But then if I'd been born three weeks later and started school at five and not four years of age that would have seemed entirely possible.

The time spent studying for a National Diploma of Design at the Maidstone College of Art brings back fond memories. I was still living at home but having to commute daily to Maidstone. I made friends, some of whom called me *spider*, a reference to my long, lean and lanky appearance. But on balance, the staff and students made for a genuinely friendly atmosphere, a contrast to the institutions I'd encountered elsewhere.

But us young people were not beyond a few pranks. On one occasion, a bunch of enterprising students got hold of the college skeleton and smuggled it into the principal's office. Quite a feat seeing they had to slip past the ever watchful secretaries of the typing pool. There, the plastic bones were sat up in the principal's chair wearing the principal's hat and dark green jacket.

There was a degree of friendly rivalry between ourselves at Maidstone and another art college in Tonbridge Wells. Our college had its mascot, a mighty set of water buffalo horns. But one day, the student body received intelligence that the rivals from Tonbridge Wells planned to steal our sacred mascot during a social function. To ward off this threat, our side set the horns into a large block of concrete thinking the sheer weight would be enough to deter the thieves. But thanks to an excellent piece of strategic planning, the Tonbridge Wells mob deftly defied the odds and made off with the horns, concrete and all. The whole thing had been snatched, passed through an open window and into an open sports car waiting outside.

I witnessed none of this, but on arriving at college the following morning, found the place abuzz. Within an hour, 120 students had taken to the roads all heading for Tonbridge Wells, an excited yours truly amongst them.

With friends I hitchhiked into the town and assembled with about 50 of my fellow raiders with yet more reinforcements arriving by the minute. There was much excited talk but no real plan, though flour bombs were being seriously considered. But then the deputy principle from the offending college boldly and bravely stepped into our midst. He addressed us as adults, appealing to our sense of responsibility. Okay, it had all been a really tremendous joke but had gone much too far. The mood changed, yes, we were grown up people, common sense set in and so we all headed back from whence we came.

During more normal days at college, I studied various aspects of design, practised lettering by hand, and learned about the working of printing presses. Also, of three colour work, of four colour work, line drawing, of photography, book binding and type setting. This was an era before computer-graphics and terms like *photoshop* were yet to enter the English language.

I became interested in a girl by the name of Hellan. She was perhaps a year older than me, a quiet sort, but I judged that if she was looking for a relationship it would be with someone older and more mature. We never went further than a few pleasant words and the odd joke in class.

I also worked with the special education teacher, Mr Edmunds, to improve my writing skills and made real progress. Later, I was to write to him on arriving in Australia, but regret not keeping that going.

One day, someone said to me words to the effect that the design diploma I was aiming for would be a nice way of rounding off my formal education. Looking back, I find that ironic. The *formal rounding off,* when it eventuated 25 years later, had absolutely nothing to do with art, design or printing.

But there were other issues. Firstly, would this diploma course that ran for four years, land me a job and set me on a career path? The end of year report from the college wasn't pointing to any outstanding talent on my part.

At that time, these sort of government funded courses were being run by art colleges across the country, but our teachers, many of whom worked in areas like advertising, were telling us things were tight in that particular job market and likely to get worse. Furthermore, if we really wanted to pursue a career in the art related industries we needed to be looking at alternative employment before seeking a way forward. With my abysmal, effectively none existent school record, that seemed a recipe for disaster.

Even with both my parents working and me contributing a little with part-time gardening, the family finances remained difficult. But me leaving home, getting out into the world, would significantly lessen the burden.

For years, my father had been talking of migrating to somewhere like Canada, New Zealand or Australia. I think the only reason he'd not pursued that further was because of his crippled condition, the fear of rejection on medical grounds. I didn't have that impediment and as my second year at Maidstone drew to a close, I started to think it was time to act. Furthermore, I'd never felt part of English society, the years spent in caravans and the experiences of school major factors.

There was a further reminder of this in a court case that involved a guy I'll call Robert. We had first met in the scouts at Weald and later we'd been in the same class in the Wilderness school. We were not close friends, but I knew him as a quietly spoken, nice sort of bloke. Back in Weald, and having left school, he'd become keen on some girl only to be caught by the father climbing through the girl's window. Silly lad he may have been, but hauled before a judge he'd been charged with breaking and entering and sentenced to two years jail. I was shocked on reading an account in the local paper. It certainly caused a stir in the district, but some of the older generation seemed to think this somehow amusing. I suspected that if Robert hadn't been a village lad, had a grammar school education and decent legal representation, he would have been treated quite differently. British justice - two years, a criminal record, but what impact was that going have on the rest of his life?

Years later in Australia, I was to hear of a similar case in a small country town, though there, the lad had been caught climbing down a drain pipe. The end result, the offender got a swift kick up the backside by the local sergeant of police before being told to go home and behave. It seems to me the impact of a policeman's boot was far preferable to being banged up in jail with god knows what for company.

At home, when I raised the issue of migration, my parents were a bit taken aback. For them, it'd come out of the blue. At first, I favoured New Zealand, but dad pointed out that Australia was bigger and in the long run much more was likely going on there. So, plans started to get underway.

Enquires at Australia House in London had me directed to an organisation called The Big Brother Movement. Their aim was to recruit sixteen-, seventeen-year old British boys, ship them across to Australia and find them their first job. The Movement would then be their legal guardian until such time as they turned 21 or a suitable relative arrived. And all this at no cost to the migrant. This seemed a good deal to me.

When I told Mr Edmunds, the special education teacher, of these plans he thought it all good. Adding, 'I can see you many years into the future managing a sheep station out there in Australia.' This never happened but at one stage there was the potential.

But not everyone thought Australia was a good idea. Marcus, a fellow student at art college who I also knew from both school and the scouts, thought I was letting my country down. Sure, things were difficult in Britain but destined to get better providing everyone stayed and pulled their weight.

I also went to see my art teacher from school, Mr Edwards, a man I'd always liked and respected. He lived in the older part of Kemsing but this was the first time I'd visited him at home. He was visibly shocked at the news. It wasn't clear if my impending departure was seen as some sort of failure on his part or if there were other reasons. Many years later, I was sad to hear of his sudden death at home. If I could travel back in time, Mr Edwards would definitely be one I'd dearly love to speak with. As it was, I left his house that day feeling embarrassed with neither a handshake nor a wish of good luck for the future.

But I can only speculate as to what my life would have been like if, as Marcus had suggested, I'd chosen to remain in Britain. The only certainty is that my life would have been different. There were push factors, reasons for leaving England, but there was also a sense of adventure that was providing a strong pull factor. Go there, try that, see where it leads.

My last entry in my English nature diary, dated 26 October 1959 reads as follows.

> *I am standing on the promenade deck of the Italian Liner Fair Sky. Across the choppy waters of the Solent I can see in the gathering dusk the white cliffs of the Isle of Wight. At the cliffs end, I can just make out the three big rocks with the lighthouse at the end, they are The Needles. As the darkness closes in the lighthouse begins to blink out its warning to shipping.*
>
> *But to me it is not a warning, it is a farewell. A farewell to England. To the oak and the ash, to the damp woods. A farewell to the song of the Blackbird and to the cold wet winters, to the spring violets. To the yew berries of Autumn.*
>
> *Now it is dark and the sea is wild. Only the little blinking light afar is there to remind me of England of the North Down of Kent my late home.*
>
> *But I must go forward into a new life, a new country, a country of opportunity. So Australia here I come!*

I was 17 when I wrote that and it would be over 50 years before I again set foot on English soil.

Chapter 11

Australia: The Early Days

AMONGST SOME WHO BELIEVE THE Earth to be flat there is a conviction that Australia doesn't exist. That is, if someone gets on a plane in San Francisco or London and flies out to Australia, they're really being taken to some place in South America where trained actors put on funny accents in an effort to fool them. A very interesting idea, but it doesn't match too well with my experiences over the last sixty years. But as a 17-year-old on that emigrant ship from England it certainly crossed my mind that Australia wouldn't be anything like what I'd been led to believe. But I'd met a couple of Australians at the Lullingstone dig and they'd seemed genuine enough, no signs of acting there.

My Uncle Jack, mum's older brother had been living in Australia for several years but we'd virtually lost contact. But the fact that he and his family were supposedly still there gave reason to hope.

On the ship Fair Sea, there were about 35 boys in the Big Brother Movement group plus two male minders. There was not a great deal to do though our minders supervised an hour of physical exercise every day. As a group, I guess none of the boys had done well at school, but all seemed to have come from stable family backgrounds. There were no bullies, no real alpha males amongst them.

There was drama off the coast of Spain when, in stormy weather, the ship was hit by a freak wave. On the ship, the meals were served in two sessions, there being insufficient space in the dining room.

The first of the evening meal sessions was underway when the wave struck. At the time, I was upstairs in the lounge room when the ship started to roll. The floor assumed a steeper and steeper angle and lounge chairs that were not bolted to the floor went sliding around. The tilt reached about thirty degrees before the ship started to right itself. Fortunately, I was in one of the chairs fixed to the floor and managed to put out a helping hand to a fellow passenger as he went shooting by. I heard later that the only real casualty was someone who broke a leg on the stairs. But in the dining room, everything on the tables had ended up on the floor, the mess had to be seen in order to be believed. It was a testament to the mainly Italian crew that the ship was back into some sort of working order within a couple of hours.

Later, the ship passed through the Mediterranean and the Suez Canal. The canal area was particularly interesting. Here was intensive agriculture, farmland growing rice, maize and date palms, intersected by crowed settlements of small flat-topped houses. And all this adjacent to sandy desert and cutting through all the great shipping canals with its associated lake system.

A few days later, down the other end of the Red Sea at Aden, the bum-boat crews came out to the ship, keen to sell all manner of bric-a-brac to us migrants. 'McGregor you buy,' they would call. 'Genuine gold figurine from Queen Sheba tomb. Yes, McGregor chance in lifetime. Just for you cheap, not to be missed.'

After leaving Aden, we crossed the equator encountering flying fish in the open ocean and on to Fremantle. My first sight of Australia was while standing on the deck of the ship and watching the eastern sky brighten over a darkened land mass. There was a small crowd silently watching our first Australian sunrise, all very quiet, all perhaps wondering what the future held. Then came a couple of hours ashore around the bustling city of Perth before setting course for Sydney.

It was on our way across the Great Australian Bight that I observed Wandering Albatross for the first time. I was impressed by both the sheer size of these birds and their ability to keep up with our ship for hours on end.

A little over a month after leaving England, we sailed into Sydney Harbour, but in those days the opera house site was nothing more than a bus depot. Here was another real city, a real bridge (known locally as the coat hanger) with not a single South American flag, nor giant ant-eater, in sight. In all fairness to the flat-earthers, it was to be a year before I saw my first kangaroo in the wild. The rumours that they were to be seen hopping along Pitt Street in and out of the rush hour city traffic simply weren't true. As for funny accents, they were everywhere and, having a sensitive ear, it wasn't long before I was emulating them. But this was a part of the world where people still referred to Britain as *the old country*. Where, being called *a pommy bastard* was not usually meant as an insult. But there were still elements of the colonial cringe – being an outpost of Britain, we couldn't possibly do that here -which I'm glad to say has disappeared from the Australian psyche in the decades since.

On arrival, our free holiday over, I remember trying to peer into the future and trying to guess what it might hold for me, but came away with no answers. Hardly a surprise there. Later on, a visit to Bondi Beach with the boys, I spied a group of giggling 13-year-old schoolgirls walking along the footpath and wondered if here could be a future wife. In hindsight, it's unlikely my wife-to-be was on the beach that day, but probably not too far away. Yet over the next 17 years, I was to have almost nothing to do with this eastern part of Sydney.

Once off the boat, the Big Brother boys were split into two groups. Those destined for the city's factories stayed in a hostel in Homebush, while the lads like myself were sent out to a small dairy farm on the other side of Liverpool, on the city's southwest fringe. We lived in a dormitory and discovered that running a dairy farm was really hard work. The cows were milked twice a day, but there was a schedule, so those whose turn it was had to be up around five am to help get the morning milking underway. But the schedule kept changing because our guardians were finding real employment, so within days, guys started to leave, many for distant places with funny names like Dubbo and Cootamundra.

After a month, there was only two of us, and morning milking part of our everyday. Then just before Christmas, I had a job interview and was off to a mushroom farm at Dural on the northern edge of Sydney.

My sense of home sickness for dear old England lasted all of two hours. What really had me enthralled on the farm at Liverpool and later at Dural was the Australian bushland. Everything was so different, the light, the smell, the insects, birds, flowers, and the lizards, wow! In England, I used to catch the local common lizards which grew to about four inches. In a creek at Dural, I cornered and captured a goanna, which must have been at least three feet. It was dark brown, almost black, in colour with very fine yellow spots. Admittedly, I got a few scratches for my trouble before I let it go, but what a find. On the farm at Liverpool, I saw my first Red-belled Black Snake, my first ever poisonous snake in the wild, but I knew to leave it well alone. With the birds, I could identify the Kookaburra but not the others. I remember sitting by a rock pool on a hot summer's day while a variety of birds came down to drink, but no clue as to what I was looking at. One, I nicknamed the grey fantail, by virtue of its appearance only to discover later that was its official title. The easily observable insects included a great variety of dragon flies and large orange and black sand wasps. These are solitary wasps, and though they look threatening, they're not normally aggressive. Apart from mosquitoes I've been stung and bitten very little during my years in Australia. Though in the north, the mossies would have included *Anopheles* and *Aedes aergypti,* both potentially dangerous disease carrying species.

Sam Moberry's mushroom farm was on the Old North Road, about a mile from a small store and petrol station that in those days constituted the centre of Dural. Apart from the house, the farm was made up of a half-dozen long low sheds and a large roofed-over concrete slab. The slab was used to prepare the compost mix, the base of which was wheat straw. This had to be fed through a mulching machine, a petrol driven spinning barrel with protruding cogs. This chopped up the straw into which fertilisers like blood and bone were added. The mulch was then watered and formed into a pile about five feet high, forty feet long. The mulch was put through the machine weekly for about six weeks. Once the compost was ready, it was loaded into large wooden trays. The mushroom seed material, mycelium cultivated on wheat, was added before being covered with damp peat. The loaded trays were stacked in the sheds in such a way that air could circulate around each tray. Maintaining the right moisture in the trays and controlling the humidity and temperature within the sheds was critical. The first flush of mushrooms would appear after ten days and cropping would continue for six to nine weeks.

Before I arrived, Sam had been running things on his own, but the business had developed to the extent that extra hands were needed. I was paid nine pounds a week and lived in a caravan. I had to do my own cooking and grocery shopping, but only had a cold shower and a very basic laundry. I could just about tolerate a cold wash in summer, but in winter I resorted to a wet flannel rub down. There was also a shed toilet with bucket that needed to be emptied regularly.

It was in the caravan one night when I had my first encounter with a Brush-tailed Possum. The animals grow to the size of a large cat, but when moving across a roof, they sound like the footsteps of someone walking. On hearing this for the first time, I was quite alarmed, but then a possum's furry brown face and pig-like nose appeared, peering in at me through the open skylight.

The mushroom farm was interesting. Sam was a good boss and this was my first real taste of independence. But I was still very much the daydreamer and not always paying proper attention as to what I was supposed to be doing. This inevitably led to numerous small mistakes. Looking back, I think my daydreaming may always have been a mental coping mechanism, but in times of stress it could both help and hinder. Help in the sense of a mental crutch, hinder in that the lack of attention led to situations that could add to the stress. But I'd always possessed the ability to turn this on and off at will.

Then after four months, Sam hurt his knee and was laid up in bed for about two weeks, though desperately worried, he would occasionally hobble out to see what was going on. But suddenly, I was in charge of the day-to-day running of a mushroom farm. Time to seriously kick the mind into gear, concentrate and remember all I'd learnt in the previous months. I'm glad to report that no great disasters occurred on my watch. The only thing that worried me was the composting pile on the slab ended up with a bit of a sideways lean, but I was told this wasn't unusual. But then with the boss back at work, the crisis over, I reverted to my normal dreamy self.

In those days, I could be socially awkward. On one occasion while at Dural, I was invited out to a party being put on by a family I'd befriended. Because I didn't have a car, I was taken there by a young couple, friends of my friends. But I had no experience of what was expected at these sorts of gatherings. I don't think there was any serious drinking, but a good party atmosphere got underway. The family were amateur musicians and able to bang out a bit of a dance tune. I sat in a corner and all was well until it was decided that everyone would participate in the dancing. Well awkward me got all silly by refusing to participate. Becoming the odd man out, I was suddenly the centre of everyone's attention, which made it worse. Then the party atmosphere simply evaporated, some people started to leave. One of the girls was crying. The couple who'd earlier brought me there now refused to give me a lift back. Faced with this rejection, I prepared to walk home, a distance of perhaps three miles. I did in fact get a lift with someone else, but the whole business had ended in utter disaster and I felt a fool.

The long-term outcome was that I tried to avoid parties whenever possible, and did so for years. When avoidance was not really an option, I liked to have an early exit plan whereby I could politely disappear.

A week or so after this, I was given the sack. Sam not happy with my overall performance had contacted the Big Brother Movement, asking them to find me another position. They didn't normally do this, but they had a job for me in the state of Victoria at a place called Marnoo. So, I left the mushroom farm. It had been an experience, hadn't really worked out but was interesting. I was being transferred to a chicken farm, the next leg of my journey. Furthermore, I would see another part of Australia and having lost friends in Dural, I thought about not repeating that mistake again.

It was mid-winter and the journey south was by steam train, the first part at night and the train carriage freezing cold. We reached Albury on the New South Wales – Victorian border on a clear frosty morning. Here, I had to change trains. Each state has its own railway gage, a left over from Australia's pre-federation days, when squabbling state politicians couldn't agree. The result is a dysfunctional national rail system that has caused endless problems ever since.

Late afternoon, I was still on a train, the third in 18 hours, but this time, looking out at the flat wheat fields of central Victoria. I saw a flock of pink, grey and white birds, and on asking a fellow passenger, was told that they were Galahs. I discovered later that Galahs are a type of small cockatoo.

My new boss, Helen Low, was waiting for me at the station at Stawell, the nearest town to Maroon. Miss Low was a large middle-aged woman with a nice smile. As we drove in the car out of town, she seemed to have been trying to impress me with talk of her extended family, owners of various sheep and wheat properties in the district. But I looked out the window thinking how flat and treeless this country was, though I could see the Victorian Grampian Mountains receding into the blue hazy distance.

Marnoo was composed of a single wide street with a line of shops and houses on either side. I say *was* because when last seen in the mid 1980s the place was a ghost town of boarded-up abandoned buildings. The two little bank buildings that once were the centre of the town's business had seemingly vanishedd. A few years earlier the banks had gone through a period of reducing the number of branches. For some small communities, the loss of the local bank branch had marked the beginning of the end.

On this day in 1961, we stopped at the post office, then around to the baker's next door. I was told the baker was new to Marnoo and hadn't quite got the hang of it. This indeed seemed to be the case, for the bread was undercooked inside but with a somewhat blackened exterior. Back in the car, we went off to Helen's place not far out of town. The house was quite large, single storey, wide verandas, car port, a leafy well-kept garden. Once inside, I met the family collie dog, an over-grown pup, and Helen's elderly mother.

The chicken farm was not very big, one long shed and a dozen other structures that could best be described as large covered pens holding about 40 chickens each. The operation of the farm was straightforward. Batches of day-old chicks were brought in and kept under a heat lamp. At a month old, the bird beaks were trimmed.

A few millimetres of the upper bill were cut away using an electrically heated cutting bar. The purpose of this was to stop the chickens attacking each other in the pens' confined spaces. They were then separated as far as possible into males and females. Some hens were kept for egg production but most were fattened for the meat market. But from remarks made from time to time, I understood the farm was too small, currently running at a loss, and Helen was largely dependent on investments elsewhere.

My working arrangements were that I would be paid four pounds a week but with full board. This wasn't as bad as it sounds because with food and lodging but no car, most of the money went straight into savings. I lived in a converted garage which had been well set up, but ate over at the house.

Helen's mother was a nice old lady well into her seventies, but subject to an almost constant bombardment of derogatory comments from her daughter. These weren't overtly outrageous, just small put-downs. I once said something to her about this and was told Helen had always been like that. I wasn't being subjected to this sort of treatment but the signs were there and I needed to tread carefully around Miss Low. But I was 17 and very naive.

One of the people I met at that time was Garry Fordham. He was a man in his seventies who did odd jobs for Miss Low. But it wasn't long before he was telling me something of his life story. After finishing school, he worked for one of the local wheat farmers. At one stage in those early years, the farmer had promised that if Garry worked for him long enough he would make Garry a share cropper. In other words, they would effectively go into business, the farmer supplying the land, Garry the labour and they'd share the proceeds. This was a society where a man's word and a handshake were seen as a done deal. The years went by and every so often Garry would remind his boss of their agreement. Then after 23 years of faithful toil, Garry was sacked over a matter that he described as totally trivial. Here was utter betrayal, leaving in its wake a bitter sense of injustice that Garry vowed to take to the grave. Certainly, when I met him, there was no holding back when it came to damning his old boss.

On several occasions, Helen took me on shopping trips to the larger towns like Donald and Horsham. On the second such trip, I purchased a copy of Neville Cayley's *What Bird is That?* At that time, the bible of Australian birdwatching, only to be roundly criticised by Helen for wasting my money. There weren't that many birds around but at least I could start matching up names, but I lacked binoculars. On my next shopping trip, I got myself a pair but kept that fact hidden. I also restarted my nature diary, notetaking with an emphasis on the local birds.

A pleasant Christmas came and went. But in mid-January, the start of a truly odd episode in my relationship with Miss Low. We drove out to Halls Gap in the Grampian Mountains, about 40 miles away. It started off as a bit of a mystery tour. I thought we were going shopping in Stawell only to taken on through the town.

The Victorian Grampians are not high by world standards. Rocky, rugged ridges, they mushroom up out of the plain. They are dissected by farmland valleys but with the lower slopes covered with eucalyptus forest with wattle understorey. Above this, towered the reddish peaks with patches of stunted vegetation perched in impossible places. I was very impressed, never having seen country like this before.

My diary says we saw Koalas and six species of bird, including a possible Painted Honeyeater. I was without my still-secret binoculars and the birds were allocated names after thumbing through my bird book that evening. But the day's real surprise was being asked if I would like to stay in the mountains for a few days. I thought this couldn't be serious, but Helen pulled up in front of one of the local guest houses and went inside. On re-emerging she announced that I'd been booked in next week, I still didn't fully believe it. I'd worked for this woman for seven months and now I was being given a week's holiday all expenses paid? Yet this is exactly what happened.

On the 21 January 1961, I was given a pre-arranged lift into Stawell by Marnoo's postmaster Mr Corrie before catching a bus out to the mountains. I returned eight days later. The holiday was great, this time I had my bird book and binoculars and I spent hours hiking through the bush. I spotted both Eastern Grey Kangaroos and Rock Wallabies and encountered my first brown snake. Unlike the grass snakes of England, here was another species worthy of respect.

But going through my head was the question of what was I doing here? None of this seemed right. I even formed the hypothesis that Helen had planned to do her mother in and this holiday was a ruse to get me out of the house. But I'm glad to report that the old lady was still in one piece when I got back.

Soon after this, Helen and I had a falling out. It was quite trivial, she told me to do something, I started questioning if it was really necessary and suddenly, I was being accused of challenging her authority. 'Just because I'm a woman you think I know nothing.' Was one of the things thrown at me. Stunned at her aggressive tone, I didn't answer back but thought, given a day or so, all this would blow over. It didn't. I was now on the hit list for derogatory put-downs and it continued day after day. And of course, the privileged shopping trips ceased.

This had all been some sort of power game, but I don't think she ever understood me. Few perhaps did in those days. On one occasion, Helen had visitors and during a meal, I mentioned that I'd worked on a mushroom farm. I was then asked how such farms worked and at this Helen shot back, 'Don't ask him he doesn't know anything.' But I proceeded to give a detailed account. Later, she said to me, 'How come you know so much about your old job, while around here you're absolutely useless?'

Helen took in a boarder, Derick, a lad about my age, who was a trainee bank clerk at one of Marnoo's two little branches. He lived in the main house, went off to work in the morning, home in the evening. He and I got on well, but Derick became Helen's new golden boy, always favoured at meal times whereas I was the evil twin.

I was regularly writing home to England and though I said nothing directly about what was going on, my parents sensed my growing unhappiness. But Helen's extraordinary generosity at the beginning of the year made me feel guilty about leaving.

However, in May, I saw an ad in the paper for apprentice train drivers and what's more, they didn't seem to be asking for any formal qualifications. I wrote to them and they replied asking me to come down to the railway workshops at Ararat for a job interview. This was the excuse I needed.

Helen seemed quite upset when I announced my departure during an evening meal and then spelt out my reasons for doing so. But Derick overhearing all this told me afterwards he'd been quietly applauding.

So, a week later, I caught the bus into Stawell and from there on, the train to Ararat, the next major stop on the line. The initial job interview seemed to go well. As an apprentice, I would be paid but there would a series of hurdles along the way. But even before I could be signed on, I'd have to undergo a medical examination and for that I needed to go down to Melbourne at my own expense.

I failed the medical examination. Train drivers, it seemed, needed perfect vision, but I was slightly short-sighted. I knew that and if anyone had asked, I would have told them. So, having spent money travelling to and from Melbourne, I was stuck in Ararat, a smallish country town, with no job. Furthermore, this was not a good time because the Australian economy was heading into recession.

I found accommodation at the Commercial Hostel near the railway station. Bed and breakfast and the couple that ran it seemed like good people. Several of the others staying there were young blokes like me, but they worked in the railway shunting yards. Could there be an opening for me after all? But I discovered this was a dangerous occupation, with much of the shunting done at night. Their job was to couple and de-couple rolling stock. But with massive machinery trundling around in the poor light, errors could be fatal. Only a few months earlier someone had been killed, run down by an empty freight wagon rolling silently through the night. When it came to work, I thought to look elsewhere.

I returned to what I'd been doing in England, going door to door looking for work as a part-time gardener. The money wasn't brilliant but I made enough to stop my savings from being run down further. One of the temporary jobs I had was sanding down and painting the side of a house, work that lasted perhaps a week. Talking to the householder over a cup of coffee, the conversation drifted onto some issue about science.

'What are you doing working like this?' he asked, 'A young fella like you should be heading off to university or something.'

'No, no that's all too academic for me,' I replied, an embarrassed laugh. I might have added that I'd effectively failed school, no point in trying to go down that road again.

However, I was coming around to the view that my habit of daydreaming had to stop. Life in the real world was full of challenges and I couldn't afford such behaviour.

On one occasion, I worked in a sawmill for a day. The mill was being run by the boss and a second guy, both real characters with a continuous flow of banter going on between them. Putting aside the all too frequent bad language, the pair were pretty witty. I don't think they needed the extra labour but this was the boss's way of helping someone looking to earn a bit of money.

Then there was the three days I was sent tidying up a badly overgrown garden. With youthful enthusiasm, I carved my way through the jungle, but in the end the elderly lady who owned the place wasn't that happy because she'd lost her privacy. The house that had remained hidden for years was now visible from the road.

Next day, another old lady said to me, 'I need some wood chopped but I can't afford to pay you.'

'Two shillings and that will do,' I proposed.

So, the work was done.

But when handing over the two bob she said, 'I thought you must be one of them on drugs or something, desperate for money.'

'No not like that,' I said. 'Just glad to help.'

The only problem was that the wood had been springy pine and a chunk of it had come up and hit me in the face. I was bruised and sore for a couple of days.

On another occasion, my efforts to find work led me down a strange path. I'd been given the name of someone who might have been able to help. This I followed up only to be referred on to someone else. This happened a couple more times but, in the end, I was confronted by a bloke who believed I was on a mission of harassment. 'Bill sent you? Well you can fucking tell Bill he can go to bloody hell!' What did I do to deserve that?

At the end of June, I saw an ad in the paper for a station hand at Old Dunaway Station near Deniliquin in New South Wales. Initial contact was by phone to a Robert McCauley. Soon, I was packing my bags and catching a bus first to the provincial centre of Bendigo. Then a second long-distance bus north across the state border.

I'd arranged to meet Robert outside the town hall at 12 as he was coming into town on other business. Two hours later, there had been absolutely no sign. I was thinking that a further phone call might be needed, though this could be another dead end. What was the potential when it came to gardening part-time or otherwise in this town? What I didn't know was that the McCauleys as a family were habitually late, sometimes exceptionally so.

I gave up waiting, set off down the street and was standing on a corner when someone behind called out my name. There he was, Robert McCauley, neatly dressed, blue eyes, in his late fifties. When we shook hands he said, 'Thought it might be you. The right age and your jacket looks like it was made in England.' I'd told him earlier I was eighteen months in Australia. So, a job interview on a street corner got underway. I was nearly 19 but he was looking for someone slightly younger because they didn't need to be paid so much. Add to that I had no experience with sheep and had never driven a tractor. However, he was impressed that I'd travelled all the way up from Ararat. It showed a keenness to work.

Later I sat in the back of a light truck as it sped through the night. With three blokes in the front cabin there had been no extra room. I was wearing an old army coat that someone had given me but being mid-winter it was freezing. Then the truck left the bitumen road for unsealed gravel and forever onwards. I thought, *I'm going to be bloody glad when we get there, wherever it is.*

Chapter 12

Old Dunaway Station

I WOKE UP FEELING COLD. I'D slept fully clothed; the borrowed blankets had helped but still not enough. Now the dawn light was coming through the only window, the panes dusty with cobwebs. The room was small and bare, with corrugated iron walls, the bed a tubular metal frame supporting a somewhat lumpy mattress. Suddenly conscious of the time, I was out of bed reaching for my shoes sitting atop my only suitcase lying on the bare floorboards.

I shot out the door. This was Old Dunaway's shearer's quarters, a long low building with an iron roof and a wooden veranda lined by half a dozen doors that opened into other poky rooms. A similar set a rooms were on the other side of the building, but was without a covered veranda. I needed to relieve myself, but not knowing the location of the toilet, I urinated around a nearby corner. Then I made my way to the kitchen at the other end of the building.

The night before, I'd arrived at another of the station's corrugated iron buildings, I'll call this the red house. In town, I had met Paul, one of Robert McCauley's sons, and on arrival, I'd been introduced to Paul's wife, Marg, plus their two young children. Robert had then left saying he lived over at Coniston Downs Station about four miles away.

I had been given something to eat, stewed mutton, carrots and potatoes. On Old Dunaway, sheep were never eaten until at least three years old. This was a Marino stud property and the culling of sheep, the selection of killers for meat didn't take place until they reached maturity.

After the meal, I was taken over to the shearer's quarters and told that the station ran on its own 32-volt power generator. The electricity would be turned off about ten or when the diesel run generator was closed down. At the shearer's quarters, I met John Spenser and was told I could take any room I liked except his. John was a big man in his early thirties and my first impression was that he didn't like me. However, when I got to know him better, I discovered he was somewhat wary of strangers but in time, we became firm friends.

On that first morning John greeted me with, 'You're late.'

'Sorry,' I said. 'Don't have an alarm clock.' Then after a long awkward pause, 'I don't have any food either. If I'd known I would have…'

'Milk in the fridge,' replied John, a casual wave toward a packet of cornflakes on the kitchen's large central table.

Having found the milk in the kerosene powered fridge, then bowl and spoon, I asked, thinking to rectify the situation, if there were any shops close by.

'Two miles down the road,' came John's reply. 'Sell most things. You worked with sheep before, drive a tractor?'

'No never,' I confessed.

'They're real short of staff and shearing starts in two weeks,' claimed John. 'Going to get bloody busy. Don't know how many shearers are coming but if there's a shortage of beds you'll have to give up your room.'

'Set up a mattress in the dining area?' I suggested, indicating the door to the adjacent room.

'You and me are just baggy pants station hands,' replied John. 'No shearer is going to tolerate the like of us camping in their dining room. It's bad enough with the other conditions, the cast iron stove, the cold-water showers, the shit mattresses. The shearers get paid a little extra to look the other way when they come here. Otherwise the

McCauleys would be up for real money but when it comes to money, they're as tight as a fish's arse.'

'Big house further over,' I said. 'Who lives there?'

'The former manager,' replied John. 'He and his family are moving out in a couple of weeks. After that Selwyn, one of the other sons, will be moving in, running this place. You'd better hurry, Robert will be over from Coniston any minute.'

I'd met Selwyn the night before, one of the others in the truck. A solidly built man only a little older than me.

But I was puzzled by this talk of a former sheep station manager. Later when John was speaking with Marg, I deduced that there had been some sort of verbal altercation between John and the manager. Something about which John was still fuming. It seemed that until recently, Old Dunaway had been part of a larger pastoral company, M H McCauley and Sons. But all this was in the process of being divided up into three different entities. In the weeks before I arrived, John had been brought in from one of the other properties and elevated to foreman. In addition, two of Robert's sons had moved or were moving in while the original manager's contract was being terminated. So, a time of transition and tension but I never found out what had happened to the rest of Old Dunaway's original staff.

Besides the shearer's quarters, there was the wool shed, two houses and several smaller building. There was also a large roofed area held up by steal pylons under which were stored hundreds of bales of hay.

The eight-stand wool shed was surrounded by extensive sheep yards. The shed's shearing floor was about twelve feet wide with the shearing stands being driven by a shaft and pulley system powered by a southern cross diesel engine. Beyond an internal divide that marked the boundary of the shearing floor was a complex series of holding pens with a wooden lattice floor through which sheep droppings could pass to the space below. At the front of the shed was the sorting floor with wool classing tables and a hand operated wool press. This was a large box-like structure with a long crack handle and iron gear wheels, seemingly a 19th century design. On the wooden casing some wag had scrawled *Rob's Money Box,* as indeed it was.

The toilet that I couldn't find that first morning was a two-seater long drop, a corrugated iron shed with wooden seats perched above a deep pit. Often, we avoided pissing in the toilet because there was a need to keep the contents as dry as possible, particularly in the summer. So being a world of men, it was a case of stand and delivering wherever it was politely convenient.

Near the toilet was the wash house with shower, concrete lined wash basins and a copper tub under which a fire could be lit to boil clothes. I resented the cold showers, particularly during the winter, and I again resorted to the wet flannel trick.

The main water supply was a large underground tank fed by rain water runoff from nearby sheds. The water was then pumped by a steel-tower windmill into a top tank which stood on a stand 30 feet off the ground. This provided the gravity fed water supply to the other buildings.

Old Dunaway Station covered about 18,000 acres. The country was flat, much of it grassy sheep padlocks, but with belts of low growing Black Box Eucalyptus. These trees marked ancient stream lines, some of which still flooded during wet years.

There was a single stand of about a dozen River Red Gums which must have been there well before European settlement. These massive trees looked to be all about the same age and were so tall they could be seen across the flat landscape for miles. Close by, or so I was told, was the site of the original Dunaway Station shearing shed, built around the middle of the 19th century, a time when the station was much larger. It was also said that there were a couple of graves in the area, shearers who'd died on the job. I didn't go amongst the trees very often but when I did, there was a sort of presence. With the great tree trunks, it was like standing in a cathedral, a church with a wire fence around it but no access gate. Apart from the ghost of long departed shearers, this place could have had some significance for the native Baraba, a sub-group of the Wiradjuri peoples who once roamed this land.

Apart from the trees, there were two extensive areas of salt bush plain with occasional clumps of lignum, a wiry almost leafless bush that grows up to four feet high. Western grey kangaroos were commonly seen around the property and during my years there, I recorded over 120 bird species. Of these, the Masked Owl and Black Falcon were birds that I would not see elsewhere.

Coniston Downs, the McCauley's other property, was on the edge of the extensive River Red Gum forests that flanked the northern side of the Murray River. The homestead, partly surrounded by pepper trees, was on the banks of the Coniston Lagoon, an anabranch of the main river. In flood years, the lagoon would fill and be a great place for waterbirds such as spoonbills and pelicans. But in dry periods, and in the absence of water, the bed of the lagoon was used for cropping. This was a gamble, for if there was a flood any crop would be lost.

Species seen around Coniston but never further out in the open country included Brown Treecreeper, Freckled Duck and Yellow Rosella (a type of parrot).

In the weeks following my arrival, I was on a very steep learning curve. Fortunately, I'd put my daydreaming habits aside and so this was now comprehensively my world, my life. As John had predicted, shearing time was hectic and the hours long. Because, at that stage I didn't know my way around the property, most of my efforts were spent in and around the shearing shed. This involved working with dogs to move sheep through the yards, up the ramp, into the shed and then on into the shearers' catching pens. A good dog could be relied on to do the work of three men, both in the yards and out in the open. However, a newcomer had to learn to work with the natural instincts, the abilities of both sheep and dogs.

Once the sheep were shorn, they were sent down a wooden shoot into each shearer's counting pens. The boss of the shed, usually the shearing contractor, would count the sheep in each pen about four times a day. The animals were then pushed along a race and branded using an iron dipped in an ink dye. The brand mark denoted ownership and the colour the mob to which the sheep belonged. From there, the animals would be moved back out into the paddocks. In an average day, five to nine hundred sheep would pass through the shed depending on the number of shearers. Elsewhere in the shed, the wool was being sorted, class and baled.

During that first shearing time, neither John or I had to give up our rooms, there being six shearers, two rouser-bouts, the cook and a wool presser. As was customary, the wool classer was billeted elsewhere. John and I ate with the shearers and we had our evening meal at one of the half dozen wooden tables in the dining room.

Then one of the shearers got up and started swearing at us, 'Why am I having to eat sitting bloody opposite a couple of fucking station hands who've no business being here?'

At this John got to his feet and declared, 'Okay we can piss off out of here but we're pretty short staffed and tomorrow don't be too surprised if the sheep are a bit slow turning up at the shed.'

After this, cooler heads prevailed, the protester was told to sit down and, 'bloody shut up.'

On the whole, I found most shearers good blokes, though some seemed to be drinking themselves into an early grave. There was a strictly enforced ban on drinking at the station during shearing time. Anyone caught doing so faced being sacked on the spot. But in town come Friday nights, some made up for lost time. They would dry out a bit on Sunday before turning up ready to go Monday morning. Then there were the cars, some were obsessed, spending their free time washing and polishing. But one young fella insisted on drive to and from work every day. That is from the shearers quarters over to the wool shed and back a distance of a hundred yards. On a couple of occasions, I found shearers washing their clothes. They'd stripped off and were standing around a steaming tub of boiling water and as in a Caravaggio masterpiece, totally naked. I supposed one way of staying warm in the middle of winter.

The thing that everyone feared most was rain, for sheep can't be shorn when wet. This could be mitigated to some extent by storing sheep both inside and under the wool shed overnight. But space was limited and prolonged wet weather a problem. When shearers were not working, they didn't get paid. Furthermore, lost working days resulted in shearing contractor schedules being thrown into chaos.

Soon after the shearing came dipping time. Sheep simply don't like being dipped and I don't blame them. No fun being made to swim through a cold toxic brew, having the head momentarily pushed under for maximum coverage. Some of the old ewes who'd been through it before would smell the brew and start digging their heels in a mile away. Even with younger animals in the race leading to the dipping trough, it was a case of grabbing the stump of the tail and shove. Pass the animal to the man next in line before reaching to grab another. This being repeated thousands of times in the course of perhaps ten days.

But sheep work was seasonal, and unlike dairy farming, there was never a set routine. Furthermore, this was broad acre farming so two men such as John and myself were looking after six to seven thousand sheep while going about our other duties. But from time to time, we did lose animals because no one was there to check. On a few occasions, a young ram would get its horns caught in some isolated boundary fence. By the time it was discovered, the crows and eagles had picked the bones clean.

John had gone straight from school into sheep station work which, when I first met him, he would have been doing for about 12 years. A kindly good-natured man, he could be quite self-deprecating and lacking in confidence sometimes. But he knew his job well, paid attention to detail. I always felt that given the right encouragement, he could have made an excellent stock and station agent, though perhaps the paperwork could have been a challenge.

At lambing time, we would check on the various flocks of ewes at least once a day. Sometimes we'd discover an ewe in difficulty and John would apply one of his tricks. The animal was caught, held down, and the lamb which might be hanging half out removed. But if the lamb was still alive, there was a further problem. On release, the ewe could well panic, run back to the other sheep abandoning its offspring. So, John would encourage the ewe to lay quietly on its side by placing a clod of turf on the animal's upturned eye. This might take a little persistence, but once the animal was lying passively, he would quickly retreat. A short while later, the ewe would start to wriggle again, the turf fall away and able to see, stand up. But the human threat was now at a distance, the flight response avoided, mother and baby safely united.

Ewes had a life expectancy of between seven to nine years and as such, many died of old age on the property. John, on passing a newly deceased animal, would often raise his hat as a mark of ironic respect and say, 'Rest in peace old girl.' But in accordance with the *stay and fertilise* policy, burying dead animals was something never contemplated.

The only way to fully restrain a sheep was to sit it up on its backside, with the back of the animal's head resting against the handler's knees. Any animal being worked on needs to be held in this way. With advancing age, sheep, as with humans, are prone to feet and teeth problems. With age, front teeth tended to drop out, but a sheep with half its front teeth missing was in danger of starving to death. In an attempt to mitigate this, we would pull what remained out with pliers. The idea being to give the animal an even surface around the hardened gum line, but I was never sure how well this worked in practise. Going back over the same flock a few months later, the animals with missing front teeth simply weren't there.

Sheep hooves are made of the same material as human toe nails and as such, grow continuously through life. With a young healthy animal walking over hard ground, the hooves needed little attention. But with age, the feet structure starts to break down and the wear on the hooves becomes uneven. Feet clipping was done with small paring shears and we tried to get to the older animals at least once a year. But it was one of those thankless tasks, hard on the back and hands and a job that tended to be put off to times when there wasn't much else to do.

Other activities included the jetting, the application of insecticide to ward off fly strike and drenching, dosing the sheep against internal parasites, such as round worm. The latter job was done with a hand operated drenching gun, the nozzle of which was pushed into the side of the mouth through a gap between the front and back teeth.

For the rams, life was for the most part relatively short and sharp. In any given year, about 1500 ram lambs would be produced on the property. Successive and severe culling for the meat market would start at about the age of two and continue until they reached their prime at three years. After this, there would be about forty rams left, those of the topmost quality. Some would be sold to other properties, even fewer used for show and stud breeding.

The culling of ewes was not so rigorous, the aim being to remove poor quality animals while maintaining overall flock size. However, in poor seasons, some of the older sheep were sent off to the butchers or for pet food.

The aim of culling was not only to improve the quality of the flock but also to hold stocking rates at long term sustainable levels. In some of the paddocks there were patches of bare ground where the topsoil was missing, the consequence of past over stocking.

In many ways, a brutal system, but one that closely mirrored herd animals living in a natural ecosystem where males battle for breeding dominance and predators keep the population in check by removing the old and weak.

During my first years on Old Dunaway, the mustering of sheep required the use of a horse pulling a sulky (a small two-wheeled cart) and dogs. Later, the horse was replaced by a small agricultural motorbike with a dog sitting up behind the rider. The bike's main advantage was that it was a lot faster getting from place to place. The two main disadvantages were that it didn't perform well in boggy conditions and riders tended to fall off fairly frequently. But unlike the human driver, the canine pillion passengers always seemed to successfully bale out when disaster loomed.

One of the jobs I never liked was the docking and mulesing of lambs. This is a process in which the tail was cut off (docked) and then a strip of wool-bearing skin removed from the breech down the back of the legs (mulesing). With a handler holding the animal correctly, a skilled muleser, using a knife and small sharp shears, would achieve all this in less than a minute, but the results look awful. But the lambs, who at that stage were still dependent on their mother's milk, would recover remarkable quickly. The wounds closed over within hours and all signs were gone by day ten. It was another cruel practise but with the aim of removing the wrinkles from the sheep's backside, thus lessening the chance of blow fly strike. But then, as is now, there was a problem with practical humane alternatives. Cleaning up a blown sheep was no fun, the sight and smell never to be forgotten, but the condition, if not caught early, produced great suffering and could be fatal.

Another job I never really liked was hand milking a cow first thing every morning. A small number of cows were run on the station and the morning milking could go well if the animal was compliant. But this wasn't always the case and there were times when I was kicked and milk buckets sent flying. But as the station's milk boy, I was spared that other nasty task, butchering sheep.

Life for a working dog on a sheep station was often hard. Sometimes they could be expected to work very long hours and a dog driving a mob of sheep may cover ten times the distance taken by the sheep walking in a more or less straight line. Add to that the food supply could vary from feast to famine. The supply could be offal when a sheep was killed, or at other times, dry dog biscuits. On arrival, I adopted a bitch who answered to the name of Lassie. She was a black and white Kelpie, short-haired and unusually tubby for a sheep dog. She was at her best when working sheep in the open but her death a tragedy that really moved me at the time.

There had been a 1080 rabbit poisoning campaign on the station. This involved putting out trails of poison carrots and then collecting up the bait and rabbit carcases afterwards. Because this poison occurs naturally in the Australian vegetation, a lot of native wildlife is not affected by it. But dogs that feed on poisoned rabbits are particularly susceptible. While baiting was going on, all dogs had been kept on their chains and when it was over we went around disposing of the rabbit carcases. The poisoning program had been over for about four months, but Lassie, it seemed, had picked up something, possibly a couple of bones, and that was enough. We were moving a mob of sheep when suddenly she let out a howl and raced off across the paddock towards the wool shed. Her body was found the next day.

Besides sheep work, there was the irrigating of pasture, rice crops and on one occasion soon after I arrived, the desperate saving of that wheat crop. With properly consolidated and grassed over check banks, irrigation, apart from the walking, wasn't usually an arduous process. Though one of my tasks on Old Dunaway was to plant kikuyu grass along newly constructed irrigation channels. This involved walking along the water's edge, pushing the stems of grass into the mud with a long stick. The sheep didn't like the kikuyu much, but in wet soil, it established quickly and was great for holding earthen banks together.

There were a number of vehicles used around the station, one of which John had christened Betsie. It was with this vehicle I learnt to drive during my first few weeks. Betsie was an A model Ford, perhaps forty years old. It was unclear if it had started life as a car or ute (pick up). But the top of the original cabin had been cut away and a tray body attached behind the driver. The original narrow wheels had been retained on the front, but on the back, broader tread drive wheels had been fitted. There were rust holes in the floor but the high clearance underneath and light frame meant it handled well in mud. However, going through water, the hot manifold combined with the ventilation holes in the floor would send a cloud of steam over the driver. There was no starter motor, it required a crank handle but had a feature not found in modern vehicles - a hand operated accelerator sitting just under the steering wheel. So here was a design feature that could pose a hazard, but on one occasion, possibly saved me from very serious injury.

Where the main track from the lower part of the property approached the road, it went over a bridge that spanned an irrigation channel. Here there was a gate that on this particular day was closed. I drove up in Betsie, stopped, got out and opened the gate. But the A model didn't have a hand brake that worked. Being such flat country, hardly any farm vehicle on the place had a working hand brake. The old car started to slowly roll forward, but fearing it would end up in the middle of the road, I attempted to dive back into the driver's seat. But alas, my right foot became jammed between the gate post and the running board. In considerable discomfort, I was stuck and if held there for more than twenty minutes, in great danger of losing a foot due to restricted blood circulation. Fortunately, I have long legs and just managed to get my free left foot onto the clutch peddle. But there was a danger that as I engaged reverse gear, the engine would stall. It was then I thanked god for the hand accelerator. I still remember that huge sense of relief as the weight came off, my foot freed. It was a bit sore for several days, but years later an X-ray revealed a metatarsal bone in my right foot showed signs of an earlier fracture. I guess it could've been far worse.

Some of the staff that came after my arrival were almost full-time tractor drivers. But John and I only became involved during peak periods, such as wheat sowing time. For me, this meant getting up at one in the morning in winter and driving some monster machine until dawn. Even with multiple layers of clothing it was often far too cold. This was another of the jobs I thoroughly disliked but I was given this dreaded dog-watch because I was deemed reliable.

There were two types of tractors, a modern Fordson and a pair of Lanz Bulldogs. The latter were really weird machines made in Germany in the 1930s. I suspected Hitler's legacy of revenge that would linger across the world long after all else had been lost. The Fordson was by comparison almost a luxury to drive, this was despite not having any sort of cabin.

The Bulldogs were built around a single cylinder diesel where the piston moved horizontally within the lower half of the engine block. This made for an extremely noisy engine. Because everything used to shudder and shake, the whole machine had to be massively reinforced to stop it falling to bits. The engine was started by sticking a blow lamp up into the heat bulb that covered the cylinder head right at the front of the engine. After heating for several minutes, a little fuel was pumped by hand into the engine which was then started by turning one of two fly wheels on either side. Sometimes the engine would start but run backwards and as a result, reverse gear would have the tractor going forwards. However, an experienced operator could tell by the noise if things were running the wrong way. But to correct this, the fuel had to be cut off and then the engine re-started.

In those days, I was a very fit young man. But to push down on a Bulldog's clutch peddle, I needed to stand up, hang onto the steering wheel and then throw my full weight onto my left leg. After this, the gear change needed to be made quickly because I couldn't hold the pedal down for more than a few seconds. But having sat on one of these monsters for half the night, I'd come home with the bang, bang, bang of the engine still going on in my head. Indeed, a machine worthy of a race of super men. Though on one occasion, an exhausted Selwyn actually fell asleep while driving one of these noisy monsters. Fortunately, he'd managed to put it into neutral before dozing off.

Chapter 13

Of the Family and Their Sheep

AS I'D NOTICED AT MARNOO, there was a class structure in country Australia with those who owned land seeing themselves as socially a cut above most others. I suspect this went back to the earliest days of white settlement. But with the McCauleys, there was nothing Robert and his sons wouldn't or couldn't do when it came to the day-to-day station work. They worked very hard and expected others to do the same.

I first met all the immediate members of the family when I was invited to spend Christmas with them at Coniston Downs during my first year. That Christmas morning, sitting in the kitchen was Robert and his wife Fran, plus Paul and Selwyn (who'd come over from Old Dunaway) and the two younger kids, Harry and Leonnie, home from boarding school. I felt here was a really strong, loyal and loving family. Over the next four-and-a-half years I was to get to know most of them really well. But I became aware of the family dynamics, their strengths and weaknesses.

The founder of the McCauley dynasty, Malcolm, had arrived in Australia during the 1880s and after working in sawmills along the Murray River, bought up land. Robert, of the second generation, had started farming Coniston Downs when he was a teenager. Old Dunaway had been a later acquisition that in turn led to the setting up of the Marino stud.

Robert was a man I particularly respected, for he'd built up a small empire, be it one started by his father. However, by developing the sheep stud which require both knowledge and skill, proclaimed he was more than the average cocky farmer. Yet day-to-day he was anything but pretentious.

However, looking back, given the labour needed to run the stud, the endless assessing of sheep for their quality, I question if it ever could have made money. What was making the business work was grain and wool production, and yet the stud was Robert's principal interest, his pride and joy.

All four of his children went through boarding school and Robert had high expectations for his sons. None of them were academically inclined, but I felt all suffered to some extent from a feeling of falling short of their father's expectations. I heard stories which could well have been true, of ten-years-olds on school holidays being sent out in the middle of the night to check irrigation pumps. A man's work expected of them before they were ready. I felt this had consequences, either in excessive shyness as in Paul's case, or a tendency to take unnecessary risks.

On one occasion, Harry and I were taking a truckload of stud rams down to Melbourne. Harry was behind the wheel and had just come over a hill. At the bottom of the slope on the two-lane highway a semi-trailer was overtaking another. Instead of slowing down, Harry hit the accelerator. Fortunately, the overtaking vehicle was travelling light, and the manoeuvre completed in time, but there weren't too many precious seconds to spare. Harry's response to all this was to laugh and call out, 'That showed 'em!'

During this period, Harry was involved in several minor traffic accidents, one when I was again a passenger. On this occasion, there were four of us in the family's Fairlane, driving through Koondrook. Up ahead, a car had gone into the back of another and stopped. Harry behind the wheel called out a warning to us passengers and then proceeded to slide into the pile up. The damage to our car was relativity light and I chose to say nothing. But if a driver has time to call out, then he has time to take evasive action, which, in this case, could have been done with complete safety, there being a wide and clear verge to the side.

The following year, Sylwin was involved in a far more serious accident but on that occasion, it seemed a case of youthful exuberance. The plan had been to take a small truckload of rams to a show and sale at Wentworth. But first, he was to call in on a party at Kerang and then drive through the night to be at Wentworth the following morning. I said to him, 'Don't you think you're pushing it a bit hard?' No, no he thought it was going to be all right. But in the early hours of the morning, he went to sleep at the wheel, went off the road and rolled the truck. The sheep in the back were full-woolled and well packed in; they were all right, but Sylwin sustained a broken leg. Later, he described how he stood on the side of the highway, supported by a hockey stick trying to flag down help. A truck driver fortunately stopped for him, but later in hospital, Sylwin almost died due to complications from a blood clot.

Leonnie, the youngest in the family, was a very nice girl, but I didn't see much of her. When we were at an agricultural show in Melbourne, she met a man I'll call Bruce. He owned a sheep stud property near Geelong in Victoria and drove a dark green sports car. A romance developed; the family thought highly of Bruce. He and Leonine were married. I'd like to report that they lived happily ever after but from what I heard years later, that was far from the case.

But it was a family with an intense sense of loyalty. Of working with each other day-to-day, displaying both tolerance and humour and of enjoying themselves when circumstances permitted. On three occasions, I went with them to agricultural shows in Melbourne and was treated very much like one of the family. And we won a few prizes with our rams that went before the judges.

In my second year, I became the station's stud groom. This meant for about four months of the year, I spent much time preparing specially selected rams for agricultural shows and sales. In any given season, I would be working with about 40 rams and I would get to know them and they me. Seven years earlier at the Wilderness school, I'd watched with passing interest a film on Australian Marinos. Now I was there, doing all that and more.

It's a common perception that sheep are fundamentally stupid, but this is not really the case. Having worked with my little flock for a few weeks, I could move among them with ease. But with a stranger, the behaviour was quite different. They'd bunch up while trying to keep clear of the intruder. For much of the time, I would be grooming a ram that had been tethered, and as a result, my back to the rest of flock. But every so often, one of the others would come up and given me a nudge in the back. At this, I would always turn around and give it a slap in the face. Lesson learnt, the animal would never do it again. But personality traits such as friendliness or aloofness towards me became apparent. This was quite apart from the bossy behaviour or otherwise towards others rams, and sometimes, I found it necessary to break up fights among the troublemakers. But meet these same animals a year or two later, after they'd been living like normal sheep, and any sense of familiarity had evaporated.

Grooming Marinos involved keeping the animals indoors during bad weather and at night. Their woollen coats could never get wet. Grooming required the animal to be standing tethered while the tip of the wool was clipped. This had to be repeated over the course of three or four months, the aim being to give the coat a nice finish. Clipping was done with a large pair of hand shears. These instruments consisted of a pair of wide, very sharp, blades attached to handles which in turn were connected by a semicircular spring. The blades, as they were called, were held in one hand and worked by pushing against the power of the spring. Even when clipping only the tips of the wool, the blades could be very exacting on the hand if the operator was not used to them.

Not all wool tips were the same, and the amount of clipping needed varied from sheep to sheep. During the early stages of grooming, another sort of clipping, deeper cutting, was done to accentuate the good point, and to some extent, cover up the less desirable ones. A badly proportioned sheep couldn't be made good, but for animals that had the potential to catch the eye of a judge or buyer, preparation was important. As for the quality of the animal's wool, there was very little that could be achieved by grooming alone. Though a little bit of gentle opening up of the wool would improve the feel prior to judgement day. Animals on show were supposed to have a year's wool growth, but in reality, it was more likely to be 13 or 14 months.

There were other positives during my time on Old Dunaway. My sister Gill had arrived in Australia and the rest of my family landed in Sydney two years later. Furthermore, after a year of looking around, my parents had bought themselves a house with money saved in England. Now my mother was talking of buying a car.

During this period, various members of my family came to visit me at the station. The first was my mother and brother, Adrian, but they arrived in the middle of their first Australian summer, the heat a real shock. Later, it was my other brother Jon, and followed a year later by Gill and her new husband Fred. Their visits tended to emphasise just how much I'd adapted to the Old Dunaway lifestyle. Fred described the countryside as being *like a billiard table with a few trees*. But it was a billiard table with a few redeeming features. Such as being able to jump into an irrigation channel on a hot day or listen to the plaintive cry of the Bush Stone Curlews on a clear, starry night.

The winter of 1964 was wet and there were all sorts of delays during the shearing. Adding to the problems, an old steam line at the western end of Old Dunaway had turned into a real waterway. Though it wasn't deep, we were having real difficulties mustering, for sheep, unlike cattle, have an aversion to wading through water. For John Spencer, it was a reminder of the nightmare he went through during the 1956 floods.

One day in the wool shed another young fellow whose name I can't remember, told me he'd had enough of the rain, the mud, the third rate living conditions and was leaving. He then said to me, 'Why are you still here? Clearly, you've got a bit of brains but all this is just a dead end. You should be getting out, doing something else.'

He was of course right, but at the time, I argued that it wasn't really that bad. But underlying this was the perception of my proven hopelessness when it came to anything even a little bit academic. When I arrived at Old Dunaway Station, I had been beset by a real sense of failure. My earlier pursuits at Lullingstone and fossil hunting expeditions had done absolutely nothing to make a substantial change in the course of my life. Perhaps Maidstone Art College had been a way forward, but I'd passed that up. What Old Dunaway had done was teach me a range of skills, of being able to do a real job and do it well.

Add to that I was physically fitter than I'd ever been or ever would be and with that had come a physical co-ordination that I'd lacked as a teenager. On one occasion, I was out with Sylwin who was driving an ute. On crossing a paddock, we came upon a mob of ewes but there was a ram amongst them, one of ours that had seemingly gotten through a fence. The sheep were running along in front of us as they are apt to do when a grazing mob is suddenly disturbed. But seeing an opportunity, I asked Sylwin to stop and then jumped out of the vehicle. Running doubled over I caught up with the ram, seized him by the wool on his back, before whipping my right hand under his chin to haul him over.

'You're like a red Indian,' said Sylwin, as he set about tying the ram's legs.

'Comes of being descended from a long line of sheep stealers,' I replied, with a grin.

But what I didn't know was that by choosing to stay on Old Dunaway I would be exposing myself to some very real dangers. Things related to lifestyle and the company I was soon to keep.

Chapter 14

Living Dangerously

AN INTERESTING STORY CAME MY way of a man and his wife who'd once worked on Coniston. I'd known them and had no reason to doubt its authenticity. The pair had found themselves another job at a station out on the Hay Plains to the north of Deniliquin. During the winter of 1964, they'd lived in a dilapidated old house in the middle of nowhere surrounded by endless saltbush plain. Then the rains had started and they'd been completely bogged in. They had enough food, but a major problem was no access to firewood needed for cooking. So, they started demolishing the wooden house around them. Finally, when rescue arrived, they'd systematically burned almost everything and were living in what was left of the kitchen.

In my experience, mishaps when droving sheep were rare but when they did occur could range from bothersome to the highly dangerous.

On one occasion, I managed to bring down the phone line to the main house at Old Dunaway. The line was carried by a series of poles that formed an interlaced part of a fence. A small mob of fully woolled rams, ones that I was about to start grooming, had gotten loose and were heading off along the fence line. I sent a dog after them, but like a rugby scrum, they jammed into the fence which promptly collapsed and then down came the phone line.

I had some experience at working with wire, so I put my skills to good use, fixing both fence and broken line. Before the accident, the phone wire had been sagging, but on joining the broken ends, I had an overlap of several inches which was just as well. Nevertheless, the wire was very stiff, difficult to manage and I had to use some ingenuity in achieving a good reconnection. But I must have done a good job for Selwyn spoke to me later saying he had been on the phone when it suddenly went dead, but now all working again. My response was, 'Oh yes, fancy that.'

On another occasion, I was bringing a mob of sheep over from Coniston Downs. As the sheep were destined for one of Old Dunaway's back paddocks, I was on a road that ran parallel with the local railway track. Though this was within the state of New South Wales, the single-track branch line was part of the Victorian network. Generally, trains were few and far between but on this particular day, a steam train hauling wheat wagons was approaching. At some distance, the train driver blew the whistle which promptly upset my horse. Then as the train slowly trundled by, the sheep suddenly stampeded back the wrong way. Again, I sent the dogs off around the front, and all might have been brought under control, but for the fence along the rail line being full of wide gaps. As a result, three hundred sheep ended up on the track right alongside the wagons. Fortunately, by this stage, the train had stopped but it wasn't clear if this was because of the woolly invasion or the need to change the points leading into the local grain solo. Then the train guard climbed out of his van and called out, 'Holy shit where did all these flamin' sheep come from?' But the mob had been trying to get away from his damned train, not cuddle up to it.

Some months later, on moving another mob between the two properties, the sheep were more lively than usual. The animals were one-year-olds and recently divested of their woolly coats. With the sulky out the front of the mob, I was waving backwards and forwards slowing them down, ensuring they made maximum use of the roadside grass. Even in good years, the resources of the long paddock weren't to be wasted and moving sheep like this a daylong activity.

Two dogs were sitting with me in the cart, all set it seemed for a quiet day.

There was the usual car or two on the road, some nudging through the sheep with no difficulty, others needing me to walk in front, clearing the way. Occasionally, during exercises like this, some idiot would try charging through at 40 miles per hour, horn blaring. They risked having a large lump of mutton through the radiator. I don't know if these people ever realised that as the sheep were under my supervision, they would have been liable for the cost of the animal they killed, quite apart from anything else. But so far on this late winter's morning, it'd been all routine.

Then I noticed a very large brown and white steer coming across an adjacent paddock towards us. I could tell by the way the animal moved it was agitated, a trot, a lifting of the feet like a race horse. What I didn't know but discovered later was that two blokes had been trying to load this great beast into the back of a truck. But the steer, perhaps sensing a grim fate, had broken free and headed off across the paddock. I thought when it reached the fence bordering the road, it would stop. It didn't. Head down and straight through almost as if the fence weren't there.

In hindsight, it's clear I should have turned the sulky around and got the hell out of there. However, I had limited experience of cattle. When I was a kid, I'd been wary of large bulls. But I was now 22 and like many young men considered myself bulletproof and no silly bovine was going to bother me. But the horse, normally a placid old thing, was starting to get upset as the steer trotted towards us. With the horse snorting and trying to back away I got out of the sulky and went around to hold the bridle. The beast stopped about six yards away snorting pawing the ground.

But for the horse, this was all too much. It suddenly backed and then violently spun around dragging me with it. Struggling to hold on, I felt something brush my left shoulder. It was the horns of the steer as it charged past. I remember glancing to my left looking along the back of the animal as it shot by. But it couldn't hold the horse and it was off, bolting for home with two dogs in the back of the sulky who were no doubt wondering what happened next.

Meanwhile, I was right out in the open with nothing more than a few blades of grass between me and a tone of very angry beef. Fortunately, the steer had had enough. It crashed through another fence and took off.

At that moment, the two farmers who'd been trying to load the animal, arrived in a green ute and I waved them down, told them the horse had bolted. I then dived in the back of the ute and we were off. The table drains on the side of the road were full of water, but we went through one before racing along the fence line. When ahead of the horse and sulky, the driver had us flying back up onto the road before shooting off in the direction of the local store, a place where the rail line crossed the road. With assistance of the storekeeper and the storekeeper's wife, we formed a human chain across the road. The horse arrived only to be diverted up a laneway. From there, we were finally able to get the situation under control.

The horse was very slow and reluctant to go back the other way, and of course, all the sheep had headed off in the entirely wrong direction. But the whole business had taken a lot out of the poor old horse which was soon thereafter pensioned off in favour of a motor bike.

At that time, station hands were never paid well, perhaps not much has changed since. Impoverished, they tended to buy cheap second-hand cars. As the mass-produced vehicles of that era where not particularly well-made, limited budgets were too often spent keeping these things on the road. During my time on Old Dunaway, I had three utilities (pick-ups) and when away on camping trips, I used to sleep in the back.

The first was a Morris Minor, grossly underpowered and totally unsuited for Australian conditions. Each time I took it away on long trips, I was almost assured of some breakdown drama, everything from burnt out ignition points to big end bearings. Even pottering around in the local area could be problematic. Unsealed roads after rains tend to be covered in puddles. But with this vehicle, when going through water, it would splash up, get caught by the fan blades and blown back over the distributor. As a result, the engine would die and I would have get out, dry off the distributor cap and coil before driving on to repeat the process ten minutes later. I supposed a plastic bag tied over the distributor may have solved the electrical problem, but by that stage Miss Morris and I had parted company.

The second vehicle, a Holden FC, was generally much better, but one night a potentially very dangerous situation developed. John Spenser was getting married at Molong, a town in the central west of New South Wales. As a guest at the wedding I planned to be there. The night before, I was approaching the town of Parks when I discovered no brakes. Letting the vehicle roll to a halt, I checked the wheel hubs and sure enough, the left rear wheel was red hot. In cars of that era, gunk tended to build up in the brake fluid and sometimes, as had happened here, a brake pad had failed to release. Friction had then led to dangerous overheating. I let everything cool down before proceeding very slowly, but didn't get far. The wheel bearing collapsed, the back axial disconnected, the entire wheel on the point of coming adrift. If this had happened at high speeds, the results could have been catastrophic.

I slept in the back of the ute that night and then arranged for a tow into town the following morning. One of the great advantages of the Holden brand during that era were that there were dealerships just about everywhere, and I arrived in Molong in time for the wedding.

Having my own set of wheels meant that during holidays and long weekends I could travel far and wide over southern and eastern Australia. Thus, I was to observe Rufous Treecreeper on the Eyre Peninsula, a Turquoise Parrot in northeast Victoria and black and yellow Regent Bowerbird on the Lamington Plateau of south eastern Queensland. I even located the mythical Green Catbird of my youthful imaginings. A rain forest species, it is green but gets its name from its cat-like yowling cry.

About a year after I arrived at the sheep station, Paul McCauley and his family moved to a new house that had been built for them down the other end of the property. As a result, John and I moved into the Red House. But with John getting married and the McCauley's keen to retain his services, they had a second house constructed. But behind the scene, John who'd married into a bit of wealth, was talking of getting a small property of his own.

By that stage, I was also seriously thinking of leaving Old Dunaway, but to a job that would give me better pay, a better standard of living and hopefully some sort of way to the future. On the other hand, there was a remote possibility that if I stayed, put-up with it long enough, I could end up managing the place. But there were Robert's three sons, all, it seemed, keen to carry on their father's legacy. Add to that at the back of my mind, the story of Garry Fordham. Like him, I'd be looking to advance on merit alone, but a wrong word at the wrong time and any ambitions could simply vanish.

One of the jobs I applied for was keeper of the animal house at the University of Melbourne. After all, I was looking after stud rams for four months of the year. I didn't even get a job interview. I also started to enquire about positions as zoo keeper and was told competition was very fierce.

It was about this time Reynold Keys and his wife, Anna, appeared on the scene. They started off living in the shearer's quarters with a couple of unmarried lads, but later moved into the Red House with me. Rey was slightly-built, middle-aged, a quietly spoken man who'd worked on properties around the district for much of his life. Though in his late teens towards the end of the war, had spent some time on a pacific island but hadn't seen combat.

Anna, I guess, was about the same age. She'd been brought up as part of a large family in the Redfern area of Sydney. Though she claimed her father was Swedish, her dark hair and facial features suggested some sort of Aboriginal heritage. This was a time when any sort of connection to Australia's first people was seen as a bad thing and those with pale skin tended to hide that fact.

I got to know them well. Here were two lives that'd been utterly ground down, though how much was self-inflicted and how much by circumstances alone was hard to tell. On one occasion, being without a car, they took the bus to Melbourne to visit some of Rey's city relatives. But on the way back, they'd missed the bus. Instead of staying overnight and catching a bus next day, they caught a taxi. That is four hours in a taxi from Melbourne to Old Dunaway and then because of the excessive distance, having to pay for the driver's return to the city. They arrived home in the early hours of the morning and Selwyn had to be dug out of bed so as to pay the driver by cheque. Rey had then to repay the money owed with deductions from his wages. Something that went on for months if not years.

Though it was never openly discussed, I gathered from a few things said that Anna had had a couple of children by a previous relationship. But these kids, for whatever reason, had been taken away from her and twenty years on, she was still grieving. She had a teddy bear and when she'd been drinking would walk around with it in her arms, tears in her eyes.

One day I said to Anna, 'It's a great life if you don't weaken.' A bit of an over-used cliché.

At this she really lost her temper which was rare for her, 'How can you say life is great! Life is just bloody terrible!' More followed in the same vein.

Anna was a good housekeeper. The place was spotless as never before. As we were sharing the kitchen and bathroom, I'd to be especially careful not to leave a mess. Anna would get upset, though rarely would anything be said directly to me.

Then on coming home at the end of a long weekend, having been off looking at birds somewhere, I walked in the door and the kitchen looked like a dirt bomb had gone off. The place was an absolute pigsty, unwashed dishes in the sink, beer bottles and muck over the floor. The stove looked to have been the centre piece in a food fight.

The pair had been into town and come home thoroughly drunk. The following day, Rey, looking like death warmed up, managed to stagger out of his room saying something about not feeling too well. It was a couple of days before he was back at work. It took even longer for Anna to resurface and set about getting the house into better order. But beset by a stomach ulcers, she was never a well woman even when staying away from the booze.

After that, all settled down on the home front for about three months. Then it started again, but this time I was home. On arrival, Anna promptly scuttled away into their bedroom and her teddy bear. While Rey had transformed into a raving monster who shouted, swore and threatened me before retreating to their room to sleep it off.

When I spoke to Selwyn about it afterwards, he expressed the hope that I'd have a steadying influence on the pair. Rey was considered harmless, but if there was any resort to physical violence to let him know. He added that by docking the man's wages on account of the Melbourne taxi business and lost days at work, this was restricting the amount of money that could be used to buy grog. But I was left with the impression he didn't take the situation at all seriously.

Close to the end of the year, it happened again.

I'd just come back from a month-long bird-watching trip through north Queensland. A few days before I left to go north, Rey had borrowed a 22-calibre rifle from one of boys over at the shearer's quarter. The idea was to shoot a few rabbits for the pot. But having been away, I'd forgotten all about it.

On getting back, the house was in good order but the next day, someone gave Rey and Anna a lift into town so they could do some Christmas shopping. No, they didn't want a lift home. They'd make their own arrangements. On hearing of this, I thought, *here we go again, why do I put up with this nonsense?*

As expected, a late night taxi brought the pair home. As expected, Rey was drunk and roaring but on coming in, headed straight for the bathroom.

The rifle I'd forgotten about was behind the door. By the time I realised what was going on, the weapon had been loaded and the business end pointed at me. I should have been terrified, but I remember being strangely calm. For almost as far back as I could remember, I'd been intimidated by bullies. But this was the ultimate in bullying, a mad drunk with a loaded gun. Now I was going to look him in the eye, face the danger and survive to see tomorrow's sun rise. He wasn't going to shoot me, of that I suddenly left sure. 'Rey be careful what you're doing with that thing,' I said and sat down at the kitchen table. The gun was waved in my face. The ranting continued for several more minutes and then he went into the bedroom to threaten his wife. I would hear her loudly moaning. Rey had his back to me but could I, should I, have acted? The rifle was a single shot, but attempting a violent intervention, who knows what the outcome could have been. In the event, the bedroom door was closed, Anna stopped moaning. I continued sitting at the table for the next hour. The house was silent. After that, I judged it safe to go to bed.

At first light, I retrieved the rifle from where it had been left leaning against a wall. It was still loaded.

But after this, I came to the conclusion that I'd simply had enough. Even if the man had been sacked over the incident which he wasn't, my time on Old Dunaway Station was at an end. Yet, I felt trapped, attempts at getting better jobs elsewhere had failed. The only alternative was to just pack up and go. But there were problems. Quite apart from no job waiting out there, I had little money, the month away and further car repairs having drained my savings. Add to that my sights were set on northern Australia, another world at least with regards to its wild life. But it was December, the start of the wet season in the north and not a good time to be travelling or looking for work. If I could keep rifles out of Rey's hands for a couple of months I might linger in the current job, leave at a better time. In the meantime, perhaps that sought-after job might still turn up.

I'd planned to be gone by Easter 1966, but this was extended to August. Though there were underlying tensions at home, the rifle incident was never openly discussed. But to their credit, Rey and Anna stayed away from the booze.

I told the McCauleys I was leaving but would stay until after the ram grooming season. I thought they may have taken the opportunity to train someone else to do this job, but Selwyn thought he could take on that role. But given the time involved and his other duties of managing the station, I privately questioned that plan.

By August, the drought that had been threatening was really starting to bite. By that stage I'd another ute, a Holden FB, with almost twelve months registration. I hoped it was going to get me to wherever I was going. It did, but only just.

A few years later I was to hear of the tragic deaths of Rey and Anna. They'd been living in humpy hut on the banks of the Edwards River at Deniliquin. Witnesses said they'd been drinking, but it seemed someone had knocked over an oil lamp. The hut went up in flames. Others had tried to get them out but were prevented by a locked door. It is to be hoped the pair were so drunk they didn't know much about it.

In more recent times, the memory of the pair formed the basis of two of the protagonists in *The Golden Man*. Though there, the *Mavis* character rises above her troubles in ways Anna in real life never did.

Chapter 15

The Transit Time

'EMILY DOESN'T LIVE HERE ANYMORE,' I was told by a middle-aged woman with dyed blonde hair, handing me an unopened letter.

'You have a forwarding address or something?' I asked.

'I've no idea where she's gone,' came the terse response. 'But nothing with her name on it gets delivered here ever again.'

With that, I put the letter in a side pocket of my post bag attached to the front of the red bicycle and continued with my deliveries down the street.

Three weeks earlier, I'd left Old Dunaway Station with the intention of driving north into Queensland, but worried by a lack of money had changed my mind. Instead, I headed for Sydney with the hope of getting some sort of job to build up my cash reserves before moving on. Looking back, I can see that having a home base in Sydney played a pivotal role, both then and in what transpired later. It was my mother who, having seen a recruitment ad in the paper, suggested I try getting a job as a postman.

So, after filling out a couple of forms, an interview and consenting to a police check, I was consigned to a post office in the nearby suburb of Wahroonga. Some very wealthy people lived in the area, but generally, more upper-middle class.

For us postmen, work started at 6.00 in the morning when the mail bags arrived. This was then sorted before we started to leave on our individual postal runs at about nine o'clock. The sorting room had a wall of pigeon holes down one side. These were divided up into nine sections. Within each of these, the pigeon holes carried the names of all the streets across the suburb. During sorting, the postmen would stand in front of their respective sections slotting the letters by streets. This completed, all the letters for each street would be gathered together for further processing, this time by house numbers. The sorter during this second stage being the one who'd make the delivery. In my case, I was delivering to nine streets and in those days, all was done on bicycles.

When delivering letters to over a hundred addresses, stuff-ups of one sort or another can occur, particularly for those new to the job. When this happened, the offender would get an official *please explain* and given five working days in which to respond in writing. Among the Wahroonga postmen, this was referred to as being *put on the rack,* denoting elements of the medieval, the painful stretching of limbs to obtain confessions. I was *racked* twice during my time there. Once, when clearly my fault, I'd misread a redirection order but the other, the business of - *Emily who doesn't live here anymore* - was different. When I was served with the resulting complaint notice, one of the more experienced postmen explained. Emily and her sister were the daughters of a famous scientist whose name didn't mean much to me at the time. But the two sisters who shared a house would periodically fallout and as a consequence, unsuspecting postmen were told forthwith to return one or the other's mail to the sender. This was by no means the first, nor perhaps the last, that a domestic problem within this particular household had boiled over, causing a public nuisance. Anyway, I thought it expedient to humbly apologise, thereby avoiding further trouble. The initial misdirection had been verbal, and though this had happened before, would have been hard to prove. Besides that, the Post Master General may have had a genuine rack hidden in a basement somewhere. Perhaps every post office had one, there not only to stretch ministrant posties, but also to obtain confessions from those who sent letters without stamps or failed to renew their dog license on time.

But the Wahroonga sorting room was well known for the camaraderie and banter that used to fly around when the mail was being processed. Someone would kick off a joke that would then roll around the room.

'Letter here address to The Red Tiled Roof north shore Sydney.'
'Really, that one again?'
'Try number six, The Front Garden.'
'Nasty dog in there.'
'Thanks, I'll wear me shin guards.'
'Mate a huge dog, more than just the legs to worry about.'
'Have me for lunch, you reckon?'
'The last postie that went there, all they found of him afterwards was a couple of undelivered letters and his whistle.'
'A whistle? Something to remember him by.'
'Where were the letters addressed to?'
'The Red Tiled Roof north shore.'
'Of course, why did I ask?'
'You tell me mate and we'll both know.'

And way back then, the good people of Wahroonga never got to hear the laughs behind their mail. Even the local council rates notices were greeted with mirth.

It was at this time I was involved with a somewhat disastrous driving lesson with my younger brother Jon. We were in my white ute the FB Holden on a gravel road and I had him stop and put the car into first gear. But when in starting off he planted his foot on the accelerator, and not surprisingly, the vehicle went skidding all over the road. We ended up crashing into an embankment. The damage was relatively slight, a bent left front mud guard.

My mother was still talking of getting a car and learning to drive. For my parents, since arriving in Australia, things generally had continued to improve, though Norman was now in retirement. One of his loves was cooking, certainly the results were marvellous, but he was starting to develop a serious weight problem.

Furthermore, drinking far too much claret. But Molly, at that time, still seemed to be adjusting to Australia. She was a full-time primary school teacher, but when I asked what she missed about

England the answer was a bit vague. Jon, on the other hand, seemed be fitting right in. But Adrian, who was in upper primary school, would have perhaps found the switch the most difficult. In those days, he seemed a bit of a lost soul as I'd been at his age, but I was to see comparatively little of him when he was growing up.

It was at about this time that we heard that our cousin Rodger had died. A young man in his early twenties at university, he'd developed an acute form of leukaemia. His passing was sudden and his parents never got over the shock. My Uncle George, an intelligent man, started drinking heavily, taking him to a very dark place, and ruining his marriage. But later, he was to devote what was left of his life to helping the poor and destitute.

While in Sydney, I was on the lookout for that special job, the sort with the potential to open the way to a genuine career. I had one job interview with what later became the Parks and Wildlife Service. Nothing, and further approaches to Taronga Zoo proved equally disappointing.

In the new year, I made the acquaintance of a very attractive young lady called Rebecca. We met at some conservationist group meeting, exchanged phone numbers and later I called in at her home. She must have been all of 18 and her mum never too far away. She'd been raised by her mother while her father, an American, was back in the states. But alas, I'd already set a date to leave Sydney, and we were as trains passing in the night.

It was about this time I explored the coast on the south side of Sydney harbour. Here in the eastern suburbs was a road on the high ground that gave a particularly good view of Bondi Beach. What I didn't know is that in one of the large houses along this street lived the grandmother of my wife-to-be and other members of her extended family.

Early March 1967, I was on the road again and this time with less chance of being stranded somewhere and desperate through lack of money. But day two out of Sydney and there was a trap for unwary travellers. I'd reached a small village on the New South Wales-Queensland border. Here there was some sort of gate, possibly to do with fruit fly or cattle tick control. I slowed down but didn't have to stop, though I noticed a brown car fall in behind as I crossed onto the Queensland side. Clear of the houses, I started to speed up, but then came a flashing blue light, the vehicle behind an unmarked police car. Furthermore, I was booked for speeding in a built-up area, even though by that stage there wasn't a house in sight.

I discovered later that this was a racket that had been going on along the border for years. Speed limit signs were set a mile or two out of town. As a result, unsuspecting interstate drivers, thinking they were out in the country, could find themselves being hit by on-the-spot fines. Welcome to the sunshine state, as it was then. But a few months after I'd fallen victim, the coppers caught the wrong guy. A lawyer who not only went to court, but publicly exposed the scam. At the time, there was quite a public fuss, but I never got my money back.

A couple of days were spent in Brisbane, staying with family friends. I contacted the Queensland Parks and Wildlife service. A phone call, a brief interview but when it came to employment, there was nothing about me that was of any interest to them.

Further up the coast, north Queensland had been hit with severe flooding and I was held up in Townsville for three days, waiting for the road to re-open. I stayed with birdwatching friends, which made a break from sleeping in the back of the ute. Later, having reached Cairns, I called in at the local employment office. They'd nothing suitable on their books, but they looked at me blankly and asked why I'd left the sheep station. This was not the sort of question that could be answered in two sentences, so I mumbled something and moved on.

I spent a couple of days further north around Daintree. Here, I stayed with the Copper family, who I'd met during my birdwatching trip 14 months earlier. In those days, Daintree was at the end of the coast road. A journey further north up the Cap York Peninsular required the traveller to take an inland route.

In a previous generation, the Coopers had come out from Cornwall and set up in north Queensland. But subsequent generations were represented by a married couple and three teen-aged children. They lived in a wooden house perched on a hillside surrounded by a few acres of cleared land that'd been carved out of the rain forest. The house was without electricity and they depended on a rainwater supply and a wood stove for cooking. The father, Des, worked as a foreman on road works construction, but liked to meet people like me - those who had reached the end of the road. Our first encounter had been a road side chat but as an interstate odd bod birdwatcher, I'd been invited home to meet the family. So, I came to hear of massive floods, of wild white men living with the natives and mad marijuana growers being pursued by giant crocodiles. But were these stories really true? Yes, sort of, but perhaps with a few embellishments along the way. Certainly, some of the rain forest around there was the thickest I'd ever seen, while the Daintree River seemed a magnificent untouched waterway. Perhaps a glimpse of what parts of east coast Australia had been like a hundred years earlier.

After leaving on this second visit, I went south to Innisfail before returning to Townsville. Along the way, some birdwatching and some job hunting. At Townsville, I briefly looked at the site of the new university which was under construction. It was to be named after James Cook. I never expected to be back.

I was preparing to leave Townsville when I collected a parking ticket, which caused much irritation. I could count on the fingers of one hand the number of times I had been caught with parking fines. If I were genuinely at fault, fair enough, I would wear the consequences. But this was one of those occasions when circumstances had conspired against me. At least that's how I saw it at the time. It started when I went to buy petrol and tried to pay with a traveller's cheque. But the guy didn't know what traveller's cheques were. Sure, I was a traveller, but the fancy bit of paper I was presenting wasn't a standard cheque. The money had already been paid and once correctly counter-signed there was no risk of it bouncing. But all to no avail, and I handed over cash, but as a result, needed to find a bank. I pulled up in front of a parking meter, thinking back in five. But the bank branch across the road was busy and it was more like thirty minutes. Then on returning, lo and behold, a ticket on my windscreen. But I had a car with an inter-state number plate, and heading off to I-don't-know-where. I tore up the ticket and left. What with having to pay a dodgy speeding fine and a shrinking budget, I'd just about had enough.

On leaving Townsville, I took the road to the west and within a day was in north western Queensland. Here was tussock grass plains and semi-desert flats. I sighted a couple of Austrian Bustards among other things. I'd travelled this country before, months earlier, but not along this particular road. It was supposed to be a highway, but after a while, the sealed road was replaced by a gravel surface.

In this type of country, I never drove at night because of the risk of hitting kangaroos or wandering cattle. On camping, I would always go well off the main road and be wary of showing a light. The vast majority of folks to be encountered in these remote areas were decent enough, but there was always the chance of meeting the odd nutter. If I'd gone missing, nobody would have had a clue where to start looking, there being a lot of wide-open spaces.

Another part of my daily routine was keeping my bird notes up-to-date. Since my days at Marnoo, I'd maintained what was effectively a nature diary but without the illustrations. By that stage, I'd six foolscap ledgers full of notes and these days looking at those yellowing pages from over 50 years ago, I can plot the course of that journey and what was seen along the way. The writing was done with a fountain pen, using the drop-down tail gate of the ute as a table.

Up until this stage, the vehicle had been running well but I was a little worried about the amount of oil it was using and was having to check the oil levels twice a day. Then some miles out of Julia Creek, I approached a cattle grid flanked by an old boundary fence that stretched off to the horizon in both directions. I reduced speed. Such grids can be bumpy and always need to be approached with care. But going over, there came a louder than expected clunk from the back. I stopped and got out. At first, there seemed nothing. But when I looked under the vehicle - what a mess.

The ute was seven years old, but in a previous life had been owned by a fruit grower. I guess from time to time, he'd been carting rotting fruit in the back. Some of the corrosive juices had leaked down into the sub floor. Now the bump over the cattle grid had caused the rusted out sub-floor to give way. As a result, the petrol tank had dropped down and the only thing stopping it from dangerously dragging on the road was the still connected inlet pipe and fuel line. In fact, if I'd kept going there would have been the risk of not only losing fuel, but of fire. Effectively, this vehicle was a wreck, and had been from the day I'd bought it.

The decision to trade in the initial Holden ute had been brought about by car troubles during my first trip to north Queensland. The back wheel bearing that had caused such trouble earlier had given way yet again. This time, I had better warning and managed to get into the town of Charleville for repairs. I reasoned the earlier episode could have produced a slight distortion of the left side back axial. Perhaps the whole rear drive assembly needed replacing? I wasn't prepared to risk it again, but in getting rid of one potential source of trouble, I'd bought into another.

Faced with the current crisis, the first thing I did was jack the fuel tank back up into place. To do this, I placed a flat piece of wood on top of the jack, thus ensuring I didn't add to my troubles by punching a hole in the tank. I'd learnt from previous car troubles that short sections of plank can come in handy. Then, with pliers in hand, I turned to the fence which was in a thoroughly dilapidated state. Here was an abundant supply of that greatest of all inventions, number eight fencing wire, also known in the trade as *cocky's joy*. With long strands of wire, I set about constructing a wire cradle under the tank using the vehicle's back springs for support. This completed, I resumed my journey.

I continued on through Cloncurry and toward evening, stopped at a very nice water hole. It was a bit off the road but there were rocks and trees. Also, birds like the Spinifex Pigeon, Painted Finch and wild Budgerigars. There had been good rains that year through northern and central Australia and I was going to see more flocks of Budgerigars. They made quite a sight, a tightly coordinated green and yellow flock coming into drink at the water hole. A noisy chatter in the evening light.

While I was there, one of the local coppers turned up, said there was a report of a horse broken down and stuck in the mud somewhere. I'd seen no such horse but he was doing his job, that is being interested in who was passing through his patch without making it too obvious. I explained my aim was to look for work in nearby Mount Isa and if nothing there I planned to cross the border into the Northern Territory.

Mount Isa was the site of a large underground copper mine, that is Cu, the metal, and not the other sort. The town was dominated by two smoke stacks, the largest being painted red and white. It had a bit more of a main street than some of the small towns I'd past through and the houses around about were numerous enough to be almost classed as suburbs. Some of the houses had nice gardens belaying the fact that this town was effectively surrounded by scrubby desert. But deserts are always interesting and this one was no exception, for here dwelt such species as the Grey-headed Honeyeater.

I had a birdwatching contact in town, Sam Caruthers. I didn't know him, all I had was a phone number. We met and spent a little time looking at the local bird life. Sam was a mining executive, a potential useful contact for someone looking for work, but I let him raise the subject at a time of his own choosing. Apparently copper prices were down and the mine wasn't putting on new people.

I passed through the little town of Camooweal on the 10th of April and pushing on across the Barkly Tablelands reached Tennant Creek in the Northern Territory. The next day, and another long drive, brought me to just north of Alice Spring. From here, I could see the spectacular rocky MacDonnell Rangers to the south. Like a lot of areas in the deserts of central Australia, the country carries significant vegetation, spinifex plains intersected with low growing mulga trees and dotted about with ghost gums. In good years, when it rains and the desert is at its best, the wildflowers are everywhere. This was one of those times.

The dream time stories of the native peoples of central Australia describe how the MacDonnell Ranges were formed by a giant reddish-brown caterpillar that had subsequently transformed into stone. But before the transformation, a mob of mythical dingo's had torn holes in the caterpillar's hide, hence the rocky canyons that can still be seen to this day. Certainly, the wild rugged caterpillar ranges were awesome, particularly at sunset.

The air in central Australia is very clear and the stars at night are truly spectacular. But I found the moonlight bothersome. In a full moon, it was bright enough to read a newspaper. Not only did it make the countryside look truly weird but the light on the face had the power to keep me awake at night. The cover over the back of the ute was essential equipment on nights like that.

The town of Alice Springs was bigger than I had expected, with modern buildings, but with a wild west feel. Perhaps it was the sight of aboriginal families camped in the dry riverbed, but after a few hours, I started to feel I really didn't want to be there. A couple of days earlier, on reaching Three Ways north of Tennant Creek, I had had two choices: turn right up the Stuart Highway and on to Darwin, or left to Alice Springs. But thinking of bird species like the long-tailed finch and rainbow pitta to be found in the territory's top end, I was fast coming to the conclusion I'd turned the wrong way. North, not south, was where I needed to be.

But before leaving town, one thing that did catch my eye was the local art shop. There were some really spectacular paintings of desert scenes. I guess at least some of this work was by that totally unknown artist (as he was in 1967) Albert Namatjira. As a former art student, I had always been attracted to work that displayed a high degree of technical competence and masterful use of colour. Some of this artwork absolutely had it all. So, there it was, twenty dollars for a small one, a hundred for something bigger.

But at the time, I was more concerned by my dwindling bank balance and the state of my car. I decided that if I really was going to reach Darwin I needed to drive more slowly. Apart from the engine, the gearbox wasn't too good either. Earlier in Sydney, some repairs had been done on the gearbox, but the same problems seemed about to resurface.

It took me four days to reach Darwin and birds seen along the way included Flock Pigeon, Banded Boneyeater and Red backed Kingfisher.

As I drove into Darwin, just at sunset, the first thing I noticed was the humidity. I'd become used to the heat, though nights in the desert can be cold even in autumn. But it had been a dry heat. The heat in Darwin was different. I discovered a small motel that didn't look like it wasn't going to be too expensive, got cleaned up and slept in a proper bed. Had I really arrived somewhere? That remained to be seen, but felt I really couldn't go on like this.

Chapter 16

Humpty Doo: The Promised Land

I FOUND THE LOCAL OFFICE OF the Commonwealth Scientific and Industrial Research Organisation (CSIRO) just off Darwin's Smiths Street. I was greeted by the girl behind the desk, and, after giving my name, was told that the farm manager would see me in a minute and to take a seat.

A short time later, a wiry figure appeared, dressed in shirt, shorts and long white socks. We shook hands as he introduced himself as Jeff Hutchins, farm manager at the Coastal Plains Research Station.

'Most of my time is spent out on the farm at Humpty Doo,' he explained as he ushered me into a poky little office. 'In town today on other business. Tell me a bit about yourself.'

This I did as we sat facing each other, before I handed over my job reference letter from Old Dunaway Station.

'So, you have tractor driving experience?' he asked, glancing over the letter.

'Yes,' I replied.

'Good I'll see you out there,' he declared with a smile. Then by way of an afterthought. 'You know where to go? We're about forty miles out of town. You'll need to report to Joe, the administration officer, when you arrive.'

'Yes, I saw the sign to Humpy Doo when I was driving up the highway yesterday afternoon,' I said, hardly believing how my luck had changed for the better.

We shook hands again and then I was on my way.

I'd been in Darwin for less than half a day but now, having been on the road for six weeks, I had a job.

First thing that morning, I stopped by at the local employment office and they had two suitable positions. One was at the Rum Jungle uranium mine at Batchelor, also out of town, and the other for a tractor driver at the CSIRO rice research station at Humpty Doo. Though the uranium mine would pay nearly twice the hourly rate, the mere mention of the word *research* had me thinking here was the place I needed to be.

So, after some grocery shopping, I headed back down the Stuart Highway (known locally as the track) to where I'd seen the turn off to Humpty Doo.

Darwin, in term of distance, is closer to the Indonesia's capital Jakarta than to any of the major cities in Australia. Its climate has been described as a desert where it rains heavily for about four months of the year. Before I arrived, it had indeed been raining, 28 inches in 28 days during February. But now in late April, the big wet was over, the country just starting to dry out.

A few shops and a petrol station at Berrimah marked the southern edge of town. From then on, open eucalyptus forest with a ground cover of spear grass, much of it over four feet high, was all that could be seen on either side of the road. People who camped out in the scrub around Darwin for whatever reason were often referred to as *long grassers*. But the soils that supported all this grass and scrubby forest were typically poor and gravelly.

That day, I passed the turnoff to Howard Springs and came to a dip in the road where creek water was still running several inches deep. Here were some Pandanus palms and low growing Melaleuca trees. I slowed down and went through the water. Then a little further and there was the turnoff to Humpty Doo, a long straight-sealed road going east. I arrived at the research station village about half an hour later. My job interview with Jeff had been so brief I hadn't even stopped to ask about pay, working hours, accommodation or anything else.

The village consisted of eight raised up stilt houses, two cottages and a line of small flats all sited around a ring road. The stilt houses were built atop platforms sitting on pylons raised to a height of nine feet, but with a small laundry compartment underneath. This was an architectural design typical of the area, but of a type that faired very badly when a severe cyclone hit Darwin some years later. In the centre of the village, surrounded by lawns, was a low sprawling building which I took to be the administration block and the laboratories.

Through the front door and into the air conditioning, I went that day and found Joe Gibson, administration officer, at his desk. Joe was in his mid-thirties, balding, a nice smile, but without a clue as to who I was or why I was there. After explaining that I'd been given a job by Jeff, who was still in town, I effectively had my second interview for the day. All very friendly and in the process of learning more of what was involved. I would be a field assistant, helping with research into rice growing. I'd be working public service hours, which meant a start at 8.30 and a finish at 4.30. So, gone were the regular 60 hour weeks of Old Dunaway. I would be sharing a house with two other blokes. The pay was more than I could have hoped for and though I had to pay rent, the cost was significantly subsidised. This was in part due to the difficult tropical climate and the research station's geographical isolation, but it all sounded great to me.

The only catch, it would take about a month before my first pay arrived, the wheels of government administration being somewhat slow. The outcome on the pay front - it did take about a month, but I ended up with two cheques. It would have been nice to start off with a double pay, but alas, honesty got the better of me and one was handed back.

After going through the details, Joe and I went over to one of the stilt houses. The interior consisted of three bedrooms, bathroom, a lounge room with a partly separated kitchen area and tables. There was an electric stove, sink and fridge. There was only one flight of stairs into the house, though I discovered later there was an escape hatch in the floor of one of the bedrooms. There were no locks on any of the doors.

The other two people I'd be sharing with were still at work. We found an unused bedroom and I proceeded to settle in. The first of the other occupants to appear was Neil and when he came in the front door, I was sitting at the kitchen table.

'You the new man?' he asked. We then introduced ourselves. Neil was about my age, bearded, fairly solidly built. He was from England like me, but was on something of an extended working holiday. He'd retained something of a cultivated English accent and I discovered later around the research station that he was generally known as *the squire*. But unlike me, he'd never really settle into Australian ways and I sensed that given a year or two he would be heading back to the UK.

I asked what was it like to work here.

'Apart from the farm manager, Jeff, and Joe in admin, there are three groups,' he informed me. 'The research people, most of whom are married, then there are the technical assistants and Alan, the motor mechanic. Finally, four farm staff which includes you and me. The actual farm is about two miles up the road, on the black soil plains of the Adelaide River. About ten years ago, private enterprise investors came in here with heaps of American money with the idea of growing a lot of rice and shipping it across into Asia. In the end, they failed and CSIRO was asked to set up a research station to see where it all went wrong.'

Soon after, Tim, the third member of the household arrived. He was fair-haired and I guessed about 18. I found him easy enough to get on with but not always able to appreciate my humour. Sometimes, I had to say to him, after being given a hard look, 'Joke mate, a joke.' and he'd give a bit of a grin and relax. His family lived in Darwin, but I discovered later that his mother, worried about the sort of company he was keeping in town, had used her contacts to get him a job out at the research station.

The road to the rice growing area led past the machinery workshop and on to the farm itself. Here was a very abrupt change in vegetation, the tall grass and open forest giving way to the black soil plains of the lower Adelaide River. Here at the end of the wet season was a green expanse of sedge stretching north and south as far as the eye could see. To the east, the trees lining the river could be seen a mile away. The farm with its narrow access roads and raised irrigation check banks had been carved out of the heavy black clay typical of these sedge lands. The experimental rice crops growing in the irrigation bays were reaching maturity but there were concerns that the ground wouldn't be hard enough to support harvesting equipment.

The aim of the research was multifaceted, but included everything from soil chemistry to assessing rice varieties, to weed control. The area had the potential to produce at least two crops of rice per year, but as I was to learn, there were two major problems. The unpredictability monsoon wet season and the availability of irrigation water in dry periods. This is best illustrated by a story I heard more than once from Sam Lassiter, the officer in charge of the research station. In the years when rice growing at Humpy Doo had been fully commercial, Sam had been based in Perth, Western Australia. But on visiting the Humpty Doo area one February, he'd been met by a desperate farm manager. The commercial crop had started to grow but the ground was bone dry and total disaster only days away. When Sam was asked what could be done, his heartfelt professional advice was, 'Pray, that's all mate just pray.'

He was on his way back to Perth when he received a telegram from Humpty Doo, 'Rice under a foot of water, what shall I do?'

His equally professional reply, 'Cease praying.'

A cyclone had gone through the area and the wet season was suddenly back.

Another major problem, and one that was to involve me directly, was keeping birds off the crop. In April of that year, this was not an issue because there was water everywhere and the two main problems Pied Geese and Little Corella (a species of small cockatoo) were elsewhere with more than enough to feed on. But as the dry season progressed, they would become a real problem and anti-bird patrols, including shooting, had to be carried out from dawn to dusk.

We occasionally had problems with water buffalo. This was an introduced species and up to a decade or so earlier, had not been considered a problem. But around the mid 1950s, some sort of evolutionary change had taken place and their numbers had started to rapidly increase. A commercial buffalo meat industry had developed around Darwin and this was keeping buffalo numbers down around Humpty Doo.

In the years to come, I was to see buffalo in Asia, but they were less than half the size of those in the Northern Territory. On one occasion, I witnessed a young bull charge through a brand-new fence, ripping three wooden posts clean out of the ground as it went. Admittedly, it was being shot at and therefore, not without reasons, but a powerful animal just the same. I could hardly have expected such a performance from its weedy Asian counterparts which almost seemed like a different species.

On a number of occasions, I would be walking through long grass only to have a buffalo the size of a small car get up out of a concealed wallow a few yards away and bolt off into the surrounding scrub. Fortunately, I never encountered a sick or wounded animal. Sometimes weekend shooters would come out from Darwin with neither the skill or the firepower to bring down a Buffalo cleanly. I heard stories of desperate shooters trying to climb up the prickly trunks of Pandanus in an attempt to get away from some maddened beast they should have left well alone.

Apart from the Water Buffalo, other introduced animals included horses, cattle and pigs. The last two species, were potentially dangerous under some circumstances. The Salt Water Crocodile was locally under a lot of hunting pressure, being shot for their skins, but I saw little sign of them though always a source of concern.

I was involved in all sorts of general farm work at Humpty Doo, everything from driving tractors to irrigating rice paddies during the dry season. The delivery of fertiliser and sometimes the sowing of rice seed was done from the air. There was an air strip near the farm on which small crop-dusting machines could land. On one occasion, I was helping to load up a crop duster with fertiliser when I discovered there was an extra pair of hands, a lad with us I didn't recognise. When asked from where he'd come, he explained he'd flown out in the plane's hopper. So, no seat, no seat belt and in a closed hopper that had been periodically used for pesticides; a brave man.

My bird notes from April 1967 showed that I wasted little time exploring. On the Sunday after arriving at Humpty Doo, I spent time around Fogg and Harrison Dams, not far from the research station village. Fogg Dam provided the irrigation water supply for the farm. An earthen wall about fifteen feet high and a hundred yards long had been built across a natural area of swamp land at the edge of the black soil plain. This had been constructed by the commercial rice growers. Though it was able to supply water to the research farm during the dry season, there would have been insufficient storage to do much else.

The second dam, Harrison, had a much greater storage capacity but seems never to have been filled. The original idea had been to pump river water into it during the wet season. Though the earth wall was substantially higher than Fogg, the catchment was smaller. So, it remained a waterbird habitat of interest but otherwise, a monument to failure.

There were other monuments around the area, such as the rusting platforms sitting in disused irrigation channels out on the river flats beyond the research farm boundary. These had once supported large electrically driven pumps, the decaying motors of which could still be seen. The idea, so I was told, had been to float the pump platforms up and down the channels delivering water where needed. The problem was the pumps were so powerful they rapidly drained the channels. They had then to be turned off while the water flowed back in from the river.

However, the greatest single problem for the commercial rice growers had been the lack of proper road access to the rice paddies during the wet season. The result was that people trying to run things spent an inordinate amount of time on foot.

But for me, this was the land not only of the Pied Goose, but also the Red-tailed Black Cockatoo and the Wedge-tailed Eagle. So those species I'd seen in the Natural History Museum all those years earlier had become a real part of my world, or, I a part of theirs.

I was now starting to think that here was a chance to push the birdwatching business much further. Not a great deal was known about the birds of the Northern Territory. So, by becoming the local expert, there was a chance that somehow in some way this might open a door to an even better future.

But if I was to seriously study the birds of the area, I needed reliable transport. andMy Holden ute was effectively falling apart. Being on a wage better than ever before, I started to think about a new car, one suited to the local conditions. Something relatively cheap, good clearance underneath, low fuel consumption plus a supportive dealership in town who could supply parts and workshop services. The colour was the least of my concerns. The car that ticked all these boxes was the Volkswagen Beetle. I was destined to live at Humpty Doo for nearly five years, but my VW 1300 was to handle well under very difficult conditions. Certainly, as good, if not better, than many four-wheel drives available at that time. Features that helped the VW were being relatively light and with the weight of the rear mounted engine distributed over the back wheels where it was most needed. Going through water, there was always a risk of the car floating. But on the other hand, providing the vehicle could maintain momentum, the water was being pushed away from the motor's electrical components. Additionally, being an air-cooled engine, there was no radiator to clog up or an exposed fan to blast water over the distributor.

The only modification needed was a reinforcement of the head frame, the large plate structure at the front of the chassis. This supported the steering and front suspension, but under rough conditions, could crack, but the VW beetles had an easy-to-bolt on reinforcement kit.

My only real complaint was with the 6-volt electrical system. This made for relativity weak headlights that became ever more of an issue as the car aged. Another aspect of this aging process - sometimes the starter motor would fail to turn over, even when the battery wasn't at fault. However, this could be overcome by twisting the fan belt pulley to set the engine on low compression, thus allowing the starter motor to overcome the initial resistance. Later models dispensed with this troublesome 6V feature replacing it with a more reliable 12 volt.

There were other issues with this type of car. Earlier models had a design fault in the rear suspension that made them prone to tipping over. Having the fuel tank at the front greatly increased the risk of fire in the event of a head on collision.

Within a very short time after arriving at Humpty Doo, I started a serious exploration of the Darwin area and its bird life. But at first, I made do with the Holden ute, but as registration time approached I switch to a brand-new Beetle and the bird work continued uninterrupted.

Apart from the open forest, which was subject to grass fires during the dry season, there was the coastal areas, low lying but with no cliffs and prominent headlands. There were mud flats, sandy beaches and a rock platform at East Point. Coastal sand dunes were typically covered with monsoon scrub, a low growing semi-rainforest. Mangroves often fringed the mud flats while behind the coast in some places were saline swamps with low growing salt tolerant vegetation. The region's sedge plains were the size of small English counties. In the dry season, they dried out, the typically black clay soil becoming deeply cracked. Around the edges of these riverine plains were stands of Pandanus palms and tall Melaleuca (tea trees) with some small patches of monsoon forest.

At the time of my arrival, the road to the iron ore mine at Mt Bundy was not open, the bridge across the Adelaide River still under construction. With its completion, this not only allowed access to the granite hills of Mt Bundy but also the open forest and grassland of the Marraki area. The grassland, with its finally granulated soils and patches of low growing trees, was of particular interest from a birdwatcher's point of view. It was a different habit from that found elsewhere in the district.

There is a substantial difference in average rainfall between the coast and areas to the south, 30 miles inland. Within the open forest this caused a marked change in the bird population with some species being common in the south but rarely if ever seen closer to the coast. The exact opposite as of what might have been expected. The underlying cause seemed to be soil type, the coast's more frequent wet season rain accentuating the problem of mineral deficiency.

Quite a number of bird species largely or completely vacated the Darwin area during the onset of the wet season. These included many of the hawks and eagles like the Black Breasted Buzzard Kite.

I started a weekly census at Fogg Dam. This was done by traversing the dam wall via a narrow roadway and counting the number of birds on either side. But in the first year, I made a fundamental error. There were two different habitsats, the relativity shallow swamp below the wall and the lagoon environment with floating pond weed on the other side. Not knowing the area, or understanding the seasonal changes, I lumped the data from both sides together. Fogg Dan was a dry season refuge area for water birds. During the first half of the dry season, June to mid-August, there could be up to several thousand birds below the dam. These would not only include birds from the surrounding coastal plains, but also, it seemed, some coming from the inland. But as the dry season progressed and the shallow swamps dried up, the birds followed the water back to make use of the lagoon environment. The overall water bird population was determined by what could survive the dry season. But by combining data I'd failed to show this all-important aspect of the local environment and the census was largely a waste of time. In later years, this was corrected.

Marvellous though Fogg Dan was in the 1960's and 70's when last seen in July 2012 is was barely a shadow of what had been. Invasive weeds and massive silting due to clearing for agriculture in the catchment had altered the ecology to the extent that the area was almost unrecognisable. Much money had been spent improving access for the bird-watching public but vastly more was needed to clean up the mess.

Prior to arriving in the Darwin area in 1967, I had had little experience with identifying migratory shore birds. These are a diverse group that breed in the northern hemisphere, some within the Arctic cycle, and then fly south, thereby avoiding the northern winter. Some arriving in Australia were still in distinctive breeding plumage. But most were in winter plumage, typically greyish, speckled brownish or off-white, posing a challenge when it came to identification. As an example, two species of Sand Plover common along the coast. Easy to identify in breeding plumage, but at other times, the only clue was very subtle differences in the shape of the bills. On one occasion, I was out with a birdwatching visitor from New Zealand. I was saying, 'The one on the left is a mongolus and on the right lechenaultii.' But he went away shaking his head, unable to recognise the difference.

It took me a couple of years of observing thousands of shore bird before I felt confident in conducting a weekly census, though this wasn't without its dangers. Though I never encountered a crocodile, I was once caught on a sand bank by the rising tide. Though I was able to wade to safety across a knee-deep tide race, this was February, and the thought of deadly box jellyfish a terrifying prospect. Several whitish blobs were seen to shoot past in the water and I was ever so thankful to be out on the other side. The beach was completely deserted and if I'd been badly stung, I wouldn't have stood a chance. But being thoroughly familiar with the area, I should have been more careful.

Around Darwin, in the wet season, no sane person goes swimming, the natural toxin from the box jellyfish being rated as the most powerful known to man. When patrolling beaches, I didn't consider washed up jellyfish the size of large dinner plates a problem, but a sharp eye was needed for the misty cup shaped medusae about the size of a man's fist. Dead they might have been, they still had the potential to kill.

On one occasion at Lee Point, a huge grouper was washed up on the beach. I don't know how old it was, but even by shark standards it was the largest fish I've ever seen.

My work with shore bird at times proved quite spectacular, for I added two previously unrecorded species to the Australian list, the Asiatic Dowitcher and the Redshank. The Dowitcher was particularly satisfying because at the time most Australian birdos didn't know such a species existed, let alone that it might occur in this country. But once people knew what to look for, it started to be recorded in small numbers in other coastal areas. The reason it had been previously overlooked was because it was an exclusively Asian breeding species and closely resembled the relatively common Bar-tailed Godwit. Australian wader watchers were largely relying in bird books from North America and Europe not realising there was a third species of Dowitcher.

In total, I recorded over 250 bird species in the Darwin area. An annotated list among other things was eventually published.

On one occasion, I decided to conduct a birdwatching marathon. That was to see how many species I could sight in one day. This required a thorough knowledge of the region, its birds and strategic planning to reduce time spent travelling. For greatest effectiveness, this needed to be done in the dry season. One day in early July, I started at dawn in the granite hills of Mount Bundy and systematically worked towards the coast. By nightfall, I'd sighted 98 species, but by no means an Australian record for this sort of thing. If a visitor from the UK had been with me that day, say someone from the village of Kemsing, then nothing of what we saw would have been familiar, all species totally new to them. But then I might have continued the hunt after dark, driving around the research station farm and likely adding Eastern Grass Owl, Tawny Frogmouth and possibly Bush Stone-Curlew to the list.

As for the two bird species that inspired my move back up the highway from Alice Springs, numerous sightings of both.

Chapter 17

Once More the Education Mountain

ON THE RESEARCH STATION AMONG the young unmarried men, including most of the field assistants, socialising often revolved around beer drinking. But I'd never been a lover of alcohol, so this and my crazy birdwatching activities, meant I was an outsider, an oddity at least in some people's eyes. But territory society at that time was full of odd bods, people who were refugees of one sort or another from southern Australia or somewhere else.

On weekends, if the weather was good, I'd often camp out in the bush or along the beach. The following morning, I would start birdwatching at first light but this also got me away from the drinkers. Though in all fairness, during the nearly five years I lived on the research station, I know of only one potentially serious alcohol related incident and that was stopped with the intervention of bystanders.

But during my first year at Humpty Doo, on at least a couple of occasions when I wasn't home, Neil had invited nurses from the Darwin Hospital to spend the weekend with him and friends. I heard stories afterwards but regarded such as somewhat exaggerated.

During that first years at Humpty Doo, a person who became convinced as to my utter strangeness was a young lady who I'll call Angela. This stemmed from an incident that occurred about three months after I arrived, but the story became part of the local subterranean chatter for quite some time.

Angela was, for a while, the research stations primary school teacher. On arrival, she caused a bit of a stir among the single men in particular because there weren't too many mini shirts to be seen around the place. One evening, she turned up at the shared house when Neil, Tim and myself were at home. Being 40 miles out of Darwin without a car, she expressed a desire to go to the beach. At that stage I'd just bought a new car and volunteered to take her that coming Saturday.

In the car we had a friendly chat. Angela was from England and like me seemed to have had her reasons for leaving, though these weren't spelt out in detail. We arrived at the mouth of the Mackel Creek. A warm July day, not a cloud in the sky, and a mile or more of broad sandy beach with not a soul in sight.

She then stripped down to her bikini and lay on the sand, baking. I was then asked to rub her back and then her legs with sun cream. She'd an excellent figure and by this stage, I was becoming seriously sexually aroused. But I hardly knew the girl and was determined to behave. With binoculars in hand, I walked off along the beach and went birdwatching for perhaps half an hour. I saw nine Grey Plover, a species I'd only ever seen once before. So, with my mind back on birds of the feathered kind, I returned to the sunbather with tales of what I'd seen. I got a mildly interested response and with this I asked if she'd like to see a bird's nest.

In the monsoon scrub that grows along the sand dunes around Darwin is the home of the Scrubfowl. The bird is a bit bigger than a chicken, but one of three mound building species found in Australia. The heat from the mound's rotting vegetation is used by the male to incubate the eggs. The Scubfowl's nesting mound at Mackel Creek was over fifteen feet high and must have been built up by successive generations of birds for perhaps a century or more. So, it was to this awesome sight that Angela and I now walked to. I took a photo of her standing next to the nest mound, but after this she seemed to become irritated by my unbelievable nerdiness and asked to be taken home. This I did, though we hardly spoke on the way.

There the matter may have rested, but within a couple of weeks, she'd formed a serious relationship with Martin, one of the technical assistants. This arrangement was such that Angela moved into Martin's flat, living with him until they broke up about two years later. But while this was going on, she started putting about stories to the effect that during the day at the beach she'd made sexual advances which I'd rejected. Furthermore, this was stated more than once to my face, in front of others. Though I do have some regrets, t buthis wasn't a question of high morals or of an opportunity lost but of common sense. This lady was simply bad news, a complication I could do without.

The pre-wet from late September to November and sometimes into the New Year is the most demanding in terms of Darwin's climate. Though hot and humid, the day will start fine, by late morning a few clouds. But these would often have developed into thunderstorms by later afternoon that would persist through the early part of the night. Next day, the cycle would start again. During this time, large ceiling fans going in bedrooms at night were absolutely essential. On a number of occasions, the mains power would go off, more often than not due to a lightning strike on a power pole somewhere. But the research station had its own back-up generator and it usually fell to Alan, the mechanic, to get it started. But waiting in bed at eleven at night for the fan to come back on could be an ordeal. However, at other times, camping out without fans was never a problem, though I avoided such activity on stormy nights.

At the research station during my first year, a hot sticky Christmas came and went, but soon after, the real monsoon set in and persistent rain made conditions more bearable. Tim had spent Christmas with his folks in Darwin, but on returning, told me and Neil that he'd had enough of the research station and was moving back into town. Neil tried to persuade him this wasn't such a good idea, but to no avail.

The last time I saw Tim was about two years later. He was sitting in a shop doorway in town, so stoned out of this mind by drugs he wouldn't have known if his arse was on fire. I didn't even try speaking with him. Later still, I heard he'd killed someone, had been charged with manslaughter and was serving five years. I guess the fears of his poor mother - him mixing with the wrong crowd, had proved well-founded.

The problem with the shared house at Humpty Doo was that if someone left, we had no say as to their replacement. But in this case, being the wet season and labour requirements low, the vacant position wasn't filled for another three months.

One day in April 1968, I arrived home to find a stranger sitting at the kitchen table just as I'd done a year earlier. A young man, dark-haired with a long black beard. In a distinctly foreign accent, he introduced himself as Milo Larcello. He seemed pleasant enough, his English was good, but having a dark complexion I thought he might be from somewhere in the Middle East. He was in fact Swiss and had spent over a year hitchhiking across the world, mixing with all types and sleeping everywhere from the decks of fishing boats to Buddhist temples.

Milo turned out to be a level-headed guy, a good sense of humour and very interesting to talk with. He would tell stories such as being abandoned in a desert somewhere by a truck driver. The man had demanded money, but when Milo wasn't forthcoming, he found himself standing on the side of the road miles from anywhere, with not a drop of water. But then hours later, he hitched a ride with a passing camel train. His only real complaint was that camel riding takes getting used to and his backside had been sore for days afterwards.

One day, Milo shaved his beard. At first, I didn't recognise him. Only when he spoke was the voice familiar, the truth revealed. The following morning, we managed to briefly fool Jeff, the farm manager, that the new Milo was the really Milo's cousin who'd turned up looking for work.

But that period in 1968 was really important for me in three significant ways. I'd enrolled to do two courses in agricultural studies by correspondence. The aim being to work towards some sort of certificate. But studying in the house was not practical so I'd been given permission to use one of the offices after hours over at the laboratories. Though the research staff and management saw this as positive, it further marked me as an oddity amongst some of the less well-educated. 'If you did badly at school why go back to that now?' I was asked on more than one occasion.

The second important step was reading an article on dyslexia and realising that this was me. At that time, the whole subject was controversial, some experts still arguing the condition didn't exist. But I'd lived with this thing, knew how it had shaped my life, how it'd come to define me as a person. But I was also angry, why hadn't I heard any of this before? What was all this nonsense about none-academic intelligence? But there was an up-side, for it made me more determined than ever to continue on the twin paths for birds and academic study.

The third revelation, the reading of another article, this time describing how the universities in Australia were being opened up to mature-aged students. Gone were the days when, if you hadn't become an undergraduate by your late teens, you were likely limited in terms of educational advancement. I was so excited on reading this one evening that I couldn't sleep and in the early hours of the morning, left the house to wander around the ring road in my pyjamas. I decided to continue with my agricultural studies and see how that worked out. However, in the coming year, I would likely turn my attention to maths and English by correspondence. But even then, during my moonlight stroll, my mind turned to the upper peaks of education, could I really go that far, me who'd utterly failed school? From now on, my work at the research station would be more than just a job, the dream I had on Old Dunaway had been partly realised. Here were further possibilities.

I'd been at Humpty Doo for a year and was due for some leave. The run of good seasonal conditions had continued across central Australia, whereas in the north the wet season appeared to have finished. Time to set out for Alice Springs again but this time under personal circumstances that had greatly improved. I had a job, no serious money troubles and an almost new car.

The desert was indeed in a wonderful condition, and I was impressed by the numbers of Bourke Parrot that seemed to be just about everywhere. I hadn't seen one the previous year.

This time, I pushed on well south of The Alice to the railway town of Oodnadatta, little more than a pub, a couple of shops and a railway station. On wandering out across sand dunes on the edge of the settlement, I came across a couple of Cinnamon qQuail-thrush, which, despite the name are neither thrush nor quail in the old-world sense. The early European settler encountering a land of strange birds had simply made up names based on what they knew. Terms like *robin* and *wren got* attached to all sorts of unrelated things. Australia has ten species of kingfisher, only three of which do any serious fishing.

On leaving Oodnadatta I came across a four-wheel drive stuck in a creek crossing. This was a problem because there was nobody around, but I needed to get past if I was to continue my journey. But there was another issue. In this part of the world, people who abandon vehicles are at considerable risk of dying. But here was water around; the creek was running, and the weather wasn't particularly hot. Nevertheless, the situation demanded further investigation.

Looking around, I sighted a house and farm buildings not far away on the other side of the creek. I then surveyed a possible alternative route to get over there. This required a drive down a steep bank, across the gravelly creek bed and up the other side. The VW beetle managed this with ease. Enquiries at the house confirmed that the bogged vehicle belonged to the woman who lived there. Apparently, her husband had left earlier that morning to drive into Oodnadatta to catch the train and had I seen him on the road? I confirmed I'd sighted a Landrover a few miles from the town, the only vehicle I passed that morning. As for the bog vehicle, she was expecting the postal delivery man later that day. There was no way I could have been of assistance and so the task of extraction was left to others.

Later that day, I camped by another creek further along the same road, observed a Pied Honeyeater, a comparatively rare species, and a herd of feral goats walking in single file across a creek bed.

Two days later I was on the Sandover Track northeast of Alice Springs. But I was worried because on looking to the southwest, I could see the very black clouds of an approaching weather front. Though the track passed through sandy spinifex desert dotted about with ghost gums, I was concerned with what the road was like further along. Heavy rain could leave me stuck for days, and, add to that the risk of running out of fuel. I was carrying supplies and spare fuel but still a concern. I kept going, reaching the black soil plains at the approaches to the Georgina River just on dark. Even a quarter inch of rain would have made progress impossible. The track itself was also becoming poorly defined, difficult to follow.

That night, I watched as heavy rain clouds passed to the south. In the morning, I found the ford that crossed the Georgina and by midday had reached the main highway at Camooweal. The town itself I remember as a general store, a couple of service stations and a few houses down either side of the highway. From there, I drove back across the Queensland-Northern Territory border. But on approaching Avon Downs on the sealed highway, I ran into heavy rain from a second weather front. Lucky not to have met this earlier.

However I wasn't entirely free of problems for next day, I became bogged in a creek crossing on the rough road to Borroloola. No amount of digging could get my car out, but then I was rescued by a scruffy looking guy in a beaten-up Toyota. He told me I may have problems further along the road at the Little River. The water at the crossing was likely to be too deep, but there was a track off to the side I might be able to use. This proved to be the case, but it was again a matter of driving down a bank across the riverbed through a foot of water and up the other side.

Borroloola in those days was a small place, a cluster of houses, a general store with a petrol pump out the front. The pump was a real antique of a type I'd seen only a couple of times before. The fuel was hand pumped via a long handle at the side, into a large clear plastic tank that sat atop of the pump stand. The tank had gradation marks indicating how much fuel had been stored. When the right level was reached, a valve was activated and the fuel gravity fed into the car.

The only problem with this was that the driver needed to estimate how much petrol the car was going to need before filling up.

The birdwatching around Borroloola was good, and the following day, I took the road to Katherine, reaching that town without further incident.

Back home, as the dry season progressed, the situation in the shared house became more difficult. Neil, who'd been tolerable to live with, decided his working holiday was at an end and returned to England. He'd never really liked Australia and couldn't understand why I loved the country.

Then Milo, who I'd always liked, was promoted to technical assistant and as such, moved into one of the flats.

Colin was the first replacement. A quietly spoken lad from Barraba in New South Wales. He was easy enough to get on with, but keen on country and western music that he would sometimes play late into the night. Normally, I didn't mind that sort of stuff, but he was a fan of a musician I couldn't stand and being a light sleeper didn't help.

However, on one occasion, Colin, who had a rather laid back attitude to most things involved me in what could have been a very nasty incident. In hindsight, one of those cases of an accident simply waiting to happen. We had an old tractor on the research station, but to get it started, a rag soaked in petrol had to be shoved up into the air intake. All this while a second person placed a metal screwdriver across the terminals on the starter motor. This was made doubly hazardous by the air intake being directly above the starter motor.

On this particular day Colin had a rag positively dripping with petrol ready to go.

'Too much,' I said.

'No, no she'll be right,' he replied.

I put the screwdriver in place and in the next second, a ball of fire. I was wearing shorts and thongs, and on looking down, discovered my right ankle ablaze. Fortunately, we were standing on the top of an irrigation channel bank and I took a flying leap ten feet or more into the water. At first, I thought I wasn't too badly injured but on getting out, the second-degree burns were only too apparent.

Colin had burnt his fingers but otherwise was not too bad. A trip to the doctor was needed and I was off work for a couple of days. It took about three weeks before I was completely healed. However, I hate to think what might have happened if the water channel hadn't been there.

Though there was some improvement to the tractor's start-up procedure, the machine didn't have any brakes and so remained relatively dangerous. It was mainly used for driving water pumps via a rear power take off (PTO), so brakes weren't quite so essential.

The second new recruit to the shared house was Dick, a big burly man in his mid-twenties. He had a really surly manner and though he never resorted to violence, there was the perception that physicality was never too far way. He played on this pushing in, leaning over but never overtly bulling. Colin and I spent much time trying to keep out of his way. Not easy when sharing a house. He was talking about getting married, some girl in town. But I thought, *Pity the woman who gets hitched up with him.*

Dick used to smoke and one night, in the back bedroom, he set his mattress on fire. Fortunately, he woke before the house burnt down. I helped him haul the still smouldering mattress into the bathroom and poured water onto it through a large burnt hole. Thinking we had it out, I went back to bed while Dick said he'd sleep on the floor.

During all this, Colin had been asleep but woke up later to find the bathroom on fire. The mattress wasn't out and after a couple of hours had flared up, this time burning a hole in the wall. The alarm was raised, the fire doused a second time, before the mattress was taken outside and set on the lawn. But by morning, the only thing left were the chard springs and a large burnt patch in the grass. It was at this point that Dick confessed that this was his second mattress burning experience and that previously, the fire had proven unstoppable. At this, Colin said to me in a low voice, 'You'd think he'd have bloody learnt from the first time, instead of trying to kill us twice in the one night.'

Within a year, both Dick and Colin had moved on, but in many respects, their replacements were far worse. The first to appear was

Hamal, another German speaking Swiss, and an old school friend of Milo's. I think Milo had been instrumental in getting Hamal the job at the research station. But having been away from Swaziland for several years and then being reunited with his old friend, he was having serious regrets.

'I pity you when Hamal comes here,' he told me.

'Really?' I replied, 'But he's your friend.'

'Yes at school, he was perhaps a bit of a hero,' confessed Milo. 'But since then, I've seen much, sort of grown up a bit. These days, Hamal isn't the bloke I thought he was. You'll need to be careful around him, because he's got a really wicked temper and by wicked, I mean just that. Once, when he was a kid, he nearly killed his own brother, and would have done so if his mother hadn't stepped in. You need to be careful.'

When I met Hamal, my first impression seemed to confirm what Milo had said. A very fit young man, English good but not perfect, but a humourless, pinched up face, hard eyes and not a bloke to be taken lightly. For the most part over the next several months, I carefully stepped around him. Yes, he admitted to having a fearsome temper, but what he feared most was lashing out - killing someone and then having to face the consequences.

The only time I came close to pressing the wrong button was when I discovered Hamal to be a raving Nazi. I've had a lifelong interest in the Second World War and the politics that led up to it. But now, Hamal was telling me that what I'd always thought of as irrefutable historic facts were simply wrong. Hitler was the victim, the hero who'd died in a failed crusade against the British, Russians and the USA. Where this re-writing of history had come from I did not know, but it deeply shocked me. But after that, I was careful not to raise the matter again.

Finally, Milo left his job as technical assistant. This left a vacancy, but much to my surprise, Hamal was offered the position which he accepted and as such moved into Milo's old flat. So, he was still around but I was no longer having to share a house with the man.

The second new comer was Barry Bricks, who was soon being referred to as *Gum Leaf* by the more disrespectful on the research station. He, too, was a young man but with an odd wrinkly face which made him look old before his time. He looked rough, was rough, and it wasn't long before he'd been given the sack. I don't know the exact reason for his dismissal, but as a government employee he would have been subject to a routine police check. I discovered later that he was using an assumed name and this may have led to his initial demise.

But whatever his troubles, he compounded the problem by taking off with my paycheque, which I'd left on a bedside table. The police were notified and then it was discovered that the cheque had been passed in a pub in town. But to do this, someone had to forge my signature. Meanwhile, it seemed Barry had got himself a job in town by claiming he knew how to weld. But his career as a welder was short-lived because he ended up in the Darwin Hospital having temporarily blinded himself from the welding flash.

Here the story might have rapidly moved on to an arrest, for the police knew where to find Barry. But the barmaid who'd accepted the dodgy cheque had described the young man who had passed it as good-looking and well-spoken. The arresting detective arrived at the hospital, took one look at Barry and walked away – couldn't be him, not with a face like that. Unfortunately, there had been another guy at Humpty Doo who'd only been there a few days and then left. His family owned a sheep and wheat property in Western Australia. It seemed he'd had a row with his father and walked out. But having arrived in Darwin was thinking that was all a big mistake. The trouble was he just might have fitted the barmaid's description and suddenly found himself having serious discussions with the police.

However, several days later, attention suddenly switched back to Barry. I think they may have gotten a sample of his very clumsy handwriting and compared that with the supposed signature on the cheque. Furthermore, they'd discovered his true identity and knew he had previous convictions. I had to be a witness at the committal hearing in which Barry conducted his own defence. Later at trial Barry pleaded guilty and given a year for forging and uttering. In my mind there has never been any doubt that he was guilty as charged. But I felt at the time that given a good legal counsel and the stuffing around that had gone on during the investigation, he just might have got off.

After this, there was a fairly quick succession of young blokes living in the house. One was Perout, a Frenchman and Sullivan a university student. Then there were the snake catchers, two guys that came from North Queensland. They didn't actually live in the house but because of accommodation shortages they were given one of the cottages. This was just as well because they brought a pet Taipan with them. The top end of the Territory has it verminous snakes including the King Brown, but the Taipan is rated as one of the most dangerous in the world. One day, their pet got loose and took to hiding in a gap behind a skirting board. After that incident the pair was asked to leave and take their precious pet with them.

Through all these comings and goings, I found the research station's administration very supportive and had a good friend in Joe Gibson. Yes, they realised that the shared house was far from an ideal. But because of budget restraints weren't in a position to do anything about it. Not that I spent much time complaining. My main strategy was to try spending as little time in the house as possible. So, I slept and ate there but the rest of the time was divided between work, studying in the labs or chasing birds of the suitably feathered variety.

One day, a silly business occurred over a letter. I'd written to a birdwatching friend, Mrs Fran Clark, who lived in Innisfail in north Queensland. But it seemed she'd moved and the post office had sent the letter back, *return to sender*. But it so happened that the bloke who was the research station's courier also went by the surname Clark. So, it was opened, even though it clearly wasn't addressed to him. But instead of admitting the mistake, he and a friend confronted me and wanted to know why I was writing funny letters to him. My first thought was, *Surely these two can't be that stupid?* So, I tried to explain that my friend was no longer living in Innisfail and that the letter had been duly returned to me. But this was brushed aside and they walked away. No doubt this was added to the stories doing the rounds among some as to my supposed weirdness.

One of the people I worked with I'll call Ron Kedgewick. A fellow field assistant, he lived in one of the cottages with his wife and four young children. A true Territorian in a society where most people originated from elsewhere, Ron had lived in and around Darwin all of his life. I got on well with him, though on one occasion I had to intervene when he was seriously thinking of, 'beating Colin's head in.' On that occasion Colin had been at fault, carelessly leaving broken beer bottles in a pool where Ron's children were apt to play. But with Ron, this was an exceptional circumstance and the threatened retaliation never eventuated.

But on one issue Ron and I were completely at odds. Australian Bustards still occurred around Humpty Doo's sedge plains, most often in the dry season. They have as much meat on them as a domestic turkey, but Ron used to shoot them, arguing they were great eating and he had a growing family to feed. In the Northern Territory, this was a legally protected bird and like bustard species across the world, under severe threat from land clearing and hunting pressures. His argument was that, illegal or not, the birds were there for the taking. But the same argument could have been made about the now extinct Passenger Pigeon and the Dodo. People can't go shooting vulnerable species and then expect them to still be around for future generations. But face with the needs of the here and now, he couldn't accept any of that.

One of the more interesting people who worked on the research station was Henrie the German. A migrant, he was married to an Australian girl and had a couple of kids. But during the war, he'd been a member of the Hitler Youth and at age 14 fought the Russians in the ruins of Berlin during the final weeks. He'd been taken prisoner by a Russian, who, it seemed, had been old enough to be his grandfather. Such was the nature of the conflict.

Sober Henrie had nothing good to say about Hitler and the Nazis. Claimed that as a kid his head had been stuffed full of utter nonsense. But on one occasion, after a few drinks, the war was on again.

'We had you English beat,' he declared, beer stubby in hand. 'That bloody Churchill, had him by the balls.'

'But your side lost,' I pointed out, but it made no difference, I was served up with more of the same.

Also, on the research station, was a Dutchman called Peter. He was about my age and therefore remembered the awful conditions, the famine that prevailed in Holland at the end of the war. He had no sympathy for even reformed Nazis, an uncle and two of his cousins having been shot by the Germans.

By this stage, Joe the admin offer, had left and his replacement was another German migrant Frank Schuster. He too had been a soldier on the other side and like Henrie, had later moved to Australia and married a local girl. But a few things he said to Peter one night indicated that Frank had, as an 18-year-old, been involved in the fighting around Arnhem in 1944. 'That man is bloody SS,' Peter darkly confided to me later, making a fist.

I found Frank easy enough to get on with, but years later I was to come across him again in a very senior position within CSIRO. But his boss at the time was a man who, during the war, had been a Polish fighter pilot serving with the RAF. I guess if the two had met as young men and Frank really had been an elite Nazi stormtrooper, they would've been doing their very best to kill each other. Such are the strange ways of the world.

The Northern Territory has a significant aboriginal population. Though they were around, I had only limited contact, but was aware of at least some of the social issues they faced.

One day at the end of the wet season, Sam Lassiter, the research station's officer in charge, asked me if I could go out collecting Pied gGoose eggs. He'd received a request from Dr Glen Storr in Perth who was trying to set up a colony of these birds. I'd never been goose egg hunting, but Sam had arranged for me to go over to Humpty Doo cattle station where one of the stockmen would assist. So later that day, I was out on the sedge plains with Jim, an aboriginal lad who may have been about 16. With his expert help we collected what we were looking for and later that day these were sent by air down to Perth. But back at the cattle station, I thanked Jim for his assistance, but got a really angry look in return. Up until that point, there'd been no hint of unpleasantness. I was left wondering what I'd said to give offence. It was only much later that I learnt that among black fellas, it's believed that when a white man says thanks he's being insincere. I'd never heard this before but could only assume it stemmed from a history of troubled race relations. But in the real world, how does a white fella say thanks to a black guy for a job well done?

On a couple of occasions, I was able to get into conversations with some of the older members of the aboriginal community. It was very interesting because they'd grown up within traditional societies. Real characters who had a positive outlook. One story was told to me by a lady from Elcho Island. Her father, as a small child, was out walking along the beach with his own father. They were going fishing, carrying fish spears. But then the older man looked back and saw that the little boy had allowed the end of his spear to drag, leaving a line in the sand. At this, the father admonished his son for disrespectfully dragging his spear through the bones of his ancestors.

But at other times, I had glimpses of the other side, the multitude of social problems that stemmed from disposition, loss of culture, hopelessness and picking up bad habits from white society. One day, I was driving along a track coming back from Cameron Beach. Passing that way earlier, I'd seen no one, but now there were three people. One was a blonde-haired white guy. He was lying face down partway across the track. The other two where aboriginal, a man and a woman. The woman was desperately waving at me to stop while the man was just as vigorously signalling me to keep going. I swerved around the guy on the track and drove on about ten yards before stopping. At this, the woman raced towards me and I let her into the car. But fearing a rock was about to come crashing through the car's back window, I sped off. I then asked the woman what was going on, but she flatly denied there was any trouble. She then propositioned me for sex, but I said I'd give her a lift to Berrimah and that was all. To this day, I've no idea what was going on, but at the time there was no news of murders or missing white men.

But among the people I worked with at the research station, were a complete spectrum of attitudes with regards to black Australians, from tolerance and understanding to extreme racial bigotry. Some of the statements that came from these fellows don't bear repeating.

But one day, I heard Sam Lassiter saying the frontier wars that had resulted in the deaths of many thousands of aboriginal people had stopped much too early. That the slaughter needed to have continued until the blacks had been exterminated. How an intelligent, well-informed person in the latter half of the 20th century could espouse such views seemed beyond explanation. Up until that time, I'd liked Sam for, among other things, his ability to spin a good yarn, but this left me utterly cold.

Once on official business in Darwin, I succeeded in stealing a vehicle and what's more, seemingly got away with it. The vehicles used around the research station were government owned and we shared a centralised car pool with Northern Territory Administration (NTA). A lot of these where white Ford utes. I had driven one such vehicle into town and left it parked on a side street. But on coming back an hour later, I discovered the door unlocked and the key in the ignition. *Getting careless,* I thought, on hopping in.

I'd got to Berrimah when I noticed a bit of a rattle in the dashboard that hadn't been there before. Then a thought stuck me and I pulled over before reaching for the vehicle's log-book. Oh dear – this was a NTA water resources vehicle; I'd grab the wrong ute. Furthermore, the key to the right vehicle was still in my pocket. I returned to the side street, yes my ute was there, and I parked the stolen property as close as possible to where I'd found it. I was tempted to write a note in the log-book, something like, *Next time do not bloody well leave your damned key in the ignition, signed CSIRO,* but thought better of it.

The irony, the stolen ute could have ended up at the research station. With log-book maintenance being such an inexact science, it could have been there for weeks. One white Ford ute was much the same as any other, though I might have wondered about the spare key. Perhaps the water resources people looking for their lost property could have helped themselves to ours and thereby completed the deal. Would anyone have noticed?

On the education front, I was struggling but getting there. Being able to study in the lab building was an absolute bonus. The two agricultural certificate units had been easy and at the end of the year, I'd sat for my first serious exam since the eleven plus. Following this, I started with year eleven English and maths (in two parts I and II). The main problem particularly with the maths was that my correspondence tutor was on the other side of the country in Adelaide. If I was stuck, it would take up to two weeks to get an answer. Most of the time, I had to work it out for myself but this led to a lot of frustration. Many were the times I simply threw down the pen and streamed off to look at birds.

With English, the number one hurdle was spelling and I used to write problem words in a notebook I carried at all times. Then, when I had a couple of spare minutes, I pulled it out to read, effectively rote learning. On occasions, I'd trawl through dictionary looking for words, but only once became totally stuck. But a day or two later, there was the offending word in the paper. Of course, I'd read it many times before but never seriously examined the nuts and bolts of its construction. Generally, words with Latin roots were more user-friendly, Greek less so, but some with an old-English backgrounds were the worst. I used to think of all this as the grind, of water dripping on a stone slowly wearing it away.

I sat for the exams with the kids in one of the high schools in Darwin at the end of the year and received a pass marks in both subjects. Not brilliant, but encouraging.

At this time, I was getting quiet encouragement from the professional staff, but this was in total contrast to people like Hamal. He had, it seemed, gained an understanding from other detractors as to what all this study could be about. He thought this too silly for words and openly laughed in my face.

The next year, 1970, I concentrated exclusively on English, this time at matriculation level. I felt that if I could get through with a reasonable mark, then I really was on the right track. After the examination I came away with a sense of achievement. One of the advantages I had over the kids was a degree of maturity that few at that age possessed. Certainly, looking back at how I was at 18, I'd come a long way. The end result was a credit. It was my feeling that if I'd not been quite so handicapped by a weakness in spelling, a distinction could have been possible. Nevertheless, a lot of hard work had paid off.

The following year, I returned to mathematics at year 11 level while attending evening classes in town to study physics. The end of the year results were again passes. I'd hoped to do better in the maths the second time around, so disappointing. But the struggle would go on.

Chapter 18

Lose Some: Win Some

HUE CLARK, THE COURIER, WAS off sick and I'd been given the task of driving his van into Darwin to deliver the outgoing mail to the town office and collect a couple of deliveries. It was the wet season and though it wasn't raining it'd been heavy overnight. I was on the Stuart Highway and approaching the creek causeway south of the Howard Springs turnoff. I came around a slight bend and sighted the causeway at the bottom of the slope. But I needed to slow down for there was perhaps two feet of water over the road. I touched the brakes and the vehicle went into a skid, in less than a second, sliding down the road sideways. My driving experience at Old Dunaway and elsewhere had taught me how to instinctively handle a vehicle under difficult conditions, but this was the worst ever. I dared not touch the brakes again as I steered into the skid, but as the van straightened up, I made that vital little flick the other way to stop the vehicle siding off in the opposite direction. A double movement in the space of seconds.

All too often, inexperienced drivers get the first bit right but miss the second, so that the vehicle remains out of control, sometimes with fatal consequences. Either that or they go into a panicked series of over-corrections which can be equally dangerous. But to do this well requires practise, for in a real situation, a driver has no time to think.

Fortunately, in this case, I had the road all to myself. I raced down the hill hoping the water at the bottom wasn't too deep. Speed was the one thing I couldn't control. With a great splash, I went through the fast-flowing water, the vehicle's weight an advantage. Going up the other side, the crisis that had lasted less than a minute, was over.

Later in the year there was good news. CSIRO Division of Wildlife Research was setting up a laboratory on the outskirts of Darwin. They were looking to employ a technical assistant. Hue Clark and I applied. The job interviews were conducted by Dr Harry Frith, the head of division. Up until that point, I'd never met Frith but knew of him by reputation, having read some of his papers. I was looking at this as a real opportunity, but this was 1969, and endeavours to improve my formal education barely underway.

The job interviews were at the research station, but in my case, didn't go well. Dr Frith was looking for someone who could shoot bird, cut them open and collect stomach contents and other things for analysis. Even though I'd been shooting at bird, keeping them away from rice crops for two years, he was not impressed. I think I was seen as just another birdo.

It was Hue Clark who got the job. He knew absolutely nothing of birds but had experience at shooting wild pigs. Good luck to him, I thought at the time, but was bitterly disappointed. Clearly, I still had a way to go.

In hindsight, losing this one was to my long-term advantage. I was in a unique situation at Humpty Doo. I was able to study the local birds, and had the time and space to confront my chronic education issues while financially supporting myself. With a change in jobs, the education side would have fallen away leaving me vulnerable in the long term, for careers in any area of science were beset by uncertainty. I would have been looking to advance on merit in a highly specialised field with no academic or any other formal qualifications. Any sort of government funding cut could have been disastrous. However, for me the real advance came six months later.

Hamal was leaving Humpty Doo and going back to Switzerland. His old friend Milo had gone his own way, getting married to a local girl. I don't think Hamal had ever adjusted to the eccentricities of Northern Territory society. However, with his impending departure, I was offered his job as technical assistant. I knew he was considerably miffed by this unexpected turn of events, certainly something neither of us could have predicted.

This promotion meant that I could at last move out of the shared house into one of the single-bedroom flats. It also boosted my pay and long-term savings plan, which in time was to prove vital for my advancement.

The scientist I would be working for was Don Avery and I'll be forever grateful at being given that chance. But with this promotion, I was leaving CSIRO and moving across to the Northern Territory Administration (NTA), though still based at Humpty Doo.

Don, an agronomist, was researching the problem of invasive weeds and the threat they might pose to a future rice industry. He'd also started on a Master of Science degree only to abandon this, before so I heard, returning to it years later.

But in 1970, there was a cloud starting to develop around the rice studies at Humpty Doo that stemmed from the research itself. CSIRO's involvement had grown out of a political quick fix by the federal government in Canberra. Under the slogan *Develop the North*, the researcher had been sent in where commercial interests had failed. However, the research was starting to show that given the vagaries of Darwin's wet season, and the absence of cheap irrigation water, rice growers could expect to have a partial or complete failure in three out of five years. In other words, commercial rice growing, given the technology of the time, wasn't viable.

Even before I started working for Don, alternative lines of research were getting underway. Then a few weeks after I started, Don announced that he was taking his family on a month's holiday and I could do what I liked during that time. This almost had shades of the week spent in the Grampians at Helen Lowe's expense. But I'd been around the research station for three years and knew how things were done and decided to take the initiative.

I'd a stack of half-grown rice plants in pots that had been discarded from another experiment. I'd been asked to throw these out, but instead turned this into a month-long experiment on water stress. The potted plants were divided into three groups. The first lot I would water and these would be the controls. The second group I had on a carefully restricted water supply and the third in total drought. There were 16 pots in each group and these would be placed in four subgroups representing four different replications. At weekly intervals, the vegetation from single pots in 4 x 3 = 12 replication were harvested. The leaves and stems were placed in paper bags and then put through a drying oven overnight to obtain the dry weight.

A simple little experiment that produced a nice graph that showed how my limited watering and drought treatments had stunted the growth of the plants when compared against the control group. Though statistically it wouldn't have held up so well because the number of replications needed to be much greater. Not that I knew anything about stats in those days, but when Don returned, he was genuinely impressed.

Attention then turned to soybeans at a place call Paddy's Creek, though the work on herbicides and other weed control methods continued at Humpty Doo. In the top end of the Northern Territory soils range, from lateritic gravels to very heavy alluvial clays, but patches of genuine fertile soils were rare. Paddy's Creek, about fifty miles south of Darwin just off the Stuart Highway, was one such place. It may once have been a patch of monsoon forest but during the war had served as a market garden.

In 1970, the Paddy's Creek patch was owned by an American called Roy. He'd spent the greater part of his adult life living in the Philippines and had a Filipino wife. He was an affable talkative sort of guy, middle-aged, while his wife, Mary, was quiet and at times struggled with her English.

They lived in a large shed that served as a workshop, but with a partitioned off section for living quarters. Roy used to tell tales about his life in the Philippines, things that suggested he'd not always kept within the boundaries of the law. But then it seemed he'd been in a wild part of the world where the law might not have had much relevance anyway.

The Paddy's Creek project was a joint venture between Roy and the Agriculture section of NTA. The plants were supplied by water pumped out of the local creek. The aim was to test out different varieties of soybean in what's called a randomised trial. Even in a small area, there could be subtle differences in soil type impacting crop yield. To mitigate any such affects, the different varieties were sown into clearly marked randomly selected plots across the cropping area.

The setting up of the trial had been done at the end of the wet season before I'd appeared on the scene, but with the crop nearing maturity, we were down there every few days. Different varieties matured at different rates and the harvesting had to be done by hand. For a while, all went well and Roy used to put on lunch for us. But then came a falling out.

Roy had a contractual arrangement with NTA, but this was due to run out in about a month. Roy was thinking that in the future he, with Don's help, could become the supplier for soybean seeds that could be sold to other commercial interests in the Darwin area. Don, as a government agronomist, made it clear that Roy was free to pursue whatever commercial activities he liked. But Roy took this to mean he wasn't guaranteed any cosy government deals in the future. The argument became quite heated.

After this, Don refused to go down to Paddy's Creek, and so it fell to me to finish up the work. During these later visits, Roy would put his case with the aim of getting me to talk to Don about changing his mind. At this, I'd point out that Don simply didn't have the authority to make deals with anyone, cosy or otherwise. Add to that the region had very little decent soil. It was uncertain if soybeans could ever be grown on a serious commercial scale. At this, Roy talked about the USA and South America but the top end of the Northern Territory isn't like those places. As Robert McCauley used to say - farm with the environment, not against it. I felt embarrassed by Roy's impractical ideas and glad when the project finish.

During the following dry season, we set up another soy-bean project at Palmerston, south of Darwin. In those days, Palmerston consisted of about two houses, though there was a newly sealed road suggesting future planned developments. The project site covered about an acre of cleared land with a reddish loam soil which looked as if it could be quite fertile. But when the soil was wet, it could be really sloppy. On drying, a hard crust formed on the top, not a good sign. The irrigation water came from a bore, but had to be pumped into a short channel with raised banks and closed at both ends. This was effectively a holding dam and water had then to be syphoned onto the crop through three-inch plastic pipes.

Syphon irrigation was something I'd never seen before. With a three inch pipe, the trick was to drive one end into the water, then as the pipe was pulled up, clamp the flat of one hand over the free end, producing an air tight seal and retaining the water within. With the pipe half-full, the free end was dropped down the other side of the channel bank and with luck the water started to flow.

Most of the irrigation work was done by myself, still based at Humpty Doo, and another technical assistant, Chris, who lived in Darwin. The hours were long, at times I would be leaving home at 4.30 in the morning so as to be at Palmerston at first light, but finished about midday. By then, Chris had arrived to take over until dark. Despite our considerable efforts, the project was a total failure. The soybean plants were severely stunted and though some beans were produced the whole project had to be abandoned. The soil had been unsuitable.

With the approaching wet season, soybean operations were moved to the NTA research farm on the outskirts of Darwin where the soils were much better.

While working at Palmerston, I played the part of the good Samaritan on a couple of occasions. The first, a lady's car that was bogged on a side track. A bit of shovelling solved that issue. The other was more serious. Coming into work early one morning, I noticed a car on the side of the road, but didn't pay it much attention. However, what I did notice was that plastic guide posts with reflectors had been set up along the road. But all down one side, these had been systematically knocked over.

When I was driving back later in the day, there was a young guy standing by the car who flagged me down. Could I give him a lift as his car had broken down? I would say by his accent he was either Dutch or German. I got out to look at his car and then drove him as far as the service station at Noonamah on the highway. But the night before, he'd been in a drinking session at one of the few houses in the area. Driving home, it would seem he'd swerved on and off the road in a game of knock over the plastic guide posts. One of these had been sited over a concrete culvert and the resulting impact had smashed his car's sump and cracked the engine block. Oh dear.

Quite apart from the work on soybeans during the dry seasons, we continued work with weed control on the research station farm. The wet season in this part of the world posed many challenges. When it really rained water -water everywhere and everything that was green including the weeds, grew like mad. Mechanical weed control, even using a four-wheel-drive tractor with huge tyres front and back, proved largely ineffective because of the incredibly boggy ground. But if an herbicide was to be used, say delivered by plane, it had to be fast acting because there was a likelihood of it being washed off by heavy rain. I think it's fair to say we made no real progress whatsoever.

While still living in the shared house, my sister Hilary had arrived in Darwin. A fully qualified nurse, she'd worked in the local hospital for a year before moving on. At one stage, I took her out to look at a patch of monsoon scrub on the edge of town. But Hilary had always been sensitive to mosquito bites and though she said not to worry, we didn't stay long.

Later, my brother Jon had arrived on his motorbike. Having completed a plumbing apprenticeship down south, he was off to see what the rest of the county looked like.

During this time with the birdwatching, I was conducting a weekly census at Fogg Dam and along the coast around Darwin. With the shorebird census that meant working with the tides. So, I would be at Sandgrove Creek close to the high tide when the birds were resting on sand banks. But be at the feeding grounds at Cameron Beach close to low water. The count at Cameron Beach always made me nervous because the mud flats had mangrove forest on one side and open sea on the other. Though I'd steer a middle course, there was always the possibly that a large crocodile could appear from either direction, but that never happened.

Another area that made me nervous was Black Jungle. This was a small patch of monsoon forest about a mile from the nearest track. It was a wonderful area but the hide-out of feral pigs, not a place to break a leg or be bitten by a snake. I reckoned if anything had happened to me, the only thing left after a few days might have been my hat and binoculars. The pigs would have gotten the rest.

But animals on roads, particularly at night, were a constant hazard. On one occasion, I came perilously close to hitting a female water buffalo. I knew it was a she by the shape of the horns. It was dark and I was travelling at reduced speed, but suddenly the animal was there half across the road. I swerved around, but it was close. The shape of a VW Beetle renders the driver particularly vulnerable when colliding with large animals, which tend to be flung back through the windscreen. I know of three fatal accidents on the roads around Humpty Doo, one of which resulted from someone hitting a cow.

Three away trips were made at this time. The first to Singapore and the Malayan Peninsular. Then the Malayan Peninsular and Kuching in Sarawak and finally, with my mother, from Darwin to Arnhem Land and then across to Kununurra in Western Australia.

For the most part, Malaysia was a completely different world with regards to its bird life. Woodpeckers and hornbills were not found on the Australasian side of the Wallace Line.

It was, of course, a different culture, but I was surprised at how many spoke at least some English. In a pub in Sarawak, I observed drinkers being entertained by a girl singing *Danny Boy*. So here was a young lady of Chinese extraction singing an Irish ballad to a room full of Dayaks and Malays. Even then, the world was becoming a multi-cultural place.

Driving a hire car coming back from Frazer Hills on the Malay Peninsular, I was involved in a road accident that-never-was, though could have been very serious. Up ahead, the road curved away to the left and on the side was some sort of market with street stalls and a crowd of locals. I saw a kid who would have been no more than nine, starting to wander across the road, head down, not paying attention.

Knowing all about day dreamy boys I started to slow. He reached the edge of the road; another step would have had him off the tarmac onto the gravel. But looking up, he saw my car. He panicked and dashed in front of me and then froze. I had the car under total control and stopped about five yards in front of him. This is the only time that I've witnessed a human with eyes like saucers and hair raised in absolute terror. Meanwhile all the stall holders were yelling at him. Then a woman, who I assumed to be his mother, emerged from the crowd, came over to give the boy a big slap on the backside before hauling him out the way. He'd been through an experience he was never likely to forget and I questioned if the slap was entirely necessary. But he'd been lucky because Malaysia at that time seemed full of crazy truck drives who'd only two speeds, go and stop.

One of the problems being a foreigner in a foreign land was not always knowing the local road signs. I was driving through Port Swettenham when the street suddenly erupted, shopkeepers and pedestrians yelling at me. Thought I must have run over a sacred buffalo or something, but with head down, I drove on and the yelling abruptly stopped. But I was lost and after wandering around in narrow back streets ended up driving along the same road again, producing the same angry response. Then I did it a third time, half an hour later, but this time a man with an Indian accent called out in a language I could understand, 'This is a one way street. You're going the wrong way.' Finally, I'd gotten the message.

In Singapore, which like all cities has its underside, I had a brush with criminals. It started when I visited a tourist theme park The Tiger Balm Gardens. A young guy approached me and for twenty local dollars offered to be my tour guide. Furthermore, this money would go to some sort of charity. I agreed, but was rushed through and not impressed by the need for haste. At the end, my so-called guide wanted more money, talked of schools and struggling families. But all this looked too much like a scam and I only paid the twenty dollars as had initially been agreed.

After this, I turned to watch some sort of street theatre. But then I just happened to move my left hand past my pocket and connected with another hand, limp and secretive. On turning around I discovered three men, two rough looking young guys and an older man standing between them, who promptly crouched down seemingly to avoid detection. My first thoughts was, *What the hell's going on here?* Then all three were off, quietly melting away into the crowd. As I came to realise later, they were pick-pockets, the young guys acting as shields while the master thief, the buzz cove, went about his business. Furthermore, they'd known in which pocket I carried my wallet.

The expedition to Kuching was not so interesting from a birdwatching point-of-view. Here I was surrounded by the jungles of Borneo, unable to travel outside the town without written permission from the local authorities. I spent a little time looking at bird skins in the Sarawak Museum. But finally, was able to take a motor boat ride with a driver into the delta of the Sarawak River. A noisy motor boat is not the best platform from which to spot birds. We went along muddy river channels flanked by nipa palm but ventured ashore for about half an hour at the fishing village of Bako.

The village was built on stilts and sitting out on the low tide mud flats with wooden walkways leading to higher ground. It was here I encountered one of the local men who gave me an exaggerated military salute and called me sir. He didn't seem to speak English, *sir* being the only word he knew. Perhaps a white man burdened with binoculars was a bit of a novelty in his world.

It was while departing Bako that I think I saw my first Asiatic Dowitcher, which a year later was to cause such a stir amongst Australian birdos. This one was sitting on a post out in the channel and I got my boat driver to circle around. The main wintering grounds for this migratory species is the east coast of Sumatra so it shouldn't have been such a surprise to find it here. But from the noisy motor boat I noted two salient points. The pinkish stripe at the base of the bill, typical of a Godwit, was absent. The tip of the long bill was straight, not up-turned and tapered. Wow, fancy that!

After leaving Bako, we sped past a river boat we'd seen earlier picking up passengers. But suddenly around a corner, our boat broke down, or at least the engine stopped and the driver announced, 'Ba-ling gone. No good.' On later reflection, I seriously doubted the broken bearing story. More a case of the boat driver spotting a petrol saving free lift back the Kuching. The river boat stopped for us, we got aboard and with the supposed broken down motor boat in tow, set off once more. Certainly, sitting in the forward deck of a genuine Borneo river boat was much more fun.

Walking around with binoculars can lead to misunderstandings. In Australia, I've had female sunbathers on beaches giving me dirty looks until they realised I wasn't spying on them, and the pocket notebook being used for something completely different. When doing census work I much preferred to have beaches all to myself. If there were more than a few people around I would cancel that part of the count and come back another day.

But it was only on the east coast of Malaysia where there was more than the occasional angry look. It's a part of the world where the coastal scenery is reminiscent of north east Queensland, with Casurina trees fringing the sandy beaches. I was doing a bit of birding when an old man and small boy appeared. Granddad had a hue sword at his side and stood in such a way that the over-seized cutlass was on show. Thinking language might be a small problem I gave a smiling wave, got in the car and drove off. I could have been a scout for the logging companies or anything, but clearly trespassers weren't welcome.

On another occasion, in an isolated spot on the west coast, I heard one of the local villagers singing. A natural tenor, he had a wonderful voice. Though I couldn't understand a word, he was putting his heart and soul into it while singing to the trees. Then he spotted me and became all embarrassed. I gave him a little clap and thumbs up but this seemed to make it worse. Though I had the binoculars, the notebook and the right sort of face, I wasn't a wandering Convent Garden talent scout.

In 1963 when my mother arrived in Australia, I'd presented her with a copy of Neville Cayley's bird book. Then eight years later, I paid her airfare so she could go birding with me in Darwin and the surrounds. She'd become a bird expert in her own right, but a lot of what I had to show her was new.

We spent several days around Darwin before heading out to the Arnhem Land Escarpment. This is spectacular country with low, rocky hills often covered with great disjointed slabs of bare sandstone that vary in colour, from orange to purple. Then there were the low cliff faces, deep stream wash gullies, patches of spiny spinifex grass, open eucalyptus forest and occasional patches of monsoon scrub. This is a land where some of the trees are deciduous, losing their leaves in the dry season.

There are four species of bird that are found in that area which occur nowhere else in the world. We encountered three of them on one very small patch of hillside. We had sat down on a large rock to look at White-ined Honeyeater, one of the species. It was a lovely blue-sky day and in front of us a small dead tree just a few bare branches. Then came a flap of wings and a Banded Pigeon had arrived. This bird has a white head and shoulders, dark blue grey wings and a similarly coloured band across the breast. Spectacular when sitting on a bare branch framed by a clear sky. Finally, we started to move from that magic place and there were White-throated Grasswrens, like brown feathered rats scampering in and out of the spinifex. My mother went home to Sydney having added 99 new bird species to her personal list.

But the following year my time at Humpy Doo was coming to an end. The Coastal Plans Research Station which had been my base for nearly five years was officially being closed. I could have remained in Darwin, but I had important business in the south.

I resigned from my job with NTA in February 1972. Said a final thanks to Don Avery who'd been such an excellent boss and set off for Adelaide.

Chapter 19

The Adelaide Student

I ARRIVED ON PORT AUGUSTA, BOOKED into a motel, had a shave and a shower, the first of either in four days. I'd been to Port Augusta in the state of South Australia before as the mad birdwatcher from Old Dunaway Station. But now, I was passing through on other business. I'd just driven from one side of Australia to the other, from Darwin on the Arafura Sea to Spencer Gulf a large inlet extension of the Southern Ocean.

There had been no car troubles, though the road south of Alice Springs had been unsealed, dusty and fairly rough. I had not stopped to look at birds for the aim had been to cover as much ground in the shortest possible time. I had given up my good job in Darwin to come south to study. I'd saved up enough money so that with careful budgeting and a bit of luck I wouldn't have to work for two years.

The aim, to study four Year 12 matriculation subjects, Biology, Chemistry and Math I and II and all this as a full-time student. I already had English, but nevertheless a big gamble. But for a mature-aged student, the criteria for entry into university was different than for a kid coming straight out of school. With the kids, there may have been academic excellence but a high dropout rate, particularly in the first year. The universities had recognised that mature-aged students tended to be plodders, people who could be relied on to work hard just to get through. So, the criteria for entry – some proven academic ability coupled with staying power. At the time I saw this as a path that needed exploring but with no guarantee of success.

Adelaide is a well laid out city, relatively easy to get around, but I missed Darwin's laidback lifestyle. The city's central business district was set out in a grid pattern of wide streets surrounded by a green belt of parkland. Beyond this, the major roads radiated out through the suburbs in predictable ways.

I was to have three different addresses during the ten months I lived in the city. The first was a single-bedroomed apartment, partly furnished. There was no lease and the landlord who came to the door once a week for the rent liked to be paid in cash. By the standards of the time, a rather an unusual set of arrangements.

The furnishing included a bed that must have been used by numerous newly married couples over the years, hence an annoying hollow in the middle. Other furnishings included two chairs, a small table, built-in cupboards and a wardrobe. Apart from that there was a small bathroom, and a communal laundry downstairs.

It was a good place to start my studies while at the same time getting to know the city while looking for somewhere cheaper. On leaving, I gave the landlord a week's notice and on the day of my departure, he briefly inspected the place and we parted with a handshake.

The next place was a two storey mansion that'd been turned into a multi-roomed boarding house that provided bed and breakfast. A quite spectacular brick building not far from the centre of the city, with bay windows, wide gardens and a grand gravel driveway. Then there were the wooded staircases, front and back, though I never ventured up to the second floor.

But it was a place where the bedroom doors needed to be locked at all times. The guests were a mixed lot. They included a middle-aged bloke who broken up with his wife, a couple of students like me and an elderly woman who seemed to be escaping from something. Then there was a lad who seemed about 17. I don't know what his real situation was, but after a short while I came to the conclusion that nothing he said could be believed. Certainly, there were stories, it's just they were full of inconstancies. So, people on the way up, on the way down or just drifting.

The young couple who ran the place seemed forever engaged in violent arguments. I had a room next to the kitchen and the language that could be heard through the wall was more than simply rough. I'd already started to look for better accommodation when they told me the whole show was closing down and everyone needed to move out. Apparently, they were on some sort of lease but months behind in rent, were themselves being evicted.

The only thing I thought sad during this time of mass exodus was seeing a set of little antique bells being unscrewed from a board fastened to the wall just outside the kitchen. In more opulent times, those upstairs would have used carefully relayed strings to ring - thereby summoning the household servants. The bells were part of the house and their removal a small act of vandalism.

The next place I called home was discovered purely by chance when driving around Norwood, one of Adelaide's inner suburbs looking for a parking spot. Unable to find anything in the main shopping area, I turned onto Essy Street. There, displayed on a small notice board in a front garden, was a handwritten note that announced room for rent. On enquiring at the single storey house, I was told that the landlord, Alf, wasn't there but if I came back in a couple hours, I might catch him.

This turned out to be an unusual situation. Alf was a kindly old man in his seventies. He owned two properties in the area that were effectively unofficial boarding houses. I don't know how he came by them, though I suspect it was through a family inheritance. Only men were allowed in these places, but the room rents were very low. I remember my room costing me three dollars a week, which even by the standard of the day, was extraordinary. The room wasn't much, a walled-in veranda, cold in winter but with a bed, wardrobe, chair and small table.

But as Alf said more than once, if he wasn't providing this service, some of the residents would be sleeping out on the streets. But what he did expect from his boarders was orderly behaviour and the ability to get on with others - so no drunks, drug addicts or lunatics. Each of the two houses had an unofficial minder, a bloke who'd keep an eye on things when Alf wasn't there. But we used to see quite a lot of Alf, the boarding houses and their occupants seemingly his main interest in life.

Dan was the minder in the house where I lived. I know nothing of Dan's background other than he'd recently left his wife of many years and had a grown-up son working nearby in a local car repair business. Given his age, he could have been a First World War veteran.

Then there was Len, not the brightest, but a nice guy. He and a friend, Ted, had gone into the courier business with two delivery vans. A business that could have been doing well but wasn't. Their second-hand vehicles were too old and a series of breakdowns with vehicles off the road, rapidly sending them broke. Ted, who I met on a couple of occasions, seemed the bright, fast-talking entrepreneurial type, one who would learn from his mistakes and move on. Not so much for Len, who'd put up some of the money, but risked becoming the real long-term victim.

Then there was Frank, a retired railway worker. Several years earlier he'd been severely injured when unloading goods from a freight car. A careless engine driver had crashed into a line of wagons and the jolt brought a stack of heavy boxes down on top of Frank, almost killing him and even now, he wasn't fully recovered for he walked with a stick.

Then there was Mike the American, a young, quietly spoken guy, a qualified geologist by trade. He'd come to Australia to work, some mining survey around Tennant Creek, but unable to stand the hot conditions had walked off the job. He'd been out of work for over a year, caught in a limbo, depressed, needing to put his life back together but unsure how that might happen. Spending far too much time sitting in his room doing not very much.

Then for a few weeks there was also Morrie, who lived in a shed in the back garden. He brought some woman he'd met at a local pub home for the night and then really disgraced himself by starting a backyard grass fire for no apparent reason. If I hadn't raised the alarm, it could have damaged one of Len and Ted's delivery vans. The consequence for Morrie was being asked to move on.

For me, the quiet orderliness of Essy Street was ideal but towards the end of the year, disaster struck. Dan had gotten up one bright spring morning, had breakfast, gone back to his room, sat in a chair and died, seemingly of a heart attack. Alf discovered him when he called in around lunchtime, the ambulance and the police were called. But in due course, this alerted the local council; here was a boarding house they knew nothing about. Not one boarding house but two, and furthermore, they did not seem to comply with regulations. The bathrooms in both were deemed to be in need of major repair and the communal kitchens were not up to standard. Real money was needed, funds Alf didn't have. The best he could do was sell one of the houses and use the money to fix up the other. Meanwhile, some guys would indeed be thrown out on the streets and when I left in November that year, there was a terrible dark cloud hanging over the place. Those left behind had been in one way or another living on the margins and now at the stroke of a council pen, rendered even more vulnerable.

A month before my final departure, I was out walking along The Parade, the main street through Norwood. It was about ten at night. Usually I didn't go out at this time, but I'd been studying hard and needed a break. There was not a great deal of traffic, but for some reason, a bus had stopped in the middle of the road. Furthermore, the driver had gotten out was standing in front of the vehicle holding the hand of a small child. He waved me over and explained that the little girl had been wandering across the road; could I look after her as he had a bus to drive?

The girl, would have been little more than two, had brown curly hair, and wore a knitted yellow top with a pink dress. I somewhat reluctantly agreed, but picking her up, I felt a sudden surge of parenthood, but wasn't sure what to do. I started walking slowly down the pavement in the general direction of the Norwood Police Station.

Then a few minutes later, a cry came from across the other side of the road, 'There she is!' Then, 'Excuse me, is that your daughter?'

I answered no, and waited by the curb while a group of five rescuers came over. Apparently, the parents had been at some social gathering and the child had been temporarily bedded down for the night. She'd gotten up and gone looking for mum and dad. When someone checked, she wasn't there. She'd headed for the bright lights on a main road, no place for a child of that age on her own.

My studies in Adelaide commenced in early March. I attended weekly evening classes for all four subjects. With Chemistry, I went straight into a compressed senior high school course, having never studied the subject before. Similarly, with the Biology, though here I felt I had some prior knowledge.

With maths, potentially my weakest subject, I had had two years of preparation at Year 11 level, which proved vital with the step up to matriculation level. Two decades later, I did a self-promotion crash course in senior mathematics and found I had retained much of what I'd learnt in Adelaide. I also discovered the subject to be relatively easy, whereas earlier it'd been a real struggle. I guess I could have acquired a few extra brain connections in the intervening years.

But in 1972, I was the student and the courses were run in the evenings at three different high schools, while at the same time I continued doing maths by correspondence. But because I'd only taken four and not five subjects in the one year, I would miss out on a matriculation certificate from the South Australia education system. Nevertheless, as a mature-aged student, I'd hopefully have enough ammunition to start applying to the universities.

There was a girl that really caught my eye during my first chemistry lesson. That evening, I didn't speak to her, thinking there may be a better time, but she was there only once and I was never to see her again.

When I first arrived in the city, I started looking around for casual work. For a couple of months, on one or two days every week, I drove a truck around Port Adelaide. When at Humpty Doo I'd acquired a C class driver's licence and being young and fit this was all the qualifications needed. The work involved moving loads of wool bales between warehouses.

Wool bales can weigh up to 400 lb and when they came off a sheep station, their squarish shape meant they fitted well on the backs of tray bodied trucks. Having worked on a sheep station, I was familiar with the bag hooks used when rolling these bales around. But when the bales are about to be shipped overseas, they're *dumped*. That is, put through a machine that subjects the bale to many tones of pressure so that they retain their weight, but are reduced to half the size. I found these misshapen dump bales difficult to handle, particularly to pack in tightly on the back of a truck, for the loads were being driven around an unsecured. As the trucks were generally travelling at low speed for short distances around the port area, tying the loads was considered unnecessary.

But the job gave an interesting insight into the working culture of the warehouses at that time. For example, it could be considered bad form to be too keen in getting from one place to another. People unloading a truck didn't like to see another in line. Therefore, it was good protocol to wait in a side alley for five or ten minutes to give the un-loaders a break before arriving. On one occasion, I was given a right telling off by a foreman who thought I was altogether too keen. On the other hand, if I were doing my own loading and unloading there were no such concerns.

In some workplaces, they had the radio tuned into the horse races. When a race started, everyone would stop, put down tools and listen. When the race finished, all the listeners would unfreeze and go back to what they were supposed to be doing. I've no idea how many were genuine punters but it all seemed like some carefully scripted comedy routine.

My career as a truck driver ended when I lost half a load of dumps off the back of a truck. Fortunately, no traffic was coming the other way, as I could easily have killed someone. A mechanical loader had to be brought in to clean up the mess. But after the event, I made a flippant remark about the incident, which undoubtedly sealed my fate. From then on, I received no early morning calls to come into work and in hindsight, I think it was for the better.

During this time, I had limited opportunity for birdwatching, but I started a regular census count at the ICI salt works on the northern side of the city and made a couple of visits to another salt works at Price, at the head of Spencer Gulf. In these places, seawater was pumped into a series of shallow bays and the water systematically extracted by evaporation. The initial bays are very extensive, but as the brine water was moved through the system, the bays became progressively smaller, while the salt concentration increased. The final product untreated sea salt.

The salt works were great places to look at the effects that salinity had on bird life, or more particularly, on what the birds were feeding on. The birds largely consisted of things like ducks, egrets, spoonbill, cormorant, indigenous waders like Banded Stilt, and migratory waders which included the more common species, like Red-necked Stint. On one occasion, I tried to point out the Broad-billed Sandpipers among a flock of stints to a fellow birdwatcher. This was another of those cases where the differences were perfectly obvious to me, whereas my companion, who had less experience with shorebirds, was struggling. I think he sort of believed me, but perhaps only just.

There were a couple of other birdo related instances while I was in Adelaide. At that time, there was a public row going on in the local birdwatching community over a migratory wader species called the Grey-tailed Tattler. A year or so earlier, this species had been officially recorded in South Australia for the first time. However, this sighting had been challenged by the then curator of birds at the Adelaide Museum, claiming that such claims could not be authenticated without a specimen being taken. While I was in Adelaide, I had no difficulty locating this species. Just a few birds and sure it was a matter of knowing its habitat preferences. But I questioned why all the fuss over something that I wouldn't even classify as particularly rare.

The other incident was more personal. While I was in Darwin, I'd been regularly corresponding with a fellow ornithologist who was the curator of the Northern Territory Museum in Alice Springs. We published a joint paper together, but never met in person. But while in Adelaide, we came face-to-face for the first time. On turning up at his door, and even before I'd introduced myself, he was giving me a *who the hell are you* look. Being a bit of a nerd, I normally felt comfortable around my fellow nerds, but this man was nothing like what I was expecting. There was to be no further contact after that one meeting.

But then, bird related activities came to an abrupt halt after someone slammed into the back of my car. By that stage, the VW was only covered by third party property insurance and it took several months to sort out the insurance issues. The other guy's insurance company did eventually pay up, but if it had gone on much longer I would have had no option but to walk away and look for a replacement vehicle.

But finally, in late October, with my restored car back on the road, I decided to take a three-day break and visit a birdo who lived at Langhorne Creek near the mouth of the Murray River. Alan and I had never met, but I knew of him by reputation. He was a sheep farmer and when I arrived, was about to start drenching a mob of ewes. So being a one-time sheep man, I offered my services and I kept the sheep up to him as he went to work with the drenching gun. As a result, a job what would've taken Alan two days working on his own, was completed in one.

After this, we went off to look at birds at Bunn's Bore in a remote part of the Big Desert, close to the Victorian border. This was a very interesting area of Mallee scrub, (heath and low growing Eucalyptus) and one of the last strongholds of the Red lored Whistler. Despite its exotic name, this is a rather drab grey bird with a bit of pale orange around the face but with a distinctive call. But the encroaching wheat fields were not far away, and I was left wondering just how long this critically endangered species had left before the land-clearing bulldozers moved in. It has always seemed strange to me that shooting protected species of wild bird for no good reason could get someone into serious trouble. But the destroying of birds through the clearing of their habitat, which was vastly more destructive, was somehow seen as something quite different.

Early December 1972, I had a last look around South Australia before setting out for my parents' house in Sydney. The examinations were finished, but I wouldn't know the outcome for some weeks.

It was election day when I called in at the polling station at Tumby Bay on the other side of Spencer Gulf. The political contest was McMahon's conservatives versus Whitlam's Labor. In the polling place, a couple of the elderly people, clearly McMahon supporters, were talking about keeping the communists from power. Furthermore, they eyed me with suspicion - could that young guy be a spy? Even with the incriminating binoculars hidden in the car, I must have looked like one of them, if not one of the others. Furthermore I hadn't shaved that morning and then there was that suspicious VW Beetle parked outside. The VW might be Hitler's ultimate revenge, but weren't the Nazis in cahoots with Stalin's Russia at one stage? I cast my absentee vote and departed, leaving a trail of speculation and suspicion in my wake.

Later, camped out in the bush that night, I listened to the radio as the election results came in. Whitlam had won, but what did that mean for my future? I guess I wasn't the only one asking that question.

On the way from Adelaide to Sydney, I'd called at Old Dunaway. I'd lost contact with the McCauleys soon after arriving in Darwin. But now, Harry, the youngest son, was married with two daughters and living in the main house at Coniston. Robert and his wife had moved across to a second house next door. Paul was still living in a house at the other end of Old Dunaway, but had broken up with his wife, Marg. However, Marg's younger brother, Greg, whom I'd previously met on a couple of occasions, had moved in to help raise the kids, who were now in their teens.

Selwyn was living in town but with a manager running the Old Dunaway, day-to-day.

John Spenser and his wife had left Old Dunaway, bought a small property and were raising a family of four. John was somewhat amused when I turned up at his door, for I had all my worldly possessions packed into the car. This included a kitchen mop propped up in the back seat. The mop was almost new and I wasn't going to leave that behind.

But for my friends in this part of the world, there had been changes; it was nice to see them all.

Chapter 20

James Cook University I'm Back

I WAS STAYING WITH MY PARENTS in Sydney when I received my exam results, a distinction in Biology, credit in Chemistry and a pass in each of the two Maths subjects. The question would this be enough to open the door to where I aimed to go? Then the university rejections and acceptances started to come in. Neither of the South Australian universities were interested in me, but I was offered a place at the ANU in Canberra, NEU in Armidale and James Cook University in Townsville. Far better than I could have hoped. I chose James Cook, as my best science work had been done in the tropics and north Queensland seemed the place to be.

Regarding my family, sister Gill and her husband, Fred, had returned to England, Hilary was nursing in Switzerland, Jon was still in Darwin and my youngest brother, Adrian, was in his last years at high school. My father was continuing with his retirement while Molly remained a primary school teacher. But again, I was grateful for that home base which helped to ease the living pressures.

My parents' house was perched on the eastern side of Galston Gorge. One of the characteristics of the northside of Sydney is the way the sandstone gorges and their associated bushlands penetrate deep into the suburbs. The gorge was a wonderful area of eucalyptus forest with steep rocky hillsides. It's not far from where I used to live at Dural. But living on the edge of the bush was not without risks, and a few summers earlier, a bad fire had swept through the area. My parents had been lucky not to have lost the house, a wall of fire coming within twenty yards. In fact, it seems that Norman was especially lucky not to have been killed, for he'd been in the back garden spraying water on the roof. Death can come simply from the radiant heat and or lack of oxygen. Some of the houses on the other side of the road, further away from the fire, had been damaged by the heat, but the house and my father had emerged unscathed. I don't think he realised just how lucky he'd been.

When I returned to the area in late 1972, the bushland was recovering, blackened trees covered with green shoots and the undergrowth starting to regenerate. But it would take eight to ten years before it would get back to something like it was.

There was a large roadside notice on the approaches to the gorge that warned that the road was totally unsuited to heavy traffic. Despite this, semi-trailer trucks would, from time to time, attempt the route. On the way down on the Hornsby side, they would knock out roadside guide posts while getting around the hairpin bends. Then on reaching the bottom, the drivers were confronted by a sharp angled approach to a one way bridge. This would defeat them and the only option would be to back all the way up to the top of the hill. Meanwhile, the road would be closed for hours and any guidepost not taken out on the way down would fall victim on the way up. This, all apart from the damage bill levied by the local council.

One time, driving up the gorge road, I came across a car that'd stopped, facing up hill just before one of the hairpin bends. I carefully went past but noticed that the young guy at the wheel had his head back and looked awful. I stopped my car on the outer edge of the bend, the only place it could be easily seen by on-coming traffic. On running back, I discovered the man at the wheel was unconscious. I flagged down other vehicles and a rescue operation got underway. The guy was having an epileptic fit, the car, an automatic, was in gear but the only thing stopping him from going over the edge was the upward slope of the roadway. The ambulance and police were called, but in those first twenty minutes it was us, the road side volunteers, total strangers, who worked as a team to pull the guy back from the brink.

February 1973, and I was on the move again, firstly along the New England Highway, then after by-passing Brisbane onto the Bruce Highway up the Queensland coast. A journey I was to make several times in the next three years, travelling either north or south.

When I'd last seen James Cook University it had been a building site. I'd left Townsville heading west in a wreck of a car with no clear plan, though Darwin was to be my ultimate destination. Now almost six years later, I'd returned, but better still as a newly enrolled undergraduate student.

I remember sitting up at the back of a lecture hall surrounded by other students, most a decade younger than me, most fresh out of high school. We were listening to the vice chancellor giving his welcome speech at the start of orientation with little regard for the sheer mountain of work and the challenges that lay before us. A mountain we were expected to climb in the next three years. But I was twenty-nine and full of hope. This was a long way from the wasted year of Hunningham primary school or the career adviser who'd decreed my working life could only be that of a farm labourer. Since my arrival in Australia, I'd perhaps become more of a gypsy than I ever would in England. Certainly, in terms of miles travelled and the nights spent sleeping under the stars. And yes, for a decade or so, I had been that farm labourer, but under the guise of station hand and field assistant. But I'd departed from the script, was in a place I would never have thought possible in my wildest dreams during my formative years.

However, I was there because the university had granted provisional matriculation to this mature-aged student,. I wouldn't achieve full matriculation status until after I'd completed my first year. Any failures could have seen my provisional status revoked and I would have been out.

During the period of time between when I left Darwin to my arrival in Townsville, I'd effectively been living off my savings. The truck driving episode contributed little. The car accident and yet another parking fine had cost me money. But the cheapness of living at Essy Street and staying with my parents in Sydney were an absolute blessing. In the coming year, the money I'd saved needed to last, even though there were university fees and general living costs, but beyond that, great uncertainty Did I really want to go into debt? If I went back into the workforce would I ever complete my degree? However, a white knight in the form of Mr Whitlam and his reformist, and many would say reckless, Labor government, seemed about to come to my rescue.

The Whitlam years in Australian politics were undoubtedly chaotic.

An idealist left-leaning government in power after 23 years of conservative rule, but one hit by major international economic crises, didn't make for a happy outcome for many. But Whitlam was proposing, in the coming year, to abolish university fees and provided all students with an allowance which, though not generous, was enough to live on. Lucky for me, but as with my grandfather, Fred, I'd contributed much to my own advancement. But now, as a full-time university student, I had to deliver if I was to take full advantage of the situation.

Having arrived in Townsville, one of the first things was to find accommodation. On my way there and on arrival, I'd continued my long-standing practise of camping out in the bush. But on enquiring at student services, I was told that all residential colleges were booked out. Though there were likely be last minute cancellations, the resulting places would go to the younger incoming students, many of whom were living away from home for the first time. However, later in the year, with students dropping out of university, residential college vacancies could become available. In the meantime, that meant accommodation off campus. A phone call was made on my behalf and I was given a name and address out in the suburbs.

Later that day I met Janet and her four-year-old son Peter. She explained that her husband Dale, a salesman of some sort, was expected home that evening. The house was three bedroomed, modern with wide verandas and a garage. The idea was that I, and another student, Garth, who was starting an economics commerce degree, would be sharing a bedroom. The weekly rent would include breakfast and an evening meal.

That evening, all five of us were having our first meal together. Friendly enough, but with an underlying tension. Fate, more than design, had brought us two students into the household, and I think, even at that stage there was questions as to how this was going to work out. Janet, who'd instigated the scheme, expected that we students would be off studying for most of the day. A reasonable expectation, but there was no facility for studying inside the house which meant that outside lecture times, we would be totally reliant on the university library. Though the extra money being brought in would help the household budget, I sensed that Dale had gone along with the whole idea but was having serious second thoughts. But having had experience of shared accommodation, I was determined to try and make the situation work.

Garth was a quietly spoken aloof sort of guy in his mid-twenties. Though I shared a room with him, he spoke little of his background. All I knew was that he'd been at Queensland University in Brisbane for a while. But after three weeks in the house, he left, and in hindsight, I should have been planning the same.

Then one Friday evening Dale and Janet had friends around for a party. I was told this would finish up about eleven, but it went on into the early hours. Unable to sleep due to the noise, I sat out in the back garden and then went for a walk around the streets. At breakfast, nothing was said, but the tension was palpable.

As a young man, I had a problem with smelly feet. Something that may have a genetic basis because I had a couple of uncles who seemed to have suffered from the same problem in their youth. Sharing a room with another student and being aware, I changed my socks every day and kept all dirty clothing in sealed plastic bags. Nevertheless, it was the smelly socks issue that became the catalyst for me being asked to leave. Dale, when he confronted me, actually had a screwdriver in his hand as if he was in danger of being physically assaulted. I was upset by all this, including the suggestion that I stank. Instead of staying until the end of the week, I packed and left that night.

I was prepared to camp out in the bush on the edge of town again, but knowing of a bed and breakfast boarding house and being early in the evening, I called in. The place was run by a large middle-age woman called Katt. She seemed quite a character who exchanged friendly banter with a couple male guests as she showed me to my room. 'We are all like family around here,' she assured me as I paid for the week.

The room wasn't a room at all, just an unlocked alcove with a bed and small table. The place was relatively cheap, a noisy but friendly atmosphere. I couldn't see myself staying long. By this stage, I was studying long hours including weekends.

The next place was a small one-bedroom flat a hundred yards down the road. The furnishings were quite spartan, fridge, bed, table, a chair, but served my needs for the next four months.

At the end of the semester, during the mid-winter break, I did the rounds of the residential colleges. This brought me to John Flynn College on the edge of the campus. At that time, the college was run by the Reverend Jim Martin of the Presbyterian Church. A student had left and after an interview, I had a room on the ground floor of one of the two storey residential blocks. The top floor was reserved for the girls, while men and boys occupied the lower level. It was a very nice accommodation and at a price I could afford. Here was a good-sized work desk, single bed and plenty of cupboard space. Two meals were served daily in the canteen, breakfast and dinner in the evening. The only stipulation was that the canteen ladies needed to be told in the morning if people were going to be in for dinner that night. On special occasions, students were expected to dress in academic gowns, otherwise smart casual clothes were fine. Respectful behaviour was expected at all times and the boys were told they needed to keep out of the girls' bedrooms and vice-versa. A rule that was not always followed. I was to live at John Flynn for the next two-and-a-half years and really loved the place.

When I first arrived at university, I had very little social contact with my fellow students. I found the first-year undergraduates with whom I attended lectures and practical classes immature. I was older than most and having been out in the real world, had seen something of its rough edges.

On one occasion, I was late for a zoology lecture so that I couldn't sit towards the front as I normally did. The lecture hall was full with perhaps 80 people, but at the back was a group of a dozen students who weren't paying the slightest attention. They were making such a noise that the lecturer at one stage addressed them directly saying, 'Those up the back who are clearly so smart they know everything, might do the rest of us a great favour by leaving.' This produced an ironic cheer from the more serious folks in the hall. But I was left thinking, *Where have these idiots come from? There are people out there who'd give their right arm to be in the privileged position you're in, but all you want to do is party and play the clown. Go and get yourselves jobs.* But I only saw things like this in first year students. By the time people had reached second year, the class sizes were smaller and it seemed those that didn't want to be at university had left.

Later, after I moved into the residential college, I got to know my fellow students better. Some of these were older like myself, but they included younger ones whom I'm glad to report matured over time.

In my first year, I took Zoology and Botany which went for the full year and Physical Chemistry and Introductory Physics in the first semester. This was followed by Descriptive Chemistry, General Physics and Electricity and Magnetism in the second semester.

In the beginning, I was perhaps a bit too casual. The lectures were reiterating a lot of what I'd encountered before, be it at a cracking pace. But then I failed my first physics test and failed very badly. After this, I started taking everything much more seriously. Fortunately, there was another physics test and an end of semester exam and I did well on these. The overall end result was a pass, but it'd been close.

I wasn't by any measure a brilliant student. I'd never mastered the art of swatting for exams, being able to absorb and then regurgitate the fine details when needed. I had to really learn, but when I did, it stayed with me. Sometimes, I would say to another student, 'We did all that last year, don't you remember?' But more often than not, they'd forgotten much of the details. Yet these were the people getting the distinctions and high distinctions that were eluding me. For me, the final outcome for the year was six passes and a pass conceded. But for all of us serious people, super-smart or otherwise, the workload was horrific. On the other hand that's what we were there for.

Towards the end of second semester, the student notice board was advertising labouring jobs for the Mount Isa mine over the coming summer vacation. Here was a chance to earn some money. I applied and was accepted. So, at the end of November, I again took the road to the west out across north Queensland as I had seven years earlier. More of the highway had been sealed, but around Julia Creek I again had to negotiate a difficult creek crossing. It was here, years earlier, that I'd seen Varied Lorikeet for the first time, but now I kept going.

At the mine, I had a cabin to myself, was well-fed and well-paid for the work I did. There were about 20 university students at the mine that summer. Some from James Cook, others from Brisbane University. Some were geology or engineering students, others like me just there for the money. My work centred around the lead smelter, a huge blast furnace set amid a great mass of complex infrastructure.

Though this was above ground, tin helmets had to be worn at all times and gas masks were an essential piece of kit. Usually masks were carried around the neck, but on a couple of occasions when toxic fumes came wafting through the works they proved their worth.

Most of my day was spent at the business end of a high pressure hose, washing extensive concrete pavements in an attempt to keep the dust down. At other times, I did a bit of shovel work or was using my hose to blast the fly ash off bulldozers. When doing the latter, I would wear both googles and gas mask to protect my face as much as possible and then blast away at close range, muck flying in all directions.

On one occasion, I'd just cause to be thankful for my tin hat. I'd grabbed hold of the hose about three feet from the end and under pressure, the heavy nozzle came up and would have hit me square between the eyes but for the brim of the helmet taking the impact. As it was, the helmet was sent flying. But apart from that, these were the days when I didn't have to think too much, a genuine relief from the hectic pace of university.

Soon after arriving, all we students were taken for a tour, a show and tell, underground. Here was a weird world a mile or more below the surface. Even getting down there was an experience, for the lift cage bobbed up and down like a weight on the end of a fishing line. We walked along tunnels with lights on our helmets being shown the various parts of the workings. There were offices down there, dining rooms, workshops and strange machines rolling around in cramped conditions in the heavy air. An underworld city unto itself.

Though Mount Isa is out in the desert, it rained and kept on raining. More rain fell that January than the town's average for an entire year, and elsewhere, floods were occurring right across the country. Then the highway to the coast was cut, followed soon after by the rail line. A cyclone formed in the Gulf of Carpentaria to the north before sweeping inland, and the rain persisted. I had to fly back to Townsville and arranged for my car to be sent by rail when the line reopened. On looking out the plane window, I observed strands of rail line track suspended in mid-air over sections of washed out embankment. I was not to see my car for two months but it did eventually arrive in Townsville atop a flat-bed courtesy of Queensland Rail.

During the year I'd been in Adelaide, I set about getting the results for the Darwin bird studies published and initially this had gone well. But it was when I turned to the data from my various census projects that I started to have difficulties. The editor of the leading bird journal I had been dealing with, a person I'll call Shane Maher, was raising all sorts of objections. This sort of material was complex, but I could see patterns in the data and knew there was a real science story to be told. But trying to present this material in such a way that it could be easily understood by others required expertise that I didn't have.

Knowing that I was definitely going to university at least for a year, I thought I'd find that help. Furthermore, I hoped all this could be sorted out, so on finishing university, this material would be either published or be in a publishable state, thereby helping me find a job. But there were two major problems. At university, my work on this project was largely confined to breaks between semesters; I was just too busy at other times. Additionally, the experts who may have been able to assist were themselves busy people. The end result was a rising tide of mutual frustration between Shane and myself. His assertion that the Darwin census work added up to nothing more than one small paper left me absolutely fuming. I saw this as a denigration, both of the genuine quality of the data and the effort put into collecting it. I had data from four distinct water bird habitats where, what applied to one, didn't apply to the others. Sure, some species moved from one to the other in accordance with the seasons, but how was I expected to get all that into one small paper? However, while working in Mount Isa with time to spare, I did attempt to put most of the material into some sort of order. The result can only be described in hindsight as a dog's dinner of a manuscript, a badly written PhD thesis. Mr Maher was not at all happy. I was accused of pretentiously trying to make something out of nothing and why did I even bother?

Having faced much denigration of one sort or another in my past, all this tapped into a very deep well of resentment. I could of course have taken my work elsewhere, a publication with lower editorial standards, but I was determined that the final product would be of the highest quality in the best possible journal.

A major factor in my thinking but never, it seemed, taken into consideration by Shane Maher, was that I was at university studying biological science. Therefore, when I got back to Townsville, it should have come as no surprise I would be seeking real answers. This time with a much clearer idea as to what was actually needed. The answers came in the form of community ecology techniques that had been well developed by botanists over several decades, but little used or understood in ornithological science. I still remember coming across these publications in the university library and realising here was the great revealing light on the stony road to Damascus.

What I'd being trying to do was use some species as indicators. But these other methods took a holistic community approach, thus cutting through the mountains of information to identify the underlying patterns. Providing the initial data collection had been done with sufficient thoroughness as was the case here applying the methodology seemed relatively straight forward. But to do this well, and in the absence of real outside assistance, I needed to become my own expert. But given my work load, the chances of any of this material being published by the time I graduated was looking less and less likely.

Chapter 21

A Student's Life

THE GREATEST GIFT THAT COMES from any worthwhile education is being taught how to think logically. Some of us may be born with that ability, but most have to learn along the way by one mean or another. The three years spent as an undergraduate was by far the most stressful period of my life. Later, I was to add a Master of Science (by thesis) to my qualifications, but being able to work at my own pace, I found that project relatively easy.

During my second year, undergraduate fees were being paid by the government, even though the country as a whole, like much of the Western world, was in recession. Oil producing countries had got together and greatly increased the price of oil. Perhaps good for them in the short term but bad for everyone else. There was even talk of war, but fortunately that never eventuated. I was also getting an allowance from the government which meant that the money management that I'd had to contend with over the previous two years were largely put aside.

Typically, my day would start when woken by the alarm clock at 7.00. The residential college dining room opened at 7.30, and while waiting outside, I'd often meet my Cambodian friend, Siem. A small man in his mid-twenties, he came from an influential family with connections to the Cambodian government. The utter horrors of the Pol Pot regime were yet to unfold, but he was deeply worried about the deteriorating situation in his country. While we waited, he spoke of this. 'Bloody communists,' he would say. 'They will kill everyone.' At the time I thought this a bit over dramatic but he was absolutely right. Unfortunately, attempts at achieving purity of one sort or another through the mass slaughter of the innocent is one of the recurring themes in human history. This seems never to have worked, but this hasn't deterred the crazy ideologues of whatever stripe from trying.

With the doors to the dining room open, we discovered there was breakfast cereals or porridge followed by poached eggs on toast. In those days, I was back with the porridge, having not eaten it since I left England. I lined up at the canteen server before joining Siem at our usual table. My friend was doing a commerce degree and we'd likely not see each other until evening. Siem's English was very good, but not entirely at home in the Australian culture. He saw me as a trusted friend. With the onset of winter, I'd driven him into town to buy a warm jacket and in the shop, he asked me if it was a good buy at about the right price.

We were joined at the table by Rick and Fay who had been serious friends since high school. They were younger people from Gladstone, and still to experience the work force, but finding their way in life. Long blonde-haired Fay was very attractive, but the more serious and sensible of the pair.

Then we were joined by Jonathan, mid-twenties, good-looking, from Burma. Again, some sort of connection to people in high places within his own country. I guessed Jonathan was an adopted name. He was quiet, said nothing of his past life and I never got to know him that well.

There was chatter around the table and the odd joke. I recall an old riddle from my childhood, 'When I was going to St Ives I met a man with seven wives.'

'Why only seven?' asked Siem.

'Five more at home,' suggested Rick.

'Shut up and let me tell this story,' I replied. 'Each wife had seven bags and in each bag was seven cats and each cat had seven kits. Kits, cats, bags and wives how many were going to St Ives?'

'A bit of mental calculation needed here,' suggested Fay.

'Seven to the power of three plus one,' suggested Jonathan. 'Leave the bags out.'

'No, no,' I declared, 'Just one - when I was going to St Ives. . .'

'Oh, go away,' laughed Rick, 'and take the awful joke with you.'

I had my first lecture at 8.15 and I needed to move anyway.

My first destination was a lecture theatre in the Botany Department and I arrived a little early to take up my seat amongst the students already assembled. The lecturer, Dr Huntington, arrived late and at the end went over time. The lecture was on marine botany and that day covered the different life cycles of the major groups of seaweeds. These are as diverse and complex as plant life on land. I took notes, trying to pick up on the salient points. Later, I'd read around the topic and made further notes. For every hour sitting through lectures I would spend that time again reading, compiling detail, and all this prior to the lead up for exam time. I needed to learn, to be fully across the details.

Lecture over, I'd rush for the chemistry building and a laboratory practical lesson on acid base titration. The resulting practical report was due the following week. Each student was given a standard stock solution of ammonia hydroxide (a base), a small bottle of phenolphthalein (ph indicator) and an individually labelled flask of citric acid solution, 200mL of unknown concentration. No two students had the same acid solution. For each student, the aim was to calculate the acid concentration for their particular solution. First using a long glass pipette, 25 mL of acid solution with a few drops of indicator had to go into a conical flask. After that, the ammonia base solution into a glass burette tube. A preliminary titration then followed in which the base solution was slowly added to the acid using a tap at the end of the burette to control the process. At first, the mixing liquid in the flask remained clear, but as more base was added, a cherry red patch started to hang in the liquid. Using the left hand to swirl the flask, this disappeared. A little more base solution and cherry red hung a little longer and then ten more drops and everything in the flask was cherry red. The chemical end-point had been over-shot. As was common practise, the process was then repeated, but this time with far greater attention to detail as the chemical end-point drew near. Once the exact amount of base used in reaching the exact end-point was known, then it became possible to calculate the concentration of the acid solution. The skills required included a steady hand when working the tap of the burette and a keen eye when reading the graduation marks on the glassware.

The practical report required an aim, method, calculations and discussion. I'd done similar practicals during chemistry classes in Adelaide, but here the standard was higher, the depth of understanding deeper. On the practical instruction sheet, it asked if other indicators apart from phenolphthalein had been used, and how might this have affected the result? This required further research. How much detail was the examiner looking for? I needed to ask to get a better idea.

Eleven o'clock, I grabbed a quick cup of coffee and sandwich at one of the canteens then off to the library. A major assignment was due. I'd nearly finished but with two more the following week. This was an age before personal computers, and all such work had to be hand written. Of course, it would look better typed, but I had neither the time nor the skill.

Two-forty, I headed over to the Computer Faculty. This was the era of bulky mainframe computers and card puncher machines. I was studying the computer language Fortran 2. The previous day, having written out a computer program as part of an assignment, I'd been on a card punch machine. The facility had a room full of these clunky clattery machines. A bundle of blank pale-yellow punch cards had to be placed into the feeder tray. A button was then pressed on the keyboard and clunk, a card was magically brought into position. Each card carried only a single line of the computer program and it was essential the cards didn't get out of order. I used to number each one in pencil. I then banged in the code on the keyboard before a final button whisked the card off to the out tray. While underneath, a rubbish bin caught tiny cut-out rectangles of cardboard.

On completion, the cards were tied with an elastic band with a piece of paper identifying name and student number. The cards were then placed on a long tray ready for a technician to run them through the card reader. This could be done in seconds, but much depended on the technicians finding the time. The jobs were done in batches of 10 to 20, but delays of up to a day were not uncommon.

But that afternoon, my cards were there, sitting in an alphabetically arranged pigeon hole. Also, with the bundle, a printout of the program and the test data that I had, had run through as a means of checking if all was working as it should. I could see from the results that something was wrong and when I had the time, I would go through and hopefully locate the problem. Often, it was some small things like a misplaced comma or an O instead of a zero.

Over in the chemistry building, they actually had a computer terminal that connected to the mainframe via an underground cable. Normally, it required a booking to get on, but it got away from the card system entirely and a task that might take a day could be done in minutes. Perhaps the way to the future?

But there was a note on the terminal saying it should not be run during thunderstorms. Unfortunately, a few days earlier, someone, some goose, had done just that and a lightning strike had effected the entire system. So, when most needed, everything was down for repairs.

But that day was a moderately busy and I had another lecture, this time on plant physiology and the talk was about xylem and phloem systems in flowering plants. In other words, how plants moved water and sap up and down their stems, processes not entirely understood. But then it has been said of science the more that is understood, the more it's realised how little is really known. Which should not be that surprising, seeing that we live in an infinitely complex world, that is a microcosm within an infinitely complex universe.

From plants, it was on to vertebrate Zoology. So, the formal working day finished with the dissection of dogfish preserved in formalin and another never-to-be-forgotten smell. On this occasion, we examined in great detail, the internal organs. We made sketches and drew diagrams, all in preparation for yet another report.

After an evening meal at the residential college, I was back in my room tidying up the notes for the day and filing them away for future reference. The next day, among other things, I had a tutorial class and some questions to ask. The tutor, Tony, was a PhD student who had a room two doors down from me, but my questions would wait.

Around 9 pm, I wandered down to the common room where a chess game was underway. I was looking forward to the coming weekend when I could make real progress with those two assignments. However, the mid-semester break was still a month away. Only then would there be any real easing of the work load. On Old Dunaway Station, I'd got used to the 50 to 60-hour weeks, but there the work pace, which was often physical, varied from hour to hour, day to day. Here, it was more like 80 hours and during term time, the mental demands were unrelenting.

My second year at James Cook University was not particularly good. Officially, I didn't fail anything, but I picked up four pass concedes in the nine subjects studied, while the much sought after credit grades eluded me.

But I did in fact fail one subject, along with half a dozen other students. This was called biological science, a course that revolved around statistical methods and its application. But the authorities came to us and said we could sit the exam again with a re-written exam paper, but with the proviso that the highest grade we could get was pass conceded. The net result was that we all did far better the second time around. This was at the start of the second semester, and not having the pressure from other subjects, I was able to prepare properly.

I was to be eternally grateful for this favour because in the following year, I repeated the subject, even though that wasn't essential. The aim being to better my grade, but the course was totally different and for many students a disaster. The course curriculum of the previous year had, it seemed, been thrown away. The new lecturer running the course was a young man who'd not long completed his PhD. Being a brilliant academic is one thing, being able to teach another. I started to attend his lectures but finding them vague, waffly and with no relevance as to what had gone before, I gave up. There was just a single exam at the end of the semester during which 70 per cent of the students failed. Not the sort of thing that could be subjected to a quick fix as had occurred the year before. In all fairness to the lecture, when it came to teaching, I think he'd been thrown in the deep end. On the other hand, a quick test after the first month, worth 10 per cent of the final mark, would have given an early warning of the pending disaster.

But many years later, the lecturer became the inspiration for the Devale character in *The Golden Man*. A brilliant academic, but in other ways somewhat naive. The fictional Devale gets swept up in a world of intrigue and criminality, but I don't expect the real man ever went around blowing up drug labs or shooting up cars with a tank rifle.

Elsewhere in 1974, one of my lecturers, I'll call Dr Hickson, had some sort of problem with mature-aged student. He seemed to find people who'd been out in the work force threatening. One day he said to me, 'Why are you working so hard? I'm going to give you a pass at the end but I feel the higher grades should be reserved for the younger students.' I was astonished, but at the time chose to say very little. Lecturers were in a powerful position when it came to the fate of students and I felt this was not the time for an argument. A couple of weeks after this, I had an assignment handed back to me which appeared not to have been marked and with no indication it had even been read. As promised, I received a pass grade, but I avoided dealing with this man from then on. Later, after I'd finished my degree, I wrote to him saying that all any mature-age student wanted was to be treated like the rest. If he found older people threatening, it was only because he'd made them so.

I also had an issue with another lecturer from the same faculty. He'd set an assignment at the beginning of the semester but warned students that if he caught anyone plagiarising, they'd automatically fail. He had a reputation for being a hard man and we all took him seriously. But he'd given us a long lead time for the assignment and at the end, I submitted what I thought was a really good piece of work. I was given a C grade, a bare pass, with the comment, 'This was not what I was looking for.' *What the hell does that mean?* I wondered at the time. I could have gone to see him, but fearing this might make the situation worse, decided against it. Only if I failed the entire subject might there have been grounds for appeal. That didn't happen, but to this day, I'm left to ponder, was he another with a thing against mature-age students or had I misunderstood what was needed?

One of the tutors told me a story about the time he'd been a student at Queensland University in Brisbane. He attended a summer school on marine biology and produced an assignment for which he received a very high mark. Back at university, he took a course that covered the same subject matter and duly re-submitted the same assignment only to have it heavily marked down. The university lecturer had simply not agreed with the methodology and theories of the scientist who'd run the summer school. My understanding was that the two academics were bitter rivals and their differences were later to spill over into the public arena. I guess the student needed to have checked first.

Toilet graffiti is something that has never interested me, being generally inane, infantile and boring. But the lavatory walls around the university, at least in the gent's department, were sometimes worthy of close examination. One would think that given the intelligent nature of the clientele, there would have been little compulsion to go scrawling on bathroom walls, but not so. Here could be genuine wit, even the occasional rhyming couplet, though I'm sad to report all was let down by the art work that left a lot to be desired.

During the long summer break, I drove down to Sydney to spend Christmas with my family. Late on Christmas day, news started to filter through that cyclone Tracy had devastated Darwin. My immediate thoughts were of the friends still living there, particularly Don Avery, his wife and two kids. Later I heard they'd survived but their stilt house had been blown away and they'd spent a night sheltering in the down stairs laundry. The official death toll from the cyclone stood at 71, but talking afterwards to people who'd been through it suggested a much higher number. There was such a lot of confusion with much of the population being evacuated after the storm. Some could have been washed away or been fishermen at sea and never reported.

My brother Jon had left Darwin about a year after I did. We'd been lucky in that none of the family had been there at the time. But Jon was planning to go back as a fully qualified tradesman to help rebuild the place.

In the new year, I drove down to Old Dunaway and Coniston stations to see the McCauleys. Some things had changed while others remained the same. The drought that had threatened the area two years earlier had lifted. The floods that caused problems for me in Mount Isa the year before had produced record summer rains in the region.

It was nice to see them all again, but there was an incident with Harry's wife, Colette. A small woman with dark hair she was never one to hold back when speaking her mind. We were in the kitchen of the main house with Robert and Harry present. By that stage, Robert was in his mid-seventies and Colette started to berate him about the work he insisted on doing, the inference being that he'd become a nuisance around the place. 'Work, work and nothing stops you,' she declared. 'But I suppose all that'll end when we're banging the nails into the lid of your coffin.' I glanced across at Harry and Robert. Neither said anything, but looked like they were about to melt into the floor with embarrassment. The social status and wealth that Colette enjoyed was in no small measure due to Robert's ambitions and lifetime of toil. But now he was being treated in what had been his own kitchen, like so much rubbish. At this I politely excused myself from the house, never to return.

At the beginning of my third year at James Cook, I started showing interest in Rosalyn, who worked in the library. She was in her late twenties and a student as well as a librarian. She was Canadian and we'd stop for an extended chat on a number of occasions. But one day, I overheard her talking to her psychology lecturer and it was clear this was more than just a teacher student relationship.

There were rumours going around as to who was sleeping with whom. But I just dismissed this as highly exaggerated and got on with what I was supposed to be doing.

Later that year, there was another somewhat scary moment. Over the previous eighteen months, Jerome, a Frenchman and one of the tutor resident at John Flynn College had been allowed to construct a boat at the back of one of the residential blocks. It was of a cement fibre-glass construction about twenty-five feet long. He also made a little row boat of the same sort of material. At the being of 1975, he had the whole thing towed away to Townsville's harbour area.

Then one day, Jerome invited Siem, Rick and me, aboard for a few drinks and something to eat. The boat at that stage consisted of a hull with a deck and little else. By the time I arrived, Siem and Rick were already aboard and Jerome came over in the row boat to pick me up. The evening went well, we all had slightly too much to drink. Then it was time to go home and in a somewhat merry mood, we all four got in the row boat. The water was very calm, which was just as well, as there was less than two inches between the surface of the water and the top of the gunnels. *I can't swim and what the hell am I doing here,* I thought as we set off. But with a considerable amount of laughter, we made our way across to the wooden jetty, but then started to slide underneath. At this, I put up my hand, seized an overhead cross beam and said to myself, *Whatever happens I'm hanging on.* With me still maintaining a firm grip of the woodwork, we managed to manoeuvre the boat around to the steps and the moment passed. Nevertheless, it wouldn't have taken much to have us all in the drink.

As part of the animal ecology course, about twenty other students and I plus staff went up to Mount Spec, an area of rainforest north of Townsville. It was a great area, though the stinging trees were a problem. I'd encountered them when I first ventured into north Queensland a decade earlier. They are the giant woody version of the European stinging nettle, have similar shaped leaves and can most certainly sting. What I didn't know, but discovered, on Mount Spec is that there is a type of lily which often grows in association with these giant stingers. When the leaves are rubbed on the affected area it does much to ease the pain. But even then, the tingling in the skin can linger for months after the initial encounter.

A much more serious problem for me at this time was waking one morning to find I had a very sore right wrist. This was my all-important writing hand. When I got back, I saw the university medical doctor who thought it some sort of arthritis. Though gout runs through the family on my father's side, this was ruled out at the time. Nevertheless, I believe this is what it was, and despite treatment and exercise, it was to trouble me for quite some time.

During my last year at university, I studied for ten subjects and was awarded four credits and six passes. When sitting for my final exams, the Whitlam government was being dismissed by Australia's then governor general, and the country was going through a major constitutional crisis. On this political issue, I think the campus, like the rest of the country, was split down the middle. In some societies, this could have generated blood on the streets, but fortunately, common sense prevailed.

During my last days at the residential college, there was a farewell dinner for those leaving the university. All the students were there wearing salmon coloured academic gowns over their normal cloths. Others were there including Jim Martin, wearing the black gowns that emphasised their PhD status. There were speeches and jokes and those leaving were presented with fun awards. Mine was for being the most unscathed student. Perhaps I had been unscathed by three years of very hard work, but I was looking forward to getting back to a somewhat normal life.

Earlier in the year, during an animal physiology prac, us students had taken turns hooking ourselves up to some sort of ECG machine that measured general nervous activity. My readings had been almost off the scale, a testament to the amount of stress I was under.

I had left Townsville and was staying with my parents in Sydney when I got my final examination results. I'd passed everything.

Chapter 22

Narrabri Science

THERE ARE TIMES IN LIFE when one stands at a crossroads wondering which direction to take. Knowing that whatever path is chosen will have profound personal consequences. In my life, there have been several such crossroads. The decision to leave England and in 1967, turning north towards Darwin having just reached Alice Springs are but two examples. But in Townsville, having completed my university final exams, I was faced with another crossroads. Head to Darwin by once more taking the road to the west, or go south to the parental home base in Sydney. By that stage, my WV beetle had serious rust problems in the floor, a consequence of time spent bush bashing in the Northern Territory. But with a recently fitted reconditioned engine, I was confident it would get me wherever I wanted to go. But Darwin was recovering from the devastating cyclone of the previous year, and though my brother Jon was back there, I didn't feel like chancing my luck a second time. Add to that I was again very short of money. This, then, left the road to the south. So, on that fateful day at the junction of the two highways in Townsville, I drove straight ahead while ignoring the turn right that would have taken me off along a different road, into a different life.

The journey south, as usual, took three days of continuous driving but otherwise, it was uneventful. On the way, I camped that first night at Webbs Creek, south of Mackay, the scene a few years later of a particularly nasty double murder. But as was my normal practise, I was well off the road where I couldn't be seen by passing traffic. Only once in years of camping, have I done so in clear sight of the road. This was in South Australia, and very tired, I'd pulled over, but I did have a mid-night visitation. Fortunately, it was a couple of the local coppers and after producing my driver's licence, all was well.

Six weeks later, I felt a job interview wasn't going well. I was being interviewed for a position for technical officer at the New South Wales department of agriculture's cotton research station at Myall Vale, just outside the town of Narrabri. The two people conducting the interview were Lyndon Fells and a more senior man, Alan King. I seemed to be making a favourable impression on Alan, but Lyndon, who would be my immediate boss, was giving me dark looks. *A younger guy who finds me threatening,* I thought. *No way am I going to make progress here.*

I was in Sydney, had been for about a month. I'd only just received news that I'd passed my finals, so I could call myself a university graduate in-waiting. The official conferring of my Bachelor of Science degree wouldn't occur until the following May.

As for this job, it was one of three technical officer positions I'd applied for in the last few weeks. One of which I knew by that stage was not going my way. In fact, the letter saying that my job application had been turned down bordered on insulting, leaving me to surmise it'd been written by some admin officer new to the job. Instead of sticking to the tried and true *I regret to inform you* formula, it went into the rigors of the selection process and the triumph at finding the right candidate. In other words, all you failures out there who didn't even reach the interview stage can get stuffed. Perhaps it wasn't meant that way, but I felt like writing back - I wish you luck, but how about engendering a bit more dignity into the process.

However, it was a surprise when Alan King rang me the day after the Narrabri interview, offering me the technical officer's position. I said yes, but was left wondering what I was signing up for.

I later discovered that Lyndon had himself been working as a technical officer at Narrabri but then his boss had left. But when no other suitable candidate could be found, he'd been elevated to

Research Officer. However, being not long out of university himself, he didn't feel comfortable or confident at having anyone working under him. But what Alan King saw in me was a somewhat older person with the right qualification, a depth of working experience and a mature attitude. So, when I arrived on the job, there was tension, but after a few days, Lyndon realised I wasn't about to challenge his authority and we became firm friends.

Lyndon was a highly intelligent guy who'd been brilliant at university and now had a job as a professional scientist. I also saw in him someone who was finding his way, who had yet to discover a lot of life experiences, and do other things. At Lyndon's age I'd been in another world, chasing sheep around Old Dunaway Station.

Narrabri is a country town in northern New South Wales. The region is unusual for inland Australia in that it has naturally fertile soils. This is because of volcanoes that were active in the area up to 18 million years ago. One of the extinct volcanoes, Mt Kaputar, lies to the east of the town and was to play a pivotal role in my story. At 4900 feet above sea level, it was not unusual to see snow on the top during winter, a contrast to the plains below which may not have experienced the white stuff since the end of the last ice age.

When I first arrived that summer, I stayed upstairs in one of the local pubs, just as cyclone David crossed the far north Queensland's Daintree River. No doubt dumping a whole heap of rain on Des Cooper and his family. However, I thought it may have my name on it, but nothing to worry about. I was wrong. As a low pressure system, it swept down through western Queensland and a week later, dumped several inches of rain on me at Narrabri. A massive flood peak then swept down the local Namoi River and two days later, the town was cut in half with about three feet of water through the main street.

Having had some warning, I'd managed to get my car onto what I was assured was higher ground at the far end of Maitland Street. That was right outside Lyndon's house.

The country around the town is flat and it took several days before the water started to go down. Though the research station buildings were unaffected, it took some time before anyone could get to work.

But there was a tragedy in the street just below my window, something that later generated a small item in the local paper but seemed to go no further. By the fifth day, water had just about gone from the street when I stepped outside. Three or four people were standing around a large open manhole, the street level entrance to the pub's still-flooded cellar. One of the people was, it seemed, the local town drunk and his friend.

'All that beer down in there and I can't get to it,' the drunk was saying.

'Ian, Ian, be sensible mate,' advised his friend, a restraining hand on his arm. 'You go into that muddy water and that'll be the end of youse. Come on, come away. Even if you could get to the barrels and stuff what you going to do?'

'But all that lovely beer.'

After further argument, Ian was encouraged away from the brink. But it seemed later that afternoon, he returned to the flooded cellar. The police and fire brigade retrieved his body the following morning.

On the same day, I witnessed the rescue of a dog under somewhat similar circumstances. With the water levels falling, I went down to look at the low bridge, at what connected the two halves of the town. The road decking was now clear, but with the water rushing underneath. There were a couple of kids and a dog that seemed little more than a pup. But the dog on the upstream side of the decking lost its footing and ended up in the rushing water. A teenage lad standing close by dashed across to the other side, and bending down, managed to grab the animal as it was swept out from under the bridge; one very lucky dog.

Looking for rental accommodation in Narrabri was proving difficult, a situation not improved by the recent flood. But then Lyndon suggested I move into the shared house with him, his partner Caroline, and Richard, who was another technical officer out at the research station.

The house in Maitland Street was rented, so we split the cost between us. It was single storey, of wooden construction with a corrugated iron roof. There were three bedrooms, one of which had been created at the rear of the house by walling in a veranda. This would be my room. There was a small lounge room at the front, with an open fireplace which we never used. The house tended to be hot in summer, cold in winter, though frosts were unusual. There was mains electricity, a wood burning stove which we used during the winter and an outside flush toilet. Chickens were run in the backyard and there was an old garage which had been converted into a chicken shed.

Richard was like me, not long out of university, but Narrabri was his first job. He was an intelligent young man making his way, but rather intense, sometimes inclined to take things a little too seriously.

Carol was tall and elegant, great looks, a good sense of humour. She worked as a barmaid in one of the pubs in the main street. At the time, she and Lyndon had been living together for about a year.

Having had very mixed experience of shared houses, I had some apprehension about this arrangement, particularly as one of the other people was my immediate boss, but it worked well. This meant cooking and spending meal times as a group, plus sharing the chores.

I had not long moved into the house when news came that my father was seriously ill. His problem left knee had really flared up, a massive infection, and there was talk by doctors of taking his leg off. Fortunately, this never happened but he was left with a legacy of diabetes and really having to watch his diet. Having just started a new job, I was apprehensive about shooting back to Sydney, not that I could have done much other than offer moral support. But I'd borrowed $500 off my parents and was now working to be able to pay that back.

Unlike Humpty Doo, only the farm manager, Bert Hanson, lived on the Myall Vale Research Station. Most of the staff lived in Narrabri, but a few in the Wee Waa, the other nearby town. But as with Humpty Doo, there was a social divide, only here it was more accentuated. I never got to know any of the farm staff and only spoke with the farm manager on a few occasions. Whereas the research and administration staff used to mix socially, both in and outside working hours. But as with Humpty Doo, there was a further employment divide in that some were with the NSW Department of Agriculture while others CSIRO employees.

Cotton was a crop grown exclusively during the warmer times of the year. The research was being concentrated into agronomy and entomology (insects). The control of insect pests was a major part of cotton growing and in the Narrabri area, the chief problem was caused by *Heliothis* moths.

Lyndon was one of the four entomologists on staff, the others being Dr Henry Crowcroft, Dr Edward Summers and Dr William Sharp. The team's overall objective was to improve insect pest management practises while working with the cotton growers in the region.

I soon discovered that William was the odd man out amongst the four, in fact not part of the team at all. He was middle-aged, a prolific publisher of papers and it seemed the ability to curry favours with people in high places. I found him pleasant enough to talk with. But he'd a reputation for cutting corners, which included jumping to conclusions based on little scientific evidence. As a result, he went about his day-to-day activities in almost total isolation. This didn't seem to worry him. He just sailed on seemingly impervious to the slings and arrows aimed at him by his critics. I suppose if someone works in the research area, educated guesses are bound to be right at least some of the time.

Another technical officer, I'll call George, had also been one of William's assistants. George came to work at Myall Vale a year after I did, but a few years earlier, he'd been at the Ord River Research Station at Kununurra in Western Australia. At the time, William had been based in the south and only periodically visiting Kununurra. But George, who had been left to his own devices, had started and ran a research project. When he showed the data to his boss, he was praised for his work, but then discovered a year or so later that William had published everything under his own name. George's contribution was acknowledged in the small print, but nothing more.

Science tends to be a highly competitive business and some scientists like nothing better than challenging the findings of others and exposing flaws in methodologies. In William's case, I heard a lot of complaints. His harshest critics seemed to be the graduate assistants who worked for him. But I personally witnessed no direct evidence of his supposed professional misconduct.

Later in my scientific career, I was to work at the Black Mountain laboratories in Canberra. While there, I came to appreciate that there was a substantial cultural difference between provincial centres like Myall Vale and Humpty Doo, as distinct from the imperial palaces of scientific excellence like Black Mountain. In Canberra, among other things, there was a very clear distinction between the professionals and semi-professional support staff. When I started work there as a tech officer, I'd already commenced my Masters, but it was then made clear that if I persisted with my studies I'd be sacked. Despite the threats, I continued to strive for that second degree. But all had to be done in complete secrecy, even though my studies juxtaposed with the sort of work I was doing for the research team. A situation that only became public after the completion of my three-year contract, but all very strange.

At Myall Vale in 1976, Henry and Edward were people who felt they could really make a difference to the local cotton industry. They had very different personalities. Henry was relatively young, newly married, abrupt, prone to irritation but with an ironic sense of humour. Edward was older more casual in his day-to-day dealings, a family man. His only real vice was a serious smoking habit. On one occasion, he told me about all his male relatives who'd dropped dead from heart attacks in their late-forties and fifties. Yet he seemed all too ready to dismiss the notion that smoking posed any sort of danger.

My work on the research station varied with the seasons. Next door, there was a large commercial cotton growing property and some of my time was spent there.

With *Heliothis* moths, it is the caterpillars that do the damage. When the plants grow from seedling up to the flowering stage, the damage caused by insect pests can be minimal, but once the plants starts producing bolls, which contain the developing seed and cotton fibre, that's when the serious damage can occur. When I was there, insect control was achieved by aerial spraying, either of chemical pesticides or a bacterial solution, which caused a disease when ingested by the caterpillars. Apart from the environmental issues, spraying was expensive and a cotton grower would aim to keep it to a minimum. Therefore, the timing of spray applications became critical.

Part of my job was to help monitor insect activity in cotton crops and sometimes in maize, where *Heliothis* can also be a problem. This included the effectiveness of various types of spray.

We also did a great deal of light trapping. The moths mainly flew at night and a typical light trap was built around a standard sized metal dustbin. The lid had a hole in the top and suspended above it, a central electric light, around which were four radiating metal fins. The insects would be attracted to the light. While flying around, they would strike the fins and fall into the bin, to be killed by a slow-release insecticide.

The night's catch would be collected every morning. Sometimes this resulted in a quarter dust bin of dead insects, but on such occasions, most of this would be by-catch, such as crickets.

We were interested in not only in the numbers of cotton pests but what else the specimens could tell us. There are two species of *Heliothis,* both medium-sized brown moths, but it was not always possible to tell them apart by the wing patterns. By dissecting the abdomens, not only could the species be determined, but also the sex and age. The abdomens of female moths, on emerging from the pupa, were full of eggs and fat storage bodies. But when the insect was nearing the end of its life, about ten days later, both eggs and fat were greatly depleted. Similarly, with the males we could tell both the species and age from their internal structures. So I, who had never used a microscope as a kid at school, was spending hours every day, staring down a binocular microscope and dissecting moths.

During the cooler times of the year when no cotton was being grown, I was involved in small-scale experiments in the lab. This meant such things as growing cotton plants and rearing insects under artificial light. I was also involved in data analysis. The research station did have a computer, but I remember it taking up to half an hour to chomp through a mass of data that these days would be done in seconds. In those days, a lot of such work involved handheld calculators. Programmable calculators, little machines that cost up to 400 dollars each, were just coming onto the market. But at this time, I bought myself one such calculator for a mere 100 dollars but could never get it to work properly. But on sending it away to get it fixed with a description as to what it was doing, I received a little booklet on standard operating procedures. Utterly useless, clearly, they were being overwhelmed with complaints and I vowed never to have anything to do with that brand again.

But the most satisfying piece of number crunching I did at this time was compiling data for Edward Summers. During the previous growing season, he and his assistant had been collecting data from a special type of light trap. In this, there were eight catching bins set on a wheel structure. At the end of each hour, the wheel would automatically move around a notch so that a new bin would be moved under the light. This device not only recorded the number of moths on the move hour by hour, but with follow-up dissections, species, age and sex being ascertained. The number of dissections carried out over the growing season had totalled many thousands.

I was handed this thick wad of data sheets and asked to start sorting. The overall pattern of moth numbers for both species showed them rapidly building to a peak in the three hours after sunset and remaining at that level until about three hours before dawn. But looking at the data by sex showed that the females were on the move during the early part of the night. After that, their numbers fell sharply while the males were taking to the air. A behavioural difference that had never been previously identified, one that had all sorts of implications with regards to the night-time spraying of cotton crops. As Edward said on seeing the graph for the first time, 'When you're up to the eyeballs in moths, day after day, the underlying trends aren't the least bit obvious. But what an absolutely great result.'

Finally in the year after leaving university and with spare time on my hands I turned to the problem of the Darwin bird census results.

The final outcome a further eight papers were published appearing in everything from *The Australian Birdwatcher* to the *Australian Journal of Ecology*. So much for Shane Maher vision of one small paper. But in all fairness to Shane he did come good in the end, some the papers were published in his journal.

But while all this was in progress, I got into a row with a prominent academic, ecologist and one-time assistant editor. I'd never met the man, but he was certainly free with his opinion. I was infuriated yet again, but when challenged, he seemed unable or unwilling to explain himself. By that I mean after an opening salvo, I was met by a wall of solid silence which could be interpreted in a number of different ways. But with more mature reflection, it became apparent the problem stemmed from mishandling by both sides. That is, I admit to some provocation on my part but on the other hand, he'd totally failed to appreciate the underlying issue. That is my frustration at being unable to get these bird papers published before I graduated. Earlier, he'd been in a position to at least point me in the right direction but had failed to do so. In the end, I offered a partial apology for some of the more unpleasant things I'd said but that gesture wasn't reciprocated.

However, the whole episode left me very deflated. Instead of being pleased as the last paper in the series was published, my thoughts were, *Thank god that's done with. If publishing material is that hard, who really wants to be a professional scientist?* In the end, it felt too much like a messy divorce.

Nevertheless, at about this time, I started to look at the census date on migratory shorebirds, most of it published by others. I concluded that there wasn't enough information to warrant a review. But 15 years later, having moved on with my life, I returned for a second look and found a huge expansion of the published database. There had been a period in the late 20th century when concerns were growing as to what the pending industrial development in China and elsewhere in Asia could do to the vulnerable migratory wader population. Groups of dedicated citizen scientists had been out there gathering data as never before. Unfortunately, these fears have been realised in the decades since, with species populations down by 70 percent or more.

With over 500 sets of published census results (approximately five million birds in total) I set to work, producing three more papers. The most comprehensive of these was published in *The Stilt* with the title, *The Continuum of Migratory Waders in South-east Asia, Australia and New Zealand: An Analysis.* At the time, I saw this as a duty not something that would be of any personal benefit. Even though it had taken two years to put together and made reference to the published works of 72 other authors, it certainly wasn't destined for the bestsellers list. Nor, given the nature of the data, was it a really elegant piece of science, but perhaps the best that might have been expected. But if it were to be read by 20 people in the next hundred years, it would have been worth the effort. Such is the nature of science.

Chapter 23

Nuts, Bolts and Bad News

SOON AFTER ARRIVING IN NARRABRI, I acquired another car. Worried about the rust problem in the old WV beetle and thinking I'd never get it passed in New South Wales, I'd bought another of exactly the same make and model. The only difference was the colour. The original VW 1300 was white, the replacement blue. The idea was to use the original for spare parts.

Three months later, on a cold foggy morning, I hit a kangaroo on the road near Mendooran. The animal had been a large Eastern Grey Kangaroo which continued on its way, but judging by the damage to the car, unlikely to have escaped unscathed. I was left with a smashed right-side headlight and buckled mudguard. But once I was home in Narrabri, I had no difficulty unbolting the damaged mudguard and replacing it with one from the original. I suspected the kangaroo hadn't been so lucky.

But I was also starting to have trouble with the replacement car's motor. On pressing the accelerator, the engine would threaten to stall before picking up again. A particular worry at intersections and in heavy traffic. The problem was traced to a worn distributor shaft but this raised the question what else was in a less than ideal state? However, the original had a better motor and while in Townsville, I had a reconditioned engine fitted. So, one Sunday morning, I thought it might be possible to swap the engines around, something I'd never attempted before. Working step-by-step with both cars in the back garden, it took about three hours and proved relatively easy. After disconnecting the fuel lines, the accelerator cables and the distributor wiring, there were just four main bolts holding each engine in place. The motors of the VW Beetle are of a light casting and once disconnected relatively easy to drag around. But strategic thinking was required when jacking things into place. This included removing back wheels to give myself sufficient room to work.

I held my breath when attempting to restart the newly fitted motor, for it hadn't run for about a year. It did start, but ran rough. But listening to the splutter, I decided the most likely cause were dried out seals in the carburettor. Sooner than trying to pull complex things apart, I solved the problem by swapping the carburettors around. A few minutes work and all was good. The project wasn't hard, but a bit of a step up from the meccano set I had as a child.

However, the absence of a Volkswagen dealership in town did at times cause problems. On one occasion, at car registration time, I had to drive all the way over to Tamworth, a round trip of 338 kilometres (200 miles) just to get a 6V bulb for an indicator light. The bulb cost about 60 cents. But the blue VW was to play an important role during the events in my life over the next several years.

Rhonda was a friend of my sister, Hilary, and we first met at a birthday party in Sydney. She was a nurse in her late twenties, a nice girl, but with her working in Sydney, and me in Narrabri, we sometimes went weeks without seeing each other. She visited me once in Narrabri and on another occasion, I stayed overnight at her parents' place at Springwood, in the lower Blue Mountains outside Sydney. I think both of us were looking for a serious long-term relationship. Liking that idea when writing to each other or talking over the phone. But face-to-face came the question – do I really want to live with this person for the next 20 plus years?

Having met the family, I sensed her father was quite supportive, but Rhonda's mother didn't approve. In the end, the mother had little to worry about, the relationship wasn't going anywhere. As Rhonda said at the end, 'No harm done.' Once separated, there was no contact, but I hoped that Rhonda found whatever she had been looking for.

Also at the house was Rhonda's 103-year-old great-grandmother, Mrs Howes, who by some strange coincidence I'd met a decade earlier when I was a postman in Wahroonga. As soon as she mentioned the name of the street, I recalled meeting this lady before. Even at her great age, Mrs Howes had retained a lively mind. In her younger days she'd been something of a champion draughts player. This is a game I'm not particularly good at, and sitting down together, I won the first round. But during a second game, the ancient cogs started turning and after that, it was all downhill for me. I was wiped out in less than eight minutes.

Soon after Rhonda and I went our separate ways, the Grandville train smash happened. This occurred when a train packed with morning commuters from the Blue Mountains ran off the rails and crashed into bridge supports, bringing the bridge decking down and crushing two of the carriages. Some of Rhonda's family could well have been on that train, but the causality list contained no one with her surname.

It was while staying at Rhonda's parents' house that I became aware of terrible news. Three days earlier, there had been reports of a light plane missing in the Riverina region around the town of Griffith. The search was hampered by dense fog. I knew that the McCauleys had such a plane because they'd brought another station on the Hay Plains and using the aircraft to commute between properties. Harry had his pilot's licence and was doing the flying. But now on this winter's morning came the announcement that the crashed aircraft had been located and there were no survivors. Only when the names were read out did I take notice. Robert McCauley, his two sons Paul and Harry, and one of their station hands, were dead.

Later on, I managed to piece together a little more of what had happened. They'd flown up from Coniston Downs to the new property near the town of Hay. But despite a warning of dense fog, had taken off heading east with the intention of reaching Condobolin where they were due to look at farm machinery.

I know the country north of Griffith quite well, having spent birdwatching time there. Though it is for the most part very flat, there are some low ridges rising perhaps a 150 feet above the surrounding plain. These ridges are covered with trees, and it was into one of these that their plane had crashed.

I suppose the thinking was that as they flew east and the morning progressed, the fog would start to lift. But there are a few days, just occasional days in that part of the world, when fog stays down all day. This had been one of those occasions. A local farmer had heard the plane go over, but in the dense fog it hadn't been sighted. It was to be another two days before the fog lifted and he'd been able to check his property. The wreckage had caught fire, but the end for those on the plane seemed to have been instantaneous. But knowing the characters involved, it's not too hard to speculate what was being said in the plane before fate overtook them. After flying blind for over an hour, Robert would have been urging Harry to turn back. Paul would have been saying very little, though agreeing with his father. While Harry, at the aircraft controls, would have been insisting all would be okay if they just kept going. Perhaps he was thinking that if fence posts started shooting by beneath the air craft, he'd have enough time to gain altitude. The trouble is moving at 120 mph with visibility less than 30 yards, there would have been no time to do anything.

A postscript to the tragedy; Coniston Downs passed into the hands of Harry's widow, Colette, but Sylwin, the only surviving brother, continued with Old Dunaway Station for the next 18 years. The property was sold in 1994 and the new owners, unable to make money from the Merino stud, switched production to fat lambs. The stud had been Robert McCauley's lifelong ambition into which he'd poured his heart and soul, but in the end, all for nothing.

When I visited the station in 2010, I found the shearers quarters had gone, the wool shed had been replaced and the hay storage area converted into a machinery shed. No one was living on the property, the houses and unused sheds falling into decay. There was long grass growing around the unoccupied buildings and all it would have taken was a fast-moving grass fire and everything would have gone up in smoke.

Robert McCauley had built an empire, but he'd only been the custodian of the land. But like the custodian that had gone before, a long line stretching back some sixty thousand years, he'd passed into history. Nevertheless, for the surviving family, it was a terrible blow to lose three members at the one time. Then later, the demise of a legacy Robert had hoped might outlive him. It did, in a way, but not by much more than 20 years.

Chapter 24

Destiny

ON THE MYALL VALE RESEARCH Station in the spring of 1976, Richard, with whom I also shared a house, had become fed up working for William Sharp with his questionable scientific practices. Richard applied for a job with a multinational chemical company and, if successful, would have been a real win for his future career prospects. I was horrified by the way he was going about it. His application letter not only included all the things that one might expect, but also a stinging critique of his current boss. 'You want this new job?' I asked. 'Among other things, they'll be looking for a team player and you going on about William just sends all the wrong signals.' But he couldn't see it that way and furthermore, Lyndon was backing him, claiming these things needed to be said. That might have been true, but a guy needs to pick the right time and forum.

Some weeks later, it came as no surprise to hear Richard had failed, hadn't even reached the shortlist for an interview. He was really disappointed and a few weeks later, resigned anyway. But poorly planned departures can generate their own burdens, so it was a relief to hear sometime later that he'd found something elsewhere.

Then one Friday night, Lyndon announced that a Jodie Hanslow, a recent graduate from New England University, would be taking up Richard's old position. Furthermore, he'd spoken with Jodie and finding her a nice girl, offered her Richard's old bedroom at the house. So, the following day, we were all out in the back garden when Jodie appeared and Carrol and I met her for the first time. She was short, blonde, in her early twenties and had a nice smile.

At this time, I'd just broken up with Rhonda. Jodie was a good, solid and sensible girl and though we shared the house for over a year, I felt she wasn't my type. In any event, she developed a serious relationship with George, who'd been William Sharp's assistant at the Ord River. He was a very tall man, so in this respect, there seemed an attraction of opposites.

In the house, the day would start with everyone seeing to their own breakfast, though we shared our food resources. Sometimes, Carrol would go food shopping for the group, in which case we would give her money. One of the characteristics of the household was both tolerance and humour. At one stage, Lyndon came home with a poster of Adolph Hitler. I don't know where he got it, but we decided inside the toilet door was as good a place as any. To be respectfully gazed at while engaged in other activities.

One day, Lyndon got a phone call from Carrol at work. I could tell something serious had happened, and later at home, there were long faces and intense private discussions between the pair. Then they declared they were formally getting married and asked if I would be the witness at the civil wedding ceremony. To this, I readily agreed. It seemed that Carrol, who by that stage had been Lyndon's partner for over two years, had threatened to leave if arrangements weren't made proper and legal. Lyndon, I suspect somewhat reluctantly, had agreed. The marriage, a week or so later, was conducted in the local courthouse by the registrar of births, deaths and marriages. There were just four of us present; there was almost nothing in the way of ceremony other than the formal signing of papers. All done, dusted and denoted within ten minutes. After that, a placeable routine returned to the household.

On a typical day at about 8.20 am, the shuttle bus would pull up outside and the three who worked at the research station would get on board. Carrol, as a bar maid, would start later in the day and would sometimes be coming home at odd hours. On such occasions, Lyndon would pick her up in his car. In the evening, someone would cook for the group while others would do the washing up. All vehicles were parked in the street and at one stage, there were three outside the house.

After a few months, Jodie bought herself a second-hand car, but soon thereafter, she asked me how to change a tyre. However, it was discovered that her car didn't have a jack, so I used one from mine but advised her to get a general-purpose jack from the car dealer down the street. One of the things I demonstrated was the need to keep the spare wheel under the body of the car whenever possible, just in case the jack slipped. In all my car adventures this was something that had never happened, but there was always a first time.

Some months later, one dark wet night driving back from seeing her parents in Armadale, Jodie had a flat tyre. While trying to change the tyre, the jack slipped. Fortunately, she remembered to have the spare wheel under the chassis. She was subsequently helped by a passing truck driver. But when I looked at the brand-new jack afterwards it was found to be faulty.

It was at about this time that Jodie told me that a group of environmentalists were having a camp on top of Mount Kaputar during the coming weekend. Some of her friends and staff from her university would be there. So, on Saturday morning, I drove on the narrow winding road up the mountain. There are three distinct bands of vegetation which were related to altitude and best characterised by the changes in Eucalyptus trees. Right on top, the area was dominated by Snow Gums *Eucalyptus pauciflora,* substantial trees unlike the typically stunted forms of the high country further south.

There was a gathering of about 50 people. As I arrived, they were going off in different directions on planned activities. I joined a group of bushwalkers and had an interesting time. Back at the assembly point, just at sunset, I discovered there was to be a birdwatching expedition on the following day.

I was about to head off down the mountain, but a group of people had stopped to look at the sunset. But one face in the crowd caught my attention. Early thirties, she was wearing a blue beanie and weatherproof jacket. The light from the setting sun catching her face somehow reminded me of Irene of my early childhood. Our eyes seemed to meet and I thought I caught the flicker of a smile. However, it was getting late and I didn't want to be driving on the mountain road in the dark.

When I returned the following morning, the assembly had gone off in various directions. But knowing the route planned for the birdos, I set off running down a nearby side track and caught up with them at about half a mile into the bush. Furthermore, the lady from the previous evening was there. This time I didn't tempt her with a piece of plasticine made to look like chocolate as I had with Irene all those years earlier. It didn't work then and no point in trying that a second time, but instead I greeted her with, 'How are you today?' Much, much better. We got to chatting and I felt from the start here was the right sort of chemistry. Her name was Ruth and she was a librarian from Canberra. She had an arts degree and was also a fully qualified English History Teacher. An only child, she'd grown up around eastern Sydney's Bondi Junction. In her childhood, this would have been a working-class area, not the gentrified suburbia it has since become. Nevertheless, the sort of young woman that I would have classed as well out of my league during my time on Old Dunaway Station. But a lot had happened since, and the time for travelling unencumbered had come to an end.

We even managed to look at a few birds during the day. I demonstrated my ability to tell the difference between female Spotted and Striated Pardalotes, small birds and tricky at the best of times. Ruth had always liked birds, used to feed them in the garden, but was never a true-blue-birdo.

By the end of the day, I was really excited by the encounter and we exchanged addresses and promised to write. The only worry was the sheer distance involved. From Narrabri to Canberra is approximately 620 kilometres (370 miles) about half the length of Britain. We didn't get to see each other again until after the New Year, three months later. From then on, I was regularly on the road during public holidays, or when I could get time off. A drive to Canberra was a daylong exercise, the blue WV Beetle with recently fitted motor doing the hard work.

The only time I had any car mechanical trouble was broken distributor point, which was fixed in minutes. In the bad old days of the Morris Minor, when I lacked the knowledge and the right spare parts, this might have taken hours if not days to sort out.

But there was a bad moment on the Barton Highway north of Canberra. Normally, I would try to avoid driving at night because of the VW's weak headlights, but on this occasion, I was running late. On a long straight section of road, another car was coming the other way with headlights on full. Normally, this was not much of a problem, but on this occasion, for some reason, my only point of reference was the oncoming lights. I slowed down, but didn't stop, too far to the right would have me over the centre line, too far left and I'd be off the road. The other car must have been moving slowly too because it seemed to take forever to go past.

Ruth had recently bought a three-bedroom house in Canberra and when we first met, was sharing it with two other girls and her pet dog, an Australian Terrier, Timmy (otherwise known as Timothy Barker). A thoroughly likeable but somewhat unruly character. He was to remain a bundle of energy right up to the day he died, seven years later.

As the relationship between Ruth and I deepened, the other girls in the house were asked to move out. Then in July, I asked Ruth to marry me, to which she said yes. But it was a couple of months before she told her parents, William and Rebecca. On one occasion, I drove from Narrabri to Sydney, while Ruth came up from Canberra, to stay with our respective parents. But I couldn't ring to check if she'd arrived because her parents didn't know of my existence.

William, my future father-in-law, was a motor mechanic who'd spent most of this working life with the maintenance of buses around the eastern suburbs. He'd started as an apprentice and rose to become a supervisor. On retirement, he'd started his own car repair business, a one man show in a back lane that was to keep him busy into his late 70s. Rebecca was the daughter of a one-time country doctor, part of a family of eight children. Bright at school, she was of that generation that had been through the Great Depression and the Second World War. One of her brothers had died fighting in New Guinea and another badly injured, lingering on in a repatriation hospital for a number of years.

Besides meeting the in-laws, I was also taken to see other members of Ruth's extended family, including the affluent out-laws on Dover Heights. So here was that road I'd driven along a decade earlier while admiring the view. The scenery hadn't changed, but my circumstances certainly had.

Ruth's extended family included five aunts but only two surviving uncles by marriage. Among her several cousins, there were two who were almost like sisters to her. Many lived in Sydney's northern and eastern suburbs.

But at this time, during the winter of 1977, came more tragic news. During the previous summer, four students from the New England University had worked at the research station. I'd gotten to know them quite well, but now came news that one of them, Bert Samuels, who'd been out taking water samples as part of an honours year project, was missing. He was a non-swimmer and it was feared he may have fallen in. An intensive search at the time was called off after several days. His body was eventually discovered about two months later. I couldn't help but reflect on my own misadventures at about his age and wondered why some of us survive while others aren't so lucky.

Ruth and I were married in a Catholic church in Bondi Junction, the area where she'd grown up. I'm not a Catholic, but agreed to certain conditions to show respect for the church. This led me on a journey over the next several years to examine my own feeling with regards to religion and faith, to look again at what Christianity had to say. For a while, I tried to put aside my doubles, questions that I'd been asking since the age of ten. It was an interesting decade-long exploration but in the end, left me even more firmly with an agnostic mindset. A true agnostic is one who recognises a higher power but questions the Gnosticism that seems to underlie all the world's religions. Nevertheless, issues of faith have certainly influenced my writing. The character Hydie in *The Threads of Time* is sustained, in a time of great danger, by her belief in God. The holy man, Hwinum, who is martyred by his own people in *Corner Spiral*, could, in the real world, be a Catholic priest.

The marriage ceremony went well. I was dressed in a new suit and Ruth looked marvellous in white. Extended families were there, including my sister Hilary, her partner, David Forster, and my brother Jon, who'd flown down from Darwin.

Our first night as man and wife was spent in a hotel a few streets back from Bondi Beach. The next day, it was on a plane off to Norfolk Island. We were there for six days, an interesting place, both in terms of its history and ecology.

The island seemed to have been uninhabited when discovered by James Cook in the 18th century, though faced with a forbidding coastline, he was unable to land. During the 19th century, it was periodically a penal colony before settlers moved there from Pitcairn Island. Ruth and I stayed at a hotel near Burnt Pine and spent several very pleasant days walking around the island.

On returning to Sydney, we went our separate ways, Ruth back to Canberra and me to Narrabri. But this felt so wrong, so totally unnatural. In the months leading up to our wedding, I'd been trying to get a job in Canberra and this was to continue for ten months after our marriage. I had four job interviews during this time, one looked like it was about to yield positive results only to have it fall through at the last moment. On another occasion, I had an interview that seemed to be going well until I produced a copy of one of my published bird papers. For some reason, this seemed to irritate the hell out of the bloke who would have been my boss. Why, I've no idea, because all I was trying do was demonstrate an outside interest. Surely not so shocking for someone with a degree?

On another occasion I was caught up in what can best be called a public service sham interview. These occurred when someone was put into a temporary position and worked there for say twelve months. But then it was decided their position was to be made permanent. But under public service rules, there had to be a formal interview. This resulted in the position being advertised and other candidates considered, whereas in reality, the job position was a done deal. Sometimes these shams could be conducted with the outward appearance of fairness, but at others, with such clumsiness it was only too obvious what was going on. They were common in places like Canberra, but not so amusing when a dummy candidate had to travel hundreds of miles with the sole purpose of occupying the interviewee's chair.

During this time, I continued with the long drive to Canberra whenever possible and Ruth drove up to stay with me in Narrabri on one occasion.

By August, Ruth was pregnant and during my visit, Ruth's cousin, Samantha, was also staying at the house. The plan thereafter was that I would go back to Narrabri while Ruth and Sam would spend a couple of days in the Snowy Mountains south of Canberra. I would have liked to have gone with them but my time was limited.

I left Canberra early that winter's morning and arrived back in Narrabri mid-afternoon. I left my bag in the house and drove out to the research station. I'd been there only minutes when I had a phone call from Ruth. They had been in a car accident and she was in the hospital at Cooma. At this, I left a message for Lyndon, who was off around the research station somewhere, and commenced the return journey. I got as far as Cowra in the central west of New South Wales that night. I camped on the banks of a creek and was on my way at first light the following morning. I reached Cooma, which is about 122 kilometres (73 miles) south of Canberra at about mid-morning.

Ruth had been badly shaken and held overnight in hospital for observations. Samantha had escaped unscathed, but the car that had been badly side-swiped was a write off. The accident had occurred on a sweeping bend on a gravel road. The young fellow in the other car coming towards them had been travelling much too fast. Ruth had seen the danger, pulled over and slowed right down, actions that probably saved her from a head on collision. The other driver was charged and later convicted of culpable driving.

Having picked up Ruth and Sam, the three of us spent two days in the snow fields at Perisher. I then drove back to Canberra, dropping off the women and from there on, to Narrabri.

By this stage, I was living on my own. Lyndon and Carrol, looking to get a home of their own, had moved out into another house in a nearby street. They were still renting but with the option to buy after a year. Similarly, Jodie had moved in with George and the two were planning to get married.

But my thoughts were on Ruth in Canberra. A couple of months earlier, I'd approached the Zoology Department of the Australian National University with the aim of starting a master of science degree in entomology. This would require me to do a masters qualifying course, the equivalent to an honour's year, before I could start on the degree. I was now thinking that I could resign from my job in Narrabri and move permanently down to Canberra, start my masters studies and be on the spot when it came to job hunting. If and when I had employment, I could then continue my studies part time. On the 29 September 1978, I closed the door on the Maitland Street house for the last time.

So once again, I was heading off into an uncertain future. My son Andrew was on his way and I needed to be there for his arrival.

After three years working for CSIRO at Black Mountain in Canberra, I completed my masters and a year later, did my teacher training. I was a science teacher for 15 years, but then became a school lab assistant for a further 15, finally retiring from the work force at the age of 73.

There are many examples of dyslexic kids going off the rails and having been touched by the condition, it's not hard to see why. Though I, as a teacher, sometimes found myself on the receiving end from such troubled children, thereby experiencing the problems from the other side of the fence. On one occasion, I asked a student if he was dyslexic. He didn't know what the word meant and I had to explain, but as a 14-year-old, he was clearly falling through the cracks. I'm told a significant proportion of Australia's prison population are, for whatever reason, functionally illiterate. Something that needs far more attention than is currently the case given the huge cost to the community of keeping people locked up. But I'd also had some real successes in teaching, particularly with the older kids. My two physics classes at Hawker College in 1988 were magnificent, but there are other occasions and other classrooms I prefer to forget.

Later, as a school lab assistant, I really enjoyed the experience, half the pay and half the stress suited me fine. But I did, from time to time during practical lessons, get in front of classes and it was like putting on an old glove, a good fit, a nice feel.

My marriage to Ruth effectively ended after twenty years. I think we both felt the first decade had been good, but less so after that. Our son Andrew, at aged twelve, was reprogramming his mother's computer and later went on to complete a computer science degree.

One of the things I never felt comfortable discussing with Ruth was my battles with dyslexia. In fact, my childhood and early working life were little mentioned during our marriage. As a bright child, Ruth seemed to have largely sailed through school and university. I sense our respective educational experiences from the beginning of primary school to university graduation were, for the most part, very different. On the other hand, my parents knew first-hand of my largely unpromising childhood though the *D* word was never used. Later, they were truly astonished as to how it was possible to turn it all around at the academic level.

As for my most recent endeavours as a writer, I'm in part returning to the imaginative mind set of my childhood but the influence of science shouldn't be under estimated. A typical scientific paper is similar in length to that of a short story and the word count of a graduate thesis about that of a novel. But such scientific projects have a lot in common with other forms of writing - organisation, discipline, word choices and creative imagination. Like many writers I look to the odd, the interesting and the unexpectedly ironic.

In the science fictional stories I put aside the humanoid model to envision space aliens that biologically couldn't be more unlike us two legged types. However despite the fetishes, foibles and a weird life cycle, I give them some human social characteristics. This is more than literary convenience but something that might be expected in a species that has an intelligence and social coordination on a par with our own. A galactic example of convergent evolution. The words below are those of Midnight one of the alien protagonists in *Corner Spiral*.

'Motherships are large. In fact the words, really, really very huge might best describe them. Their many functions include bossing people like me around, madly procreating when required and all this while whizzing across space between star systems. I respectfully must say that I'm still in the process of discovering who I am and what role I'm expected to play and right now taking all this very seriously. You must understand that I was born and only became fully conscious a few weeks ago. Since then, you will be pleased to hear, I've stopped growing and had my first space-walk. It felt odd and wobbly, moving off on my own for the very first time but in the last few days I've had a bit more practise; yes practise, practise.'

But the *Corner Spiral* story is set in a parallel world where ancient prophecy predicts the destruction of a unique civilisation. A prophecy that by a terrible irony becomes self-for-filling but not all is lost. The theme of survival against great odds is revisited in *The Threads of Time* – another of the sci-fi series but set in a later period. The human character Ghem ponders the links between the past and present.

Standing by the shore he recalled the words of an ancient poem, words that now seemed more than ever related to that great disaster of long ago and yet still resonated in the present. It spoke of Eluma, heroin and beautiful sister of the philosopher Melsum.
We are but threads before the winds of time
Mehel's passing has filled our minds with tears
The centuries are long but we remember still
But now again we are doubly cursed
Our spring of truth is dry, though life flickers yet

Out side the sci-fi sphere the character Memie in the satirical *The Deadly Serious Republic,* is almost the classic bird in a gilded cage. However she breaks free, forsake the constraints inherited with her great wealth and goes in search of vengeful revolutions. *Memie wanted to be there. Yes there, waving the big red flag and storming the very Winter Palace in which she'd been brought up.* But her bodyguard and faithful friend Max is forever pulling the wayward Memie back from the brink, but alas not always successfully.

> *To Memie's way of thinking, this was what red rebellions were all about. Here in the room were business men, property tycoons, banking executives, and billionaires. But unlike the general run-of-the-mill filthy rich they'd been imprisoned, tortured, robbed and for all the threat of imminent personal extinction was very real. These were her sort of people, the abused wealthy, the victims of adulterated decadent capitalism, and this was, at long last her sort of rebellion.*

This story has its sequel *The Edible Machine Gun,* but with different protagonists. In the quote below Roman Brasco is inspecting a warehouse consignment of dangerous confectionery.

> *After removing the clear plastic wrapping, Roman concluded that the weapon, if it could be called that, was modelled on a belt-fed Fincha FC 919 machine gun. According to the box, the primary ingredients were cane sugar, stiffened with vegetable gums plus chocolate attachments. The bullet belt-feed was made of pliable liquorice implanted with boiled sugar candy bullets backed by tiny compressed air canisters. The only non-edible part the canisters, were described as dangerous if mishandled.*
>
> *He loaded the belt-feed and pressed the trigger; there was a clunk, a slight hiss and then a sharp*

bang as a candy bullet smashed into a nearby wall to fragment into a thousand pieces. 'Rate of fire low,' he muttered, as the used air canister was ejected. 'Aim I guess pretty poor but at close range could still do some damage.'

Edible Machine Guns can be fatal but no where near as dangerous as say chocolate-coated hand grenades.

In *The Golden Man* at one point the story describes a meeting of criminals trying to resolve their differences. Jack Sammalanno was presiding over the preceding and had just asked the leaders of the opposing sides to formally state their names.

'George Gromberg,' declared the older man in the wheelchair. 'Queensland and northern New South Wales Marijuana Grower's Cooperative and the complainant in this case.'

'Bullshit you are,' cried a man from the second group.

'Shut up,' ordered Sammalano, arm outstretched, gun pointed. 'You open your mouth, your overused north-and-south, when I says and not before. Now give us your name.'

'You knows damn well who I am,' complained the other.

'Respect for the law is what I'm on about,' stated Sammalano, gun now back on the table. 'Either we do it right or we all go home and you lot can sort out your differences any which way.'

'I'll speak for him,' interjected the man in the wheelchair. 'Ken Braunside, retailer of prostitutes, standover man and city drug dealer.'

'And car stealer,' insisted Braunside, a large hairy man in his late thirties, red shirt and blue jeans. 'I've spent a total of three years in jail for car

> stealing and that's very much part of my resume or whatever they calls it.'
>
> 'Stick with CV, you'll find it easier to spell,' advised Sammalano. 'Now I'm the judge here and as such I need to be bribed. Both you lot have your bribe money handy?'
>
> Two brown paper bags were promptly handed over. For the next few minutes Sammalano carefully counted the contents, before announcing, 'You, Mr Braunside, are two hundred dollars short. At the start of proceedings if the scales of justice are to be truly balanced there needs to be equal amounts of dough from both sides.'
>
> At this Braunside begrudgingly produced the missing money from his pocket.

Good Evil is my most openly political work and written in the year after the 2003 invasion of Iraq. In the quote below the main character Byron Jones is talking to his torturer Jim about Byron's friend and charity worker Margot.

> 'Margot is a nice lady who wouldn't hurt a fly and has done absolutely nothing but raise money to help people in this region,' claimed Byron, trying to stop the emotion in his voice betraying him to the enemy.
>
> 'She's seen things and talked and that's doing somethin' real bad,' replied Jim. 'In the War with Terror people who talk out of turn don't get to live too long. You is either with the terrorists or with us and there can be no in-betweens, not for nobody.'
>
> 'Whose terror I wonder, our side's or the real terrorists?' thought Byron. 'Oh, good-evil, what crimes are committed in thy name?'

Apart from paraphrasing Dickens the stories continue.

So, despite a few of life's little pot holes, I have travelled a long way from Old Dunaway's muddy wheat field. Even further from the Wilderness school and Mr Silverside's long division sums. Furthermore, I converted my keenness for birdwatching into an interesting exercise in statistics and got to teach science at matriculation level. However, I was never officially a maths teacher, though I did tutor after hours in that subject. So, the calculus I'd never heard of as a kid along with algebra and geometry absent from my youth, were part of my day for a while. But no man is an island and all this had been made possible including my efforts as a writer, with the help of many others along the way.

As for Miss Cramer not wanting to hear of me ever again, perhaps the lady sensed, as no one else did, that the sleeper would one day awake. And in doing so, go against the grain of her class-driven social philosophy, which even by the standards of the 1950s, was way out of step with mainstream British society.

In this day and age with a specialist's help, a child with my sort of condition might expect to experience a hiccup in their educational progress. Though in practice this is clearly not always the case. But whatever a person's allotted time in history, dyslexia, if left unchecked, has the power to define personalities and chart the course of lives. Certainly, it defined me but fortunately, the pathway I took, though not without its trials and tribulations, was largely positive.

But onto a truly dreadful thought - how is that word *dyslexia* spelt? Did I get it right this time? Certainly, that would once have been a real challenge. But these days a dyslexic who can spell *dyslexia* must count for something.

Printed in Australia
AUHW011421210920
334351AU00072B/825